LANDSCAPES OF TRAUM. .

Integrating trauma studies with historical research and social psychology, *Landscapes of Trauma* examines a range of battlefields from across history, including Waterloo, the Battle of Sedan, the Battle of the Ebro and the Battle of Normandy, to bring to light what these battlefields say about our collective and individual psyches.

Hunt explores how war shapes the nature of trauma, not only by its innate horror but also by the historical and societal contexts it is fought in, from the cultural and social conventions of the period to the topography of the settings. This book provides a deep analysis of how war is experienced and remembered in different eras and by different generations. Moving beyond the clinical concept of post-traumatic stress disorder, Hunt discusses how trauma can be understood socially and historically, as well as through the lens of individual suffering. This book also investigates the psychological foundations of memorialisation, remembrance and commemoration that shape the legacy of the battles discussed.

Using interviews with veterans, their letters, journals and diaries, as well as literary and historical sources, Hunt locates the battlefield as a place where humans explore the parameters of human behaviour, thought and emotion. This book is an important resource for students and scholars interested in the psychology of trauma and war, as well as military history.

Nigel Hunt is an Associate Professor at the University of Nottingham. He is a Docent in Social Psychology in the Swedish School of Social Sciences, University of Helsinki. He is a Chartered Health Psychologist (HCPC Practitioner), and an Associate Fellow of the British Psychological Society, a Fellow of the Royal Historical Society and a Senior Fellow of the Higher Education Academy.

LANDSCAPES OF TRAUMA

The Psychology of the Battlefield

Nigel Hunt

LONDON AND NEW YORK

First published 2020
by Routledge
2 Park Square, Milton Park, Abingdon, Oxon OX14 4RN

and by Routledge
52 Vanderbilt Avenue, New York, NY 10017

Routledge is an imprint of the Taylor & Francis Group, an informa business

British Library Cataloguing-in-Publication Data
A catalogue record for this book is available from the British Library

Library of Congress Cataloging-in-Publication Data
A catalog record has been requested for this book

ISBN: 978-1-138-28771-6 (hbk)
ISBN: 978-1-138-28772-3 (pbk)
ISBN: 978-1-315-26817-0 (ebk)

Typeset in Bembo
by Nova Techset Private Limited, Bengaluru & Chennai, India

CONTENTS

PREFACE

This book arose out of an interest of mine that goes back to my childhood, when my father told me stories of his World War II experiences, giving me his mementos from the war and taking the powder out of 303 bullets and exploding it in his shed. He was a joiner by trade, and the shed was full of wood, shavings and sawdust, so highly inflammable. I sewed his corporal stripes on my army jacket that I bought in a little shop full of World War II surplus, from water bottles to bandages. As I grew up, I played at war, as did most boys, digging trenches in the garden, arguing over who would be British and who would be the Germans. We had all the (imaginary or wooden) weaponry and fought long battles, with the British always victorious. On rainy days we played the board game Escape from Colditz. Many years later I found my way around the actual castle in Southern Germany by remembering the map of the game. When I played, I never thought I would ever visit Colditz as it was behind the Iron Curtain, protected by the terrifying Red Army.

As I got older I started reading about the war (*the war* was of course World War II, which still dominated society; even now it is still *the war* to me), and then *The World at War* came on television, which was a key moment of my childhood when I became absorbed – some might say obsessed – by the subject. My father, though a veteran of World War II, was obsessed with World War I, so naturally I developed an interest in that too. The words *Somme* and *Passchendaele* were (and are) naturally emotive to people of my generation, though we were born long after World War I had ended. There were few World War II equivalents. The only emotive term was *Japs* and anything to do with the Japanese, as the experiences of the Far East prisoners of war was prominent. The words *Dunkirk* or *D-Day*, while important, did not have the emotive context of the World War I terms. While I followed the wars that were being fought as I grew up, be it relating to Northern Ireland, Vietnam, Israel and the Middle East or the final throes of British colonialism, I was not particularly interested in wars fought before the twentieth century.

I grew up with the classic stereotypes. Apart from fear of the Russians (which was real at the time, the Cold War blew hot and cold, and we youngsters didn't really understand the power of Western propaganda), we overplayed the surrendering capabilities of the French and the Italians, the efficiency of the Germans, the plucky Brits, the cruelty of the Japanese, and the childish but swollen-headed people from the USA. All our childhood games reflected these stereotypes.

I point these things out because the social and master narratives we grow up with are important; they are critical in the formation of our identities. While I now have a more nuanced understanding of the war and of the people of the world, it is true that *the war* and its effects were a central part of my childhood. Those contested narratives do still exist. The English – perhaps to their shame or perhaps it is just human nature – still bring up war-related jibes when playing Germany at football. There are still comments about the fighting capabilities of the French and Italians, the efficiency of the Germans, and the childish egotism of the USA. Perhaps the cruelty of the Japanese is the narrative that dare not speak its name in modern liberal society.

For some reason I did not become an historian; I became a bricklayer, a lorry driver and eventually a psychologist. My PhD examined the long-term psychological problems faced by aging World War II veterans. I interviewed many and have the stories of hundreds. I quickly realised that the psychological effects of war are complex and permanent. Out of nearly a thousand World War II veterans in my studies, around one fifth were experiencing war-related traumatic stress 40 to 50 years later. Since doing this research I have worked with veterans of many different wars and found – perhaps not surprisingly – that war is often not good for one's psychological health. On the other hand, many people come through war with only positive memories of their experiences. Whatever the outcome, war has profound effects.

Since adulthood I have had an interest in exploring battlefields. As a psychologist I became intrigued about the importance of studying battlefields in order to understand the psychology of war. These are the places people fought, were wounded, and died; where friends and comrades died, where people were brave or cowardly (terms which themselves need a lot of unpicking), where many different emotions were felt, where people learned to control or not control their reactions and behaviours, where there were victories and defeats. They are places of extremes of human behaviour, thought and emotion; as such they should be able to tell us something of our psychological make-up.

Others have explored battlefields and attempted to understand something of the human psyche. I have tried to bring some examples together from a range of battlefields across history. It is a very narrow range. All the examples relate to the British experience. Most of them are in France, with examples in Spain, England and Russia (Crimea). I make no excuses for the lack of international variety.

They are all battlefields I have visited (often more than once), and I have accessed written accounts by or about the participants.

The battlefields themselves are from very different time periods, and the amount of information about them varies enormously. I start in 1346 with the Battle of Crecy, for details of which I rely more or less on contemporary accounts, such as Froissart through to fictionalized accounts by Shakespeare, that well-known psychologist. We really do not know much about the psychological aspects of the participants in battles at this period. I finish with the Battle of Normandy, a subject closer to my heart, as during the 1980s and 1990s I collected many accounts from participants in the battle. I interviewed numerous veterans, and many others sent me letters, journals, diaries, photographs, and accounts they had written about their experiences.

I would like to thank everyone at Routledge for taking the risk in publishing this book, and my thanks to Georgina for drawing the excellent maps that I hope make the nature and extent of the various battles clear to readers. I would particularly like to express my appreciation to my long-suffering wife Sue, who has visited these and many other battlefields with me over the years. She has no real interest in the subject, and so when I am at a battlefield she is at a field. She is very good at pretending to listen when I tell her what happened at these places. Fortunately, she likes the great outdoors. For all this, I would like to dedicate this book to her.

1

INTRODUCTION

This book explores something of the psychology of war from an unusual perspective – that of physically exploring old battlefields and reading accounts of these battles and their consequences. We may more easily understand the impact of war on its participants if we tread in their footsteps, go to the places they fought, and take note of the landscape, the topography, the archaeology and the movements of the fighting troops, not just written interpretations, but incorporating written interpretations.

Most research by psychologists has focused on the negative personal impact of war: war trauma. While that is a critical part of this book, other factors will also be considered. There are a host of these factors, psychological and otherwise, that add to our understanding of the psychology of war. These include the impact of fighting on individual soldiers, training effectiveness, automaticity of behaviour resulting from training and experience, obedience and discipline, leadership and camaraderie. There are also the difficulties faced during war, the hardships, punishments, diet, general privation, health and illness, and the morale and strength of the enemy. These factors will be considered at various points throughout the book, along with the psychological aftermath of war, such as trauma and memory. The book is not intended as an exhaustive account of the various battles and the psychological understanding that may arise out of them, but rather as an introduction to such an approach.

Psychologists have long been interested in the impact of war and war trauma, with the latter usually being over-simplified and labelled as post-traumatic stress disorder (PTSD; APA, 2013). The impact of war is more complex than PTSD. There is no single set of symptoms experienced by a veteran. Their reactions vary widely, and while many if not all people are profoundly affected by their war experiences – and some do experience mental health difficulties – they are not all negative. Many veterans have positive and happy memories of their war experiences; the people they met, the places they went, the things they learned, and the things they did, remembering that a war is not all about fighting the enemy. If we are to understand the trauma of war, we need to have a more nuanced understanding of how war affects people and not just focus on mental disorders, though these are critical.

We have complex narratives about war and remembering war. It is not just about the narratives of individuals, but also about how those narratives are affected by the broader narratives held at the societal level and how those societal level narratives develop and change over time. Our experiences and what we remember are influenced by the people around us and the places we go. We are essentially social animals, and so the way we think, feel and act is determined by other people and the environment as well as our own personalities. This is often missing from explanations of the impact of war and war trauma, which largely focuses on the problems faced by individuals. Indeed, this ignorance of culture and the social world is a problem with a lot of mental health research generally. Not only individuals but societies are changed because of the experience of war. World War I did not cease to have an effect on its participant countries after the armistice in 1918 (apart from the fact that many countries were fighting well into the 1920s). The longer-term impact of the war carried on for decades, not just in the traumatised and maimed veterans and their family members, friends and society, but in the grief of the families, the communities who had lost a significant number of their young men, and in the economy and politics in general. It takes decades for a society to recover from war, and in parallel with the notion that once someone is traumatised they can never regain their pre-trauma self (and some remain traumatised for life), societies that have been at war are changed forever, both in positive and negative ways. Erich Maria Remarque described both the impact of World War I on German soldiers (*All Quiet on the Western Front*), and the difficulties they faced on returning to Germany after the war (*The Road Back*). He made the important point that the older men who went to war had wives, families, homes and jobs to return to, and could take up where they left off. The younger men had none of this. They were taken to war before they had fully grown up and knew nothing of civilian life, so they would be the ones who would not be able to adapt to post-war life, the implication being that they would profoundly affect that society for years to come. As a novelist, he effectively described the psychological impact of war (Hunt, 2004).

By visiting the battlefields themselves (whether just in this book or in reality) we can try to understand participants' experiences a little more. We can extend our psychological knowledge by exploring the reasons for the battle, the topography, the dispositions and movements of the troops, the archaeology, and by attempting to see the perspective of the participants. By being on the ground, walking where possible, but perhaps driving around some of the larger sites (the D-Day invasion in 1944 was across over 50 miles of beaches), travelling in the footsteps of the soldiers who fought, it is possible to gain a deeper understanding of what happened. This is not to claim that those without battle experience can understand the experiences of those who fought, but that it does broaden one's perspective.

In order to do this effectively we need to go beyond traditional psychology, with its experiments, surveys and interviews. Psychologists are not the only ones who understand something of the effects of war. Novelists, playwrights, artists and historians – among others – have also written about or illustrated war, both factually and through fiction (though much fiction by ex-soldiers is often autobiographical), through science and art, showing how war affects people in many different ways. This book attempts to illustrate a small part of this, exploring the impact of war on people using the sites they fought at and the varying accounts of their experiences. The historical element is that the book tries to draw on people's understanding of war across the centuries, using a range of different methods, such as journals, novels, and historical accounts, along with more traditional psychological methods.

My speciality is traumatic stress, and in particular the ways in which people respond to war experiences and the ways in which they get better or can be helped to get better. I have worked with people from all over the world who have been involved with a variety of traumatic events, from World War II (Hunt & Robbins, 2001a,b) to more recent conflicts such as The Falklands War (Burnell et al., 2006), Bosnia (Hunt & Gakenyi, 2005) and Iraq (Al-Hadethe et al., 2015). I have also been involved with projects relating to non-war-related traumatic events such as earthquakes (Zang et al., 2013) or fires (Alghamdi et al., 2015). This has been interesting and stimulating work, and it involves understanding fundamental human behavioural processes, but it *is not enough to understand the response to traumatic events simply by being a psychologist.* You also have to be a politician, a sociologist, a geographer, and many other things, but most importantly, certainly in relation to war experience, you need to be an historian with some depth of understanding. If you are studying the effects of war and are interviewing people who took part in a particular war or battle, it helps tremendously if you have some knowledge of the battles in which they fought. In relation to my early work with World War II veterans this was not really a problem for me. I was interested in the subject from an early age. My father fought throughout World War II in the Royal Air Force, and so I grew up with the war a part of me even though I was born nearly two decades after it ended. As a psychologist I began to understand the impact of the war on individuals. As a social psychologist this inevitably also means focusing not only on war and the individual, but the effects of war socially, between people and across society, and then, as an extension of this, understanding the need to explore the battlefields themselves, the topography through which these people fought. An understanding of these three functions, the self, the social and the landscape, can lead to a better understanding of war.

Visiting battlefields

Over the years I have visited many battlefields relating to wars that have taken place across the centuries. I have been to the battlefields of Crimea, to the places with names that British people usually know as street names – Alma Street or Sevastopol Road or that eminently useful Balaklava helmet. The sites are little visited by British tourists, but there are memorials dotted around the battlefields, and some museums, (A particularly good one is inside an ex-Soviet secret submarine base in Balaklava.) Sevastopol was fought over even more savagely during the Great Patriotic War of 1941–1945, and the remains, the guns and the trenches are scattered around the landscape, making it difficult at times to identify Crimean War remains. This is common to many battlefield sites, for instance in northern France and Belgium, through which numerous armies have marched and countermarched. Even during World War II, some of the battles were fought on World War I cemetery sites, as evidenced by damage to gravestones or to monuments.

The battlefields of the U.S. Civil War are usually much better preserved than many sites elsewhere as they are often national parks, with monuments to the generals still facing each other across the fields and strict codes of behaviour for visitors. It is odd but perhaps understandable that the Northerners have their generals and their guns facing south, and the Southerners have their generals and guns facing north, as though ready for further battles. In Chile, the site of the Battle of Maipú, just north of Santiago, where patriot rebels defeated the Spanish forces and enabled the independence of the core central area of Chile contains very little evidence of the battle apart from a monument. In Crimea, the sites of the Crimean War battles are strewn with the detritus of more recent wars, particularly the sieges of Sevastopol in the 1940s. Northern France and Belgium have many battle sites, with monuments, trenches and cemeteries. Bosnia in the 1990s still had mines along the sides of the roads, the villages were destroyed, and men with Kalashnikovs were blocking the roads. During one visit NATO forces were busy firing missiles and dropping bombs on nearby Serbia, clearly audible from our hotel, and we were being woken each morning by machine gun fire. The older battlefields are safer.

All the battles contained in this book took place in Europe. There is no logical or rational explanation for this, but it does make it easier for European readers to visit the sites. My apologies to readers from non-European countries. There is also no logic to the choice of battlefields. They are all from the last six or seven centuries, with the focus on more modern wars. This is not a coherent history of war, but a glimpse through the eyes of participants and others who have tried to understand particular battle experiences.

This is not intended to be just another psychology book attempting to understand war trauma. It is broader than that. It is hoped that those with an interest in the history of the countries included, and the history and politics of war, will also find it interesting. I have attempted to weave a coherent narrative through the book, and I regularly depart from the central theme in order to provide what I hope is a deeper understanding not only of the effects of war, but also the broader context of the relationships between countries, the nature of the countryside and the present day. After all, if we visit these battlefields, we are seeing them in the context of today, with people living their everyday lives on or near them. Sometimes – at least at the popular sites – the visitors get in the way or intrude into these lives. Sometimes the visitors provide a key part of the economy, particularly for the battlefields of World War I, though at the same time they can annoy farmers by wandering across ploughed fields in search of war material. (This is illegal in some countries, so do not do it!) A key difference in this book is trying to understand the psychology of war through the battlefield tour. Several of the battlefields are described so that the reader can take a real (or virtual) tour of the areas where the fighting took place, either walking or by car. This is what provides a key different experience in terms of battlefield understanding for psychologists.

Narrative and war

My academic research into traumatic stress has also made me realise the importance of the story – the narrative – if we are trying to understand something related to the human condition. We are storytellers and storymakers in most things we do. We try to make sense of things that happen to us; we want to tell other people about it, and we like listening to other people's stories. Octavio Paz argued that it is language that makes us human (Verani & Clarke, 1982). Jane Goodall went a little further and suggested: "What makes us human, I think, is an ability to ask questions, a consequence of our sophisticated spoken language" (Kamrani, 2007). This is partly true, but it is the way we put the words together, the narrative or story, that really makes us human. Questions are there to help us build this narrative, to gain a greater understanding. Without narrative, language is nothing. As far as we are aware, we are the only species that can make up stories and tell them to others. It doesn't matter whether these stories are written down, thought about while out for a walk, or discussed in the café, the pub or at home. Sometimes we ourselves are the only audience, sometimes it is many people. Narratives can be informal, like a conversation between friends, or they can be formal, such as this book or giving a lecture. The essentials are the same.

Psychologists became interested in narrative in the 1980s. Theodore Sarbin (1986) introduced it and suggested that human behaviour can best be explained through stories and using qualitative research methods. Jerome Bruner (1986) proposed a more empirical approach to understanding narrative, suggesting that there are two fundamental types of psychology: paradigmatic psychology, which is the traditional approach using traditional methods, and narrative psychology, a storied approach. Bruner suggested that both approaches are important, indeed fundamental to psychology, but that they are irreducible to one another – a debatable point.

One key aspect of narrative is construction. When we talk about events that have occurred in our lives, we do not simply recount what happened, we talk about what it meant. We confabulate, we make things up, we add detail to enrich the story and give it meaning. We remember things and we forget things. For life stories we contextualise our memories of our lives with meaning that might relate to our personalities, jobs, family or friends. Critically, the narrative is not just personal, it is social. The audience matters. The way we build and structure our stories depends on the society in which we live, so they are cultural. These stories or narratives build up into a complex narrative that we call our life story or autobiography. This is a socially constructed account of our lives. Actually, it is a whole series of constructed accounts. If I wish to describe my past to my wife, it will be a different past to the one I describe to my students, which is still different to the one I tell my friend in the pub. Depending on our audience we highlight certain things that have happened to us; we *forget* to mention other things; often we genuinely do not recall. Our mood and personality also affect how we construct our stories. If we are depressed, we tend to remember the sadder, more negative events; if we are optimistic, we over-emphasise the happier, more positive things (or our positive interpretation of things). This sense of meaning making, and the need for confabulation, is critical to understanding how we live our lives and how we make sense of them. It is similar for war stories, except sometimes people cannot help focusing on certain events – or are unable to mention or even recall other events.

The book brings together several different important elements to try and understand something of the human psyche and behaviour in relation to war. Many accounts begin and end with the person. In order to fully understand trauma, we need to know more about the person, about their habits, their personalities, but also their relationships and the meanings these relationships have for them. We also need to know about their cultures, how culture affects the ways we think, and that includes historical culture, how culture changes over time. We need to understand their experiences, what these experiences mean to them. We need to understand where these experiences took place, and this is where we get to the heart of the book, the notion of landscape, of the battlefield, of the site of memory, and how these impact on the narrative.

War and trauma

A traumatic series of events such as war is, by definition, something that is disruptive to a person's autobiography. It is a life-threatening event that causes people to experience negative emotions and feelings such as terror, fear or horror. They have bad dreams, can't sleep, can't stop thinking about what happened, and when they think about it, they again feel those negative emotions. For some people – thankfully the minority – these symptoms are so severe that they experience post-traumatic stress disorder (PTSD), a disorder characterised by intrusive thoughts and nightmares, avoidance and emotional numbing (the inability to feel emotions, any emotions, not just bad ones), and high levels of physical anxiety and arousal (this will be discussed in greater depth in Chapter 3). People with PTSD often need psychological help in order to come to terms with what has happened and the symptoms they are experiencing. This psychological help aims not at curing someone of their PTSD in the way certain drugs cure illnesses by removing the symptoms and returning the person to their previously healthy state, but by helping them with their memories, helping them to become able to live normal lives and have normal relationships. No one is cured of PTSD; they just learn to deal with their memories and the emotions associated with those memories. But this is not a book about treatment, so I will not go into details here.

The notion of trauma as a mental disorder like PTSD, a disorder that is coherent and found across many individuals expressed in similar ways, is problematic. While for convenience sake it is useful to say someone has or does not have a particular disorder, it does not reflect the reality for the person. It may be better to think of trauma as an injury. Many military personnel do, though perhaps because mental illness in itself is stigmatising, whereas an injury is not. An injury can have a greater or lesser effect. For instance, both scratching a finger and having a leg cut off are injuries, but the latter usually has much more severe consequences. People are affected by trauma in different ways (different sets of symptoms) and to different extents, and this should be taken into account.

Many people are troubled by their memories of war, but we do not want to necessarily label them as having a mental disorder. War is a fact of life for many, and the memories of war, though troubling, are a part of that life. They may be profound memories, ones which the person recalls regularly and perhaps with emotion, but most of the time they can be dealt with. Other memories decay and are lost over time, but many war-related memories stay with the person throughout life and may or may not be shared with others (they are often not shared with family members, as the home should be a safe place). These memories are more than visual, they can be auditory, tactile, olfactory or relate to taste. Not all can be put into words. Memories such as these might 'pop up' at unexpected times and have an impact on behaviour, thoughts and feelings. It is these that – in the worst cases – we label traumatic, as the person may not be able to manage them.

PTSD is not a sufficient explanation of the psychological problems associated with war. It is a personal disorder, a medicalised disorder, a disorder restricted to certain symptoms. While such simple classification has clinical and research benefits, it doesn't take into account the full effects of trauma, and it also oversimplifies in terms of one either having or not having the disorder. It is not as simple as that. War trauma (as we should perhaps call it) is not just a personal disorder, it is a social problem. Someone who is traumatised affects the people around them, their friends and relations, their work colleagues, people they meet in the street, and these people in turn affect the traumatised person. Trauma is a very social disorder; it impacts on many people. If it arises out of war, particularly a war that affects much of a population, such as one of the world wars, or an intense civil war, then it not only affects individuals and their friends and relations, but it can also affect the whole of society. There is little doubt that the nations of Europe were traumatised after World War I or that Iraq as a nation was traumatised by the last few decades of war. Trauma is beyond the individual; it affects everyone. There is also an argument that it affects people across generations, but again, that is for discussion in a later chapter.

What do we mean by data?

I have a problem. Being a psychologist, I am always being told how to be a good scientist, what are the right types of data and how they should be collected and analysed. The concept of data is, to a psychologist, something precious. It is usually numerical, often collected via experimentation, and often subjected to complex statistical procedures. Other psychologists accept the legitimacy of the spoken word and carry out interview studies to look at aspects of behaviour. I am happy with both approaches, but still that is not enough. In focusing only on traditional forms of data we are missing some very important areas. Science is about knowledge; not about particular methods, but about using appropriate and systematic methods to further that knowledge. Psychology is the science of behaviour, so we should be employing all means necessary and appropriate (i.e., ethical) to obtain knowledge about behaviour. As such, data can be anything that is produced by people that may provide insight into behaviour. This may, among other things, include historical documents, letters, journals, novels, plays and artistic productions.

War and the effects of war are ideal topics to explore these areas. First, the way we often describe the impact of traumatic events, through PTSD, is – as I have already stated – not an adequate explanation of the negative effects of war, so we need to look at other ways of obtaining knowledge. Second, war has been with us throughout history, and people have always written about it, produced narrative accounts, and many of these are still available. The book is a response to this, an attempt to understand people's responses to war in a more complex manner through exploring different wars and battles using different kinds of data. One further difficulty is that the language of psychology has only recently evolved, so it is problematic to extrapolate from early writings to an understanding of the response to war. Stress and trauma are relatively new terms, both derived from engineering. Even Shakespeare does not use the terms psychologically.

As I hope is already clear, any understanding of war trauma has to take into account both the individual and the social world. In other words, there are universal things that happen to the human body when it is placed under a great deal of stress, as in war, and then there are social or cultural factors which determine how a person might respond to this same stress. The classic British example is the so-called stiff upper lip. In World War II, while it was recognised that people do struggle to cope with war experience, there was a sociocultural expectation that they would carry on. While this is still the expectation of societies experiencing difficulties, there is a greater recognition of the problems people might face *after* their war experience.

The book is in two parts. The first part provides the background to developing our understanding of the impact of war. It has chapters on methods, the history of our understanding of war trauma, memorialisation and commemoration, and the landscape of battlefields. The second part moves on to explore the battles and wars in turn. Some of the battles took place hundreds of years ago, others are more recent, and the chapters are presented in chronological order. The final chapter draws the findings together and looks at how we may understand the impact of war better because of this wide-ranging examination of different battles across history.

Why these battles and not others?

There is no clear rationale for the choice of countries apart from personal interest and experience, and the ease at which, at least for many Europeans, the sites can be visited. If someone from outside Europe is interested, they could easily explore several of the battle sites in one trip.

The countries involved have seen many wars over the centuries, with France, particularly northern France, being the battleground between east and west, north and south – often battles fought by non-Frenchmen. Spain has been the battleground between Christians and Muslims, and between the extremes of politics. The United Kingdom, as a series of islands, has been relatively lucky over the last few centuries in that, apart from the bombings of World War II and the Northern Ireland Troubles, it has experienced little fighting on its own territory (apart from the Empire, but that is beyond the current discussion). The Crimea has seen very heavy fighting on numerous occasions. The Crimean War was a difficult time for its inhabitants, but World War II saw much more intense fighting that severely impacted on the civilian population as well as the troops.

The UK has not been properly invaded since 1688, and even then, it was a relatively bloodless invasion. Any fighting the British have done has – except for air battles – been in other people's countries. That is not to say we do not have our war-related remains, from the castles of the Norman invaders or the Edwardian invasions of Wales through to the fortifications built at times of threat, such as those posed by Napoleon or Hitler. The example in the book is of the Civil War, perhaps the most deadly war in British history, but one with relatively few remains around the country. The key battles were generally out in the open, and many of the besieged sites have either disappeared or been rebuilt.

France's troubled history of invasion, civil war and strife has left many remains across the country. There are the older remains, those of Cathar Castles or Vauban fortifications, and the newer destruction of the Western Front, with its innumerable trenches and dugouts, remaining concrete bunkers and extensive cemeteries. This extends from the Vosges through into the South Western corner of Belgium. In Normandy there are the cemeteries, the remains of the Atlantic Wall and many tanks on plinths commemorating the battle, but the fields and villages are back to normal; though I spoke to French survivors of the battle who described living in wooden huts for 15 years after the war was over before their houses were rebuilt.

The wars of Spain have a different complexion. The Romans invaded and conquered, they were ousted by the Visigoths, but for many centuries the main wars were between the Christians and the Muslims, the latter having invaded in the early eighth century and conquering effectively the whole of the Peninsula, gradually losing it to the advancing Christians until the final loss of Granada as late as 1492. Since then, apart from the gold wars of expansion to the Americas, Spain has had a series of intensely political civil wars, culminating in the Spanish Civil War of 1936–1939, which was not only a total war for the population of Spain, it also involved many thousands of troops from other countries on both sides.

Spain, the UK and France are also very diverse, and there are political arguments about social and political identity in all of them. The notion of the nation state is hardly stable and is a relatively temporary phenomenon, developing in importance through the medieval age, and now perhaps waning as economic, political and social globalisation comes to dominate the world, along with mass migration. The notion of being French, British or Spanish are concepts that are not universally accepted, particularly in parts of Spain, but also in parts of France and the UK. France contains Burgundians, Bretons, Basques, Alsatians, Normans and others, some of whom are happy to be called French, some less so at various points in history. The Spanish have a much stronger and more recent sense of separatism, with the Catalans and the Basques strongly arguing – and sometimes fighting – for separation from Castilian Spain. While Andalusians and others are not currently arguing for separation, the sense of unity with Castile is relatively weak. The constitution of 1978, formed after the death of Franco and the end of the Fascist state, allowed for a federal state, and while this might have been the best thing to do after Franco's death, the unity of the country is getting more problematic as time goes on. In the United Kingdom, there are separatists, particularly in Scotland and Northern Ireland, but also elsewhere.

All these countries have beautiful scenery and spectacular remains of war and war-related buildings. In France there are the castles and the Vauban forts ring the country; in Spain the Moorish and Castilian castles are perhaps the most spectacular of all; Crimea has Russia's main southern naval port (Sevastopol) and the remains of the recent Cold War defences alongside World War II and Crimean War memorials.

Battlefields vary enormously in how well they are recognised or kept. Many of them are unrecognisable as such unless you know where they are. In contrast to the British and French memorials and cemeteries in Northern France and Belgium, many battlefields in the United States are kept in superb condition, with markers and explanation boards everywhere. Of course, the more recent wars generally have better preserved sites.

The chapters

This chapter has briefly outlined some of the topics of interest in the book, and begun to address the aims, relating to understanding the reaction to war across a range of subjects and data types. The next chapter, "Methods Used in the Book," focuses on what is understood by data, data collection and data analysis, with the focus on developing psychological understanding. Rather than focus on traditional psychological methods such as experimentation and quasi-experimentation, surveys, and observational techniques, there will be a longer discussion of alternative forms of data – accepted by some but not all psychologists – such as novels, historical accounts, plays, poems and art. The one traditional psychological method employed is the interview, where I draw on a series of interviews I conducted with Normandy veterans in the 1990s. There is also a section on the walking interview, a relatively modern approach to interviewing, but one that has relevance for people intending to walk battlefields.

Chapter 3 provides a concise account of how traumatic stress has been represented in literature, history and elsewhere – including psychology and psychiatry – to show what we already know, and to highlight the advantages and disadvantages of the relatively narrow medical term PTSD and other more nuanced explanations regarding the impact of war on humans. There have already been explorations of trauma in history, showing that people were aware of the impact of war from the earliest times, including soldiers' dreams in Mesopotamia in 1300 BCE, Achilles in the *Iliad* in 800 BCE, Herodotus describing an Athenian soldier with an hysterical reaction at the Battle of Marathon in 490 BCE, Shakespeare's plays (which will be discussed in more detail in a later chapter), Pepys and the fire of London, French soldiers in the Revolutionary Wars, Dickens' experience of an early plane crash, soldier's heart during the U.S. Civil War, the Russo-Japanese War, and then the plethora of material that came out of the two World Wars and later wars. The chapter will end by showing how psychologists and psychiatrists developed the construct of PTSD from research into war experience, and how that construct has developed over the years. Finally, the problems with the construct will be explored to highlight the need to have a more detailed and complex construct of war trauma and the general psychological impact of war, taking into account not only the personal, but also the social and the cultural, along with individual differences.

Chapter 4 focuses on memorialisation, commemoration and remembrance. While these will be considered in the light of specific battles throughout the book (particularly Waterloo), this chapter will have a general discussion of the importance of memory regarding war, and the relationship between memory and history. This has implications for the role of commemoration in the contemporary world, and what it actually means, rather than what we are told it means. There is some psychological need for remembrance and commemoration, though perhaps such events should be time limited to the remembrance of events within living memory. Mass commemoration in the UK and elsewhere really started after World War I, and there are few communities in the UK that don't have some kind of memorial to the dead of that war. We have annual remembrance services where we are supposed to *remember* the dead of World War I (and later conflicts) though none of us alive knew anyone who died during that war (and it will soon be the same for World War II), so in what way are we remembering? Why do we continue with these services, and why do we continue with a service that has hardly changed since the first events straight after World War I? How relevant is a ceremony based on a Christian god, monarchy and militarism in modern Britain that is characterised by secularism and migration? This chapter will attempt to address these questions.

Chapter 5 focuses on the landscape of battle and on acknowledging that memory is related to the places around us, something that is enhanced where battles have taken place, where many people have been killed, where significant political change has sometimes occurred. While the previous chapter focuses on memorials, this chapter goes beyond the memorial to explore where they are placed (or not placed): the battlefield itself. If we want to understand battles better, we need to visit the sites where they took place and explore them, take the positions of the soldiers, look where the enemy was positioned. Think about how positions changed as the battle progressed. Depending on the battle, remnants, the trenches and gun emplacements, sometimes the ruins may be seen and sometimes explored. For other battles, nothing obvious remains, sometimes not even the knowledge of exactly where the battle took place. For example, it was long thought that the Battle of Bosworth was fought at Ambion Hill in Leicestershire, but recent evidence demonstrates it was fought a mile to the south west. Battlefield archeology helped establish the site of this battle and has enhanced our understanding of many battles across the ages. The context of place, of landscape, is essential to the narrative of battle.

Part Two of the book moves on to look at the battles and wars themselves. This forms the main part of the book, with each chapter developing what we know about the human experience of war, the complexity of the human response. The battles and wars chosen are deliberate attempts to cover a range of historical periods, though with more emphasis on more recent history, as our understanding has grown exponentially since the late nineteenth century. The focus becomes more on standard psychological approaches from that point, though the battlefield tours still play an important role. While each chapter focuses on a particular battle or war, in order to ensure a readable narrative, and to highlight particular ideas, some will contain information relating to other battles or wars. The wars and battles are presented more or less chronologically, so we flit between the three countries that are the sites of the battles.

Chapter 6 focuses on the Hundred Years War between England and France. This series of wars lasted 116 years and consisted of several conflicts, ending with England being ejected from most of what we now know as France. The focus will be on key battles such as Agincourt and Crecy, discussing some of the main characters such as Henry V and The Black Prince. We know very little about the ordinary soldiers of this war, though it was chronicled in detail by Froissart. Classically, this account details the key people and events, including the killing of soldiers and civilians, but there are few details on the impact these events had on anyone. In an attempt to understand war trauma during this period, historical accounts, novels, and Shakespeare's *Henry V* will be used. Visiting the battlefields can help develop our understanding of the psychology of battle, and this will be described, though inevitably our constructions, both in terms of where and how the battles took place and the effects on the people involved, will be limited by the lack of contemporaneous detailed accounts of the type we now produce. This chapter is a good example of how we can prove very little about the impact on people partly because such accounts don't exist and partly because contemporaneous accounts don't have the language of the modern psychologist.

Chapter 7 is the only one that focuses specifically on battles in the UK. The English Civil War was fought between 1642 and 1651, and proportionally more lives were lost in this country than in either World War I or World War II. People not only died in battle, but civilians were killed by troops or disease, and people starved through famine caused by the failure to collect crops. The focus here will be on the sieges of Wingfield Manor, minor sieges in terms of the war as a whole, but important to those who fought in them. There are numerous documents, accounts written by participants of the wars (not specifically Wingfield Manor), which will be used to illustrate war trauma, though again the language of the psychologist is lacking.

Chapter 8 brings us towards the modern age, the industrial age. By the early nineteenth century weaponry had developed to kill and maim people far more effectively, though battlefield medicine had started to make progress as well. The Peninsular War was fought between Britain and its Spanish allies against the French. It was the key focus of fighting for the British during the Napoleonic era. The chapter will again focus on sieges; in this case the sieges of Badajoz and Ciudad Rodrigo, which took place in 1812. Both were victories for the British armies, but they ended very differently for the civilian population. The killing and raping of civilians after the siege of Badajoz in 1812 has had a significant long-term effect on the population's views about the British Army. The people of Badajoz refused, even in the twenty-first century, to allow a memorial to be erected to the British regiments which fought here, whereas the army was more controlled after Ciudad Rodrigo. Material relating to the effects of war are obtained from the numerous first-hand accounts written after the war.

Chapter 9 is slightly different from the other battle chapters. While it focuses on the Battle of Waterloo in 1815, the main discussion will be about memorialisation and commemoration, as this was one of the first battles to be heavily memorialised. After a short account of the battle and the battlefield, the chapter will focus on some of the memorials to Waterloo both in Belgium and in the UK and, as in the chapter on memorials, explore the reasons why we commemorated this battle after 200 years.

Moving to the middle of the century, Chapter 10 focuses on the Crimean War, fought between Russia on one side and the UK, France and Turkey on the other. Basically, we did not want the Russians having access through the Dardanelles to the Mediterranean and beyond. Most of the fighting took place on the Crimean peninsula, and then mostly in the south west of the peninsula. There are memorials to the key battles. You can still go down the Valley of Death (though look out for the vines as the whole valley is covered by them), and you can see where the *Thin Red Line* held Balaklava against the Russians. The remains of the siege of Sevastopol and the Battle of Inkerman are largely overlaid with the remnants of the battles of the 1940s, but the layout of the land is clear. The chapter will examine some of the accounts of the battle written by the participants.

Chapter 11 focuses on the Franco-Prussian War of 1870–1871, specifically the Battle of Sedan. The town of Sedan, very close to the Belgian border in northern France, is unusual in that if someone was born in the 1860s and lived to be in their 80s they would have experienced three German attacks through the town, in 1870, 1914 and 1940. This chapter explores Sedan and the reasons why the French were defeated on all three occasions before focusing on 1870, exploring our understanding of the individual in war using Émile Zola's novel, *La Débâcle*., This fictional account portrays French soldiers and civilians in the lead up to the battle, the battle itself, and afterwards in the siege of Paris and the Commune. The complexity of the impact of war is evident in this novel and can be seen because we have a complex understanding of the characters. Zola researched his subject well, exploring the area around Sedan and talking to people who had been involved in the battle. He also lived through the siege of Paris and the Commune.

Moving into the twentieth century, Chapter 12 focuses on World War I, particularly the town and environs of Ypres[1], an area fought over from virtually the beginning of the war during the rush to the sea in late 1914 to the end of the war in November 1918. There are many reminders of the war in this area, from sites that were left as they were after the war to the numerous memorials and cemeteries. This chapter uses a variety of data types, as we have so much information about World War I. Apart from touring the main sites of the battles that took place in the area around Ieper and examining some of the memorials and discussing the meaning of the soldiers' cemeteries, an understanding of war trauma will be examined from the perspective of some of the doctors and psychologists who began to understand what was happening when soldiers broke down in battle. It was in 1915 that the term *shell shock* was first published, and the chapter will contain a discussion of this disorder or injury and related problems. We also have a great deal of information about the longer-term effects of war on soldiers and society. Many thousands of veterans remained in asylums for decades after the war, with many others living at home but receiving a trauma-related pension.

---

[1] Ypres is used when referring to the battle and Ieper is used when referring to the town.

The Spanish Civil War of 1936–1939 was, like most civil wars, particularly brutal. Many people were summarily executed, many civilians starved, and many thousands died in battle. Chapter 13 focuses on the Battle of the Ebro, which was the last great attempt by the Republicans to defeat the Fascists, and it failed. The area where the battle took place, around a bend of the river, is only now having modern memorials and museums developed to aid our understanding of the battle. This chapter has two aims: first, to examine the impact of war through the International Brigades that fought in Spain, and second, to examine social memory. Why was it that people were not allowed to remember the battle? Franco's Spain was, until he died in 1975, clear that the surviving Republicans should not be allowed their interpretation of what happened in the Civil War. It was only in the 1990s that Spain started to think about the atrocities and to dig up some of the mass graves of people shot by the fascists. This chapter will focus on what we mean by memory and how it is affected by living in particular types of society.

The Second World War saw a dramatic increase in our understanding of war trauma. Chapter 14 focuses on the Battle of Normandy, fought from June to August 1944. Over the years I have collected numerous first-hand accounts of the battle, along with many interviews with participants. Apart from some quotations in journal articles, most of the material is unpublished, and it provides an interesting insight into the experience of battle, including the psychological elements, not all of which is specifically about war trauma, but also about the excitement of battle, the boredom, comradeship, and so on. This chapter also explores the significant long-term effects of war trauma and how a person is often traumatised for life.

Chapter 15 concludes the book. This chapter draws together what we have learned from exploring battlefields and trying to understand the impact of war and war trauma from a range of perspectives and data sources. It will specifically show how PTSD provides an inadequate explanation for war trauma and that the disease model is fundamentally flawed. Many people talk now of injury rather than disorder, and that is a good word to use to illustrate how trauma can be damaging at different levels (e.g., from a scratch to losing a leg) and how it can be temporary or permanently disabling. The emphasis will again be on narratives and how narratives of war and war trauma are developed through not only the individual but through interactions between people and at the societal level.

2

METHODS USED IN THE BOOK

The notions of method, data, data collection and data analysis are important in scientific psychology. Data in psychology usually refers to numbers or to the words of an interview. In this book it is extended to include works of fiction, diaries and other accounts of war. This chapter includes a short discussion of standard psychological approaches – mainly to show that they are not adequate for the needs of this book – and a longer discussion of the alternative forms of data. I discussed some of these issues in a previously published book (Hunt, 2010), but this chapter provides a broader perspective. Some of the suggestions here might be controversial, but traditional scientific psychology still largely ignores much of the value that comes from understanding the mind and behaviour, particularly the creations of people, whether that is in the spoken or written word, various art forms, architecture or influence on the landscape. Human behaviour is at the heart of all these subjects and more, and so how we describe, evaluate and understand such behaviour should be part of scientific psychology. In recent decades, methodological psychology has broadened to incorporate a range of qualitative methods – based on words written and spoken. This is a fundamental and positive advance, but we should go further.

Statistics in psychology

Human behaviour is complex, difficult to understand, and even more difficult to break down into its component parts and study, yet this is what many psychologists do on a regular basis. In order to do this they turn human behaviour into numbers. This is not the place to go into the history and philosophy of why we do this, but it does stem at least in part from an erroneous understanding that to do good science is to quantify. We have, over the last century and a half, devised ever more complex ways of turning human behaviour into a numerical form, from simple counting of the number of items we can hold in short-term memory (with the classic answer: 7 plus or minus 2; Miller, 1956) to extremely complex statistical analyses of complex data through exploratory or confirmatory factor analysis, or multilevel regression techniques. These may involve the collection and analysis of thousands or even millions of data points to enable us to understand something of personality characteristics or the relationship between various mental health predictors. Over the years, the development of increasing numerical complexity has both psychologists and statisticians egging each other on to come up with ever more complex systems, so that in the end the psychologist often does not really understand the statistics and the statistician often does not really understand the psychological theory that is being tested. There is a clear relationship between the development of ever more powerful computers and ever more complex numerical explanations of behaviour – though it is not clear that there has been any added understanding of how the human mind works. The cynic might argue that some psychologists seem to believe that as long as the numbers are complex they are doing good science. That does not necessarily follow.

Without undermining the significance of the quantitative approach, which has – sometimes despite the statistics – produced many important psychological insights, it is important to briefly challenge this approach. There are problems at several levels. First, there are assumptions about statistical testing, such as power or probability, that at one level recognise the limitations of the statistical approach, but at another level ignore its pitfalls, which we ignore at our peril. Take a simple example. Compare men and women on a reaction time task. We do our statistical testing and decide that men are faster than women at the reaction time task at a probability level of 0.05. But there are several problems with even this simple conclusion. First, the probability level suggests that we are not certain about the finding. There is a small probability (5%) that we are making a Type I error, and that actually there is no real difference between men and women on the task. Good science says that we can sort this out by replicating the experiment. If we again find that men are faster than women, then we can be more certain (but not totally certain) that there is a difference. The problem here is that most psychological findings are not typically replicated. We publish a finding and it is accepted as *true*. We do not get grants to repeat what has been done before; we get grants to be *innovative*. Therefore, we are never certain about our findings. The next – and more critical – problem is using groups, bunching people together because they share a certain simple characteristic (man or woman) and ignoring every other variable. Real data on reaction times will show that even though the means differ, there are many women who have faster reaction times than many men, and that reaction times vary according to the task; perhaps women are faster at some tasks and men at others. We ignore these subtleties at our peril. What if we wanted to hire people who had a fast reaction time? If we just took the main finding, we will only employ men, missing out all those women with fast reaction times. The problems demonstrated in this simple example are everywhere in the literature – and the findings are accepted. This is not to say that such findings are not valuable, just that they have serious limitations when it comes to understanding behaviour. And through all this, reaction time is a very simple behaviour. Real human behaviour is usually much more complex.

At another level, many psychologists and statisticians will argue that they use techniques that do not have this fundamental flaw of grouping disparate people together. They use forms of regression or other techniques that take into account individual variation across many variables. This is a good thing, but it is also problematic. There is still the issue of turning the behaviour into a number so that it can be analysed. This is often done using questionnaires, where people are asked about their personality, attitudes, about such and such a subject. The items that make up these measures may use Likert scales or similar, a five- or seven-point scale indicating agreement or disagreement with a particular item. The flaw lies in the individual's interpretation of both what the item means and what each response means, and this may differ from the psychologist's understanding. What is the difference between strongly disagreeing and just disagreeing with a comment? Another flaw with questionnaires is that their structure reflects the theoretical assumptions of the researcher, and these may not fit the thoughts of the person completing the questionnaire. For instance, I used a battery of measures to assess British World War II veterans' mental health and coping (among other things). I had a theoretical view about different types of coping and structured the questionnaire accordingly. After administering the questionnaire several veterans pointed out that I had not included religion as a coping strategy. It was not on the questionnaire, and therefore it could not be measured (Hunt, 1996), even though it was important.

They were right. I was wrong. By not measuring religion, my theoretical structure was missing a key component. Years later, in support of what these veterans were saying, speaking at a conference in Iran, it became clear that for Iranian veterans of the Iran-Iraq War of 1980–1988, religion was probably the most important coping variable, with veterans, many of whom were badly injured and usually poor, stating that they were pleased they had fought in the *jihad* and that they were happy with their lives because God had willed it.

I do not really have a problem with using these psychological methods. I just wanted to point out a number of flaws. This does not mean they have no value, but it does mean we need to recognise their limitations and acknowledge the value of alternative approaches to understanding human behaviour and that psychology does not have a monopoly on trying to understand human behaviour.

Many of the studies my research group has carried out have used quantitative methods. For instance, our studies in Iraq demonstrated, through the use of standardised questionnaires that measure mental health status, that a large proportion of young people in Baghdad during the war had psychological problems. We then administered clinical techniques that – according to our later measures – had a positive impact on their mental health. The measures were all questionnaires. The analyses were all statistical. At no point did we employ any other form of data (Al-Hadethe et al., 2015). Much of the research relating to traumatic stress employs a series of standardised questionnaires that purport to measure some aspect of mental health such as PTSD, anxiety and depression. They are used very widely, and are generally accepted as valid. One potential problem with such measures is that if a measure is standardised according to Western ideas about mental health, it may not be necessarily appropriate to simply translate it and use it in other cultural contexts. There is no clear right approach to this, but it is important to be aware of the potential problem. We have used the same measures (translated as appropriate) across many languages and cultures, such as those of Iraq, Saudi Arabia, China, Bosnia and Chile. Whether this is entirely appropriate I am not sure, but when we have studies employing clinical techniques to reduce mental health problems, the scores do tend to reduce, indicating something is changing.

Qualitative methods

Over the last few decades psychologists have increasingly used qualitative methods, mostly some form of interview, where the questions may or may not be pre-specified (though there is usually some sort of interview protocol) and the responses are recorded verbatim and then analysed using one of the various techniques available. There are many approaches to this, but (as in quantitative psychology) there is a lot of overlap. Analytic approaches usually entail the selection of interesting passages – words, sentences, paragraphs, and the grouping of these together in some thematic structure, using this as the basis for the analysis and interpretation of the data.

Qualitative methods have their own problems, again at several levels. The interviewer might word the questions in a way that leads the interviewee to provide answers that are biased in certain ways – that gives the researcher the answers they want.

Another potential problem arises when conducting interviews in different languages. It is difficult enough transcribing and analysing interviews in a single language, without having to add translating into the mix. It is important to ensure that the translation is accurate – and there are times when a concept is not perfectly translatable into another language.

Another problem with interviewing is that most of the work is retrospective. It is asking participants about something that has happened in the past and that they have interpreted, perhaps changed, in some way. Causality is less powerful than with experimentation, though the understanding may be deeper and more sophisticated. As we shall see in the chapter on the Battle of Normandy, where I discuss interviews with many veterans, there are problems with retrospective data, but that does not mean it is of little worth.

Value of these methods

I am not attempting to denigrate any of these methods or claim one approach is better than another. I just note that none of them are perfect. They all have their flaws, and as long as they are recognised by the researchers this is not a significant problem. This chapter is not a critique of current methods. They are all very useful, help build useful theory, and provide good information for practicing psychologists to use with their clients. The point of the brief critique is to encourage the reader to think critically about these methods that are widely used, and perhaps consider the following methods using the same eye, seeing that there are both benefits and limitations to these methods, as there are to traditional methods.

Novel forms of data

Psychologists do not have an exclusive understanding of the human mind and behaviour; novelists, artists, historians, sociologists and archaeologists, among others, use different approaches to understanding behaviour. Later chapters in this book make use of what some of the people working in these areas know about behaviour and apply it to our understanding of the effects of war and war trauma. Sometimes the accounts of battle, particularly when we go further back in time, contain little or nothing of the thoughts and feelings of the participants, except perhaps the generals and leaders; and the other problem is that the language of psychology has only recently evolved. No one spoke of psychological trauma until towards the end of the nineteenth century.

Nevertheless, it is argued that these forms of data are legitimate, that we can learn about the effects of war from people in other disciplines. Just as we need to be critical of our usual types of psychological data but still draw valid conclusions, we need to be critical of the forms of data used in this book, but we do not need to reject them.

The concept of data is itself flawed when we consider it in terms of language. Data implies the ability to express basic understanding at a very low level, often a number. Human complexity is such that this argument, reduction to a very basic level, is itself flawed. We cannot examine aspects of human behaviour in isolation; we need to study the complexity. As language is the basis of human thought and – perhaps – behavior, the most effective way of trying to understand thought and behaviour is through the exploration of language. Clearly, individual words usually tell us very little, it is a sentence or more often a whole account that needs to be examined.

Narrative

Narrative is at the heart of being human. We naturally create and tell stories to each other. It is how we understand ourselves and the environment, how we give meaning to the world around us. The narrative turn in psychology, which came about partly through the work of Sarbin (1986) and Bruner (1986), has fundamentally changed some aspects of the discipline. While most psychologists still ignore narrative, others have recognised its importance in terms of theory, method and practice. Narrative psychology is concerned with the stories we tell each other, their structure, content and function (Murray, 2003). For the purposes of this book, the accounts that are used are narratives about war, stories about the participants, sometimes factual (e.g., journals) and sometimes fictional, as in Zola or Shakespeare.

Narratives are often personal accounts of life, but they can also reflect society. Most communities and societies have what is called a master narrative, a kind of narrative that permeates the individual narratives of members of the community. If there are conflicting narratives, such as whether we believe it is right or not for the UK to be in the European Union, then these two master narratives may conflict. It is similar when there is a civil war.

Data in the book

The specific data that are used vary from chapter to chapter and vary in the level of analysis that has already been used by others. Much of the data was generated before there was a notion of scientific psychology, and the language used over the centuries has changed fundamentally. The psychologisation of language has only taken place over the last century or so. Veterans now do talk of mental health, PTSD, anxiety, substance abuse, and so on, which in a way makes it easier to understand and interpret what they say. Veterans of earlier conflicts rarely talk about psychological trauma or distress, or they talk about it in a roundabout way. Sometimes we need to look at how others describe the battle scene. This is where the novelist and the playwright have something to say.

Shakespeare seems to have said it all. Through his works, his plays and poems, he has described just about every facet of human behaviour, thoughts and emotions. This includes the emotions of war, as we shall see in a later chapter. Many novelists have written about war. Some of them have experienced it themselves, others have described it without having personal experience, but it is not essential to have personal experience in order to create something meaningful, and this leads back to the argument about the centrality of society, the interactions between people, and how knowledge demonstrates synchronicity and the master narratives we share in society. We all develop an understanding of things beyond our experience because they are written about or they are on the television, radio or Internet. In a way, developing an understanding of something like war is like psychologists piecing together an understanding of behaviour through quantification. A single experiment or TV programme is not enough, but exposure over months and years gives one a type of understanding. There is only one novel used in the book, *La Débâcle*, by Émile Zola (1892/2006), which describes, among other things, the Battle of Sedan, 1870. Zola drew on his skills as a novelist, his experience of the Franco-Prussian War (he was involved in the siege of Paris), interviewing people who took part in the battle and, importantly, he travelled the ground on which the battle took place. This created a deep understanding of the battle. Indeed, by just reading the book it is possible to follow in the footsteps of those who fought there. Zola wrote the book in such a way that only someone who has been to the battlefield could.

Several of the chapters use extracts from diaries and journals. While these are often very information as to what happened (or what the writer wants you to think happened), they are often sparse on the psychology of war. This is partly because psychological language has only really developed since the late nineteenth century, but also partly because soldiers and veterans don't generally talk about the impact of their war. There is also the purpose of the writing, which was often to convey facts about the war rather than feelings. This does not mean the writings are of little use to psychologists. They are still telling us something of value. There are also exceptions, as we shall see in some of the writing from the Civil War and certainly in Shakespeare.

Analysing qualitative data

There are a variety of methods for the analysis of qualitative data and many books and papers that have provided detailed explanations of the philosophy behind the techniques and the practical application of these techniques (e.g., Howitt, 2010 for a good example). For the purposes of this book, which is not an attempt to expound in detail the various approaches used by psychologists and others, the focus will be on basic thematic and narrative analysis. For much of the book, even these are not used in detail, but it is helpful to understand something of the approach to the written word as data.

Thematic analysis

Thematic analysis is the most common form of qualitative analysis used by psychologists. It has been described widely. The most comprehensive account currently is that provided by Braun & Clarke (2006; Clarke & Braun 2013). They propose a system that is similar to many other systems, namely reading the text, extracting appropriate quotations, linking them together and developing themes. These elements are used across most qualitative methods. Braun & Clarke suggest six clear phases of analysis but emphasise that analysis is not a linear process. It is perfectly normal and acceptable to move back and forth between the different phases. The phases are:

1. Familiarisation with the data – reading and rereading, becoming intimately familiar with the material.
2. Coding – selecting appropriate elements of the text and providing it with labels, ensuring that the analysis is not just conceptual, but also semantic, and that there is a sense of the meaning of the selection.

3. Searching for themes – looking for meaningful pattern across the codes, finding ways of linking them together in more coherent common patterns (or themes).
4. Reviewing themes – determining whether the themes tell a coherent story about the data. This involves grouping the data and starting to write up the meaning of each theme, developing a deeper meaning for the analysis.
5. Defining and naming themes – writing a detailed analysis of each theme, identifying its essence, where it belongs in the overall analysis and providing an appropriate name for each theme
6. Writing up – this is integral to the analysis and involves providing an overall narrative that weaves the themes together and provides appropriate examples from the text.

Braun & Clarke provide a useful framework for the analysis of the written word. That is not to say a full analysis is conducted for all data when used in the context of this book. There are examples across the chapters where I simply extract a single quotation to illustrate a point that is being made. On the other hand, sometimes only a complete analysis will enable a deeper understanding of the psychology of war in a specific context. Thematic analysis is useful when considering a narrative analysis.

Narrative analysis

Unlike thematic analysis, narrative analysis does not tend to focus on the individual words and phrases people use, but on the text as a whole. There is no agreed system of conducting narrative analysis, and that is not important for the purposes of this book, but narrative analyses generally focus on how people construct their lives, their self, their identity and their attitudes to life and events (Howitt, 2010). It is about how people see their own reality as they live it. That can mean different things depending on the context, and is part of the explanation of why veterans who write about their experiences in the ways they do. They want to put forward a certain image of themselves, it may be an image that is positive, shows courage in the face of the enemy and so forth, rather than being terrified and wanting to run away from the enemy. In any narrative analysis the audience has to be taken into consideration. If I am writing to a friend, I will probably say things in a different way to when I am writing a book.

Forms of narrative analysis

There are many forms of narrative analysis, but all are involved with developing a better understanding of the process of meaning making or the meanings that have been made by people. For those who are interested, there are useful books and resources for examining the breadth of narrative analysis (e.g., Laszlo, 2008; Andrews et al., 2013; Andrews, 2014). For the purposes of this book, which is not a methods book but only presents this brief outline to provide the reader with an indication of how data were extracted and analysed, we will take a basic approach to understanding the techniques of interest. McAdams (2008) suggests there are six principles which most researchers would agree on, and these are useful to keep in mind when reading this book:

1. The self is storied.
2. Narratives integrate lives and provide a coherent account of the individual *scenes* in the narrative.
3. Narratives are told in social relationships.
4. Narratives change over time.
5. Narratives are cultural texts and reflect the culture and the culture's ways of talking narratively.
6. Some narratives are better than others in that narratives are intrinsically intertwined with morality and that some personal narratives reflect psychologically more healthy lives.

Caution

The methods used in this book rely to a great deal on first-hand accounts, often written with a specific purpose in mind (to make the writer look good, or make someone else look good or bad), and often written years after the event, when a person's narrative may have changed quite dramatically. Over the years people forget the details of events, but many writers pretend to remember the actual words spoken in conversations and the details of what happened across the course of a day, a week or several years. We know that traumatic memories are often imprinted on the mind, but these are usually fragmented, isolated memories of particular parts of a scene. Later, people may attempt to make sense of these memories by filling in the gaps. It is normal; it isn't that people are deliberately lying, but much of this detail may be historically inaccurate. As psychologists, we don't care too much about the inaccuracy of memory if it is helping the traumatised person deal with what happened, but when we are trying to provide an historical account of a battle then we need to proceed with caution, accepting that what people are saying may not be accurate or even close to accurate. Sometimes we are made aware of this through conflicting accounts such as the contested nature of the taking of one of the French eagles at the Battle of Waterloo. The capture of the 105eme Regiment de Ligne was contested by two soldiers, Captain Clark and Corporal Stiles. Both claimed to have captured it, and eventually – against the run of things where the officer generally wins a dispute – Stiles was promoted to sergeant and then to ensign, suggesting that the Regiment accepted his view of the matters, as there were several witnesses attesting to the case (Glover, 2015).

The representation of the *truth* can change over a short period of time, depending on circumstances. Glover (2015) describes how the French newspaper

Le Moniteur changed its stance through the period from when Napoleon escaped from Elba to when he arrived in Paris:

> 10 March: The Corsican ogre has landed at Cape Juan.
> 11 March: The tiger is in Gap. Troops are on their way and will stop him. He will end his miserable adventure as a homeless refugee in the mountains.
> 12 March: The monster succeeded in proceeding to Grenoble.
> 13 March: The tyrant is now in Lyon. Horror has caught the people.
> 18 March: The usurper is some days' march distant from Paris.
> 19 March: Bonaparte approaches in a hurry, but he will not succeed in advancing to Paris.
> 20 March: Napoleon will be in Paris tomorrow.
> 21 March: Emperor Napoleon is in Fontainebleau.
> 22 March: Yesterday evening His Majesty celebrated his arrival in Paris. The jubilation cannot be described.
>
> *(from Glover, 2015, pp. 23–24)*

Another example of how the truth is manipulated according to the author's wishes. Victor Hugo's *Les Miserables* (1862) contains a long account of the Battle of Waterloo. He recognises that most accounts are written from the perspective of the victor – nothing unusual about that – and decided to focus on the individuals (usually French) who stood up for their values. He writes as a novelist, not worrying too much about accuracy. Unfortunately, his account has been represented as truth, and it is only painstaking archaeological work that has demonstrated that he was actually writing as a novelist (and perhaps a propagandist).

Another useful example is the inscription on an information tablet at a viewpoint of the Battle of Agincourt. The information is clearly provided from the French perspective:

> It was eleven in the morning 25th October 1415. Lightly clad, the English archers were more supple in their line of command. Using time well, they dug their stakes into the ground to give even stronger protection and allow them to shoot arrows over the top.
>
> The bugles and trumpets of the French then began their loud calls. Each group was under its own banner, its leader at its head. The well equipped French first succeeded in pushing back the English, but progress was difficult because the ground was muddy. The shooting of the English archers did nothing to reduce the disarray amongst the French ranks.
>
> At the same time the support troops were becoming less orderly, continually pushed on by those behind them. The soldiers were so squashed together that they could barely lift their arms to fight.
>
> The arrows of the English archers badly frightened the horse, the cavalry having been strategically placed on both flanks. The panic amongst the horses did not help morale amongst the soldiers.

> Taking advantage of the situation, the English left their refuge of stakes, taking their swords, axes and other arms, they hurled themselves upon the first French line. This resulted in a tremendous slaughter of the throng. The French being too restricted to reply or defend themselves.

It is helpful to do a little analysis of this document, written of course from the winning (English) side:

1. *The well equipped French.* The French were mostly in full armour, which was very heavy, and while on a horse a soldier was well-protected but once he came off it was difficult to move, and thus he became vulnerable to the archers, who skipped forward and finished them off with their daggers. The armour was also vulnerable to the arrows of the long bowmen. The weight of the armour also meant they were more likely to slip in the mud.
2. *The shooting of the English archers did nothing to reduce the disarray amongst the French ranks.* The wording is excellent. Surely it would have been simpler to write: *the shooting of the English archers caused panic amongst the French ranks?*
3. *The arrows of the English archers badly frightened the horse, … The panic amongst the horses did not help the morale amongst the soldiers.* So the arrows frightened the horses but not the men? I think the men might have panicked and been frightened even if there were no horses on the battlefield.
4. *The soldiers were so squashed together that they could barely lift their arms to fight.* Was this the real reason they lost the battle, or was it that they never had an opportunity to fight because the archers killed them before they could get near the English?
5. The *slaughter of the throng* was largely the result of good discipline among the English archers after the English feint forward had encouraged the French to attack through a bottleneck between the woods. It was a shooting gallery. After one group was killed, the next were slowed down by having to climb over the bodies. While they did this they were killed, and so on. Any wounded were finished off by the archers who presumably had to also retrieve some of their arrows, having shot so many into the thousands of French casualties.

At least they didn't mention Henry's order to kill the French prisoners….

Limitations

As with all analyses there are limitations to what can be achieved when considering accounts written many years ago. The accounts were produced for different reasons, and so may not be *true* at all. A chronicler may be looking after his own health by praising the performance of a king on the battlefield. A diarist might overplay the danger to make himself look good in the eyes of the reader. Someone who tries to write an accurate account is not like Shakespeare, who wrote to entertain the watching and listening public. But with these limitations in mind, I hope we will see over the course of the book that there are consistencies throughout the ages which may suggest reliability, and when we interpret the material through modern theoretical eyes, then hopefully there is some validity too.

3

THE PSYCHOLOGICAL IMPACT OF BATTLE

While the previous chapter has argued that psychological language did not evolve until relatively recently, there is evidence from antiquity regarding the existence of the impact of war. People do not change; they have had the same emotions for thousands of years; it is just that they are described in different ways.

The impact of war is not just about traumatic stress, though that is an important part of the story. There are many other factors involved, including other negative factors such as stress, burnout, the lack of control and difficulties coping; but there are also more positive factors, and veterans will often talk about these, the social support and comradeship, visiting interesting places and getting to know the people. Others talk about how the armed forces provided a better life than they had previously – a family, friends, a roof over their heads. Many like the routine, the learning of new skills, pushing themselves further than they ever would in civilian life. These positive factors are just as important; in modern psychology they are just less written about.

Where do soldiers come from?

Soldiers come from all walks of life and from a range of ages. Increasingly they are both men and women. The actual criteria for selecting soldiers is outside the scope of this book except insofar as soldiers have been selected in different ways across the ages. Many soldiers have at all times been forced into the armed forces. It matters little how this happened, apart from whether this was done either against the person's will (pressed into the forces; in Britain that was very common for the naval forces) or through devious means such as plying the person with alcohol to take the King's shilling. This can be compared to when there was conscription and every able-bodied man (in Britain's case military conscription has always been about men) was liable to be called up into the forces. The latter was seen as acceptable for both World War I and II, with conscription starting in 1916 for World War I and 1938 (before the war actually started) for World War II. Other countries have had different approaches.

If an army is a purely voluntary force, it is more likely to just consist of those people who see themselves as suitable for military activities. What this means will not be considered here, but any form of compulsion will necessarily bring into the forces those people who (a) do not want to be there, and (b) are not suited for the military life. A conscripted force is very different from a voluntary force. The WWII British Army was considered by many to be largely a civilian army.

Another important factor is age. Many people join the armed forces directly from school and stay for a number of years – only a minority will serve more than a decade – so most soldiers are in their 20s. They are young people. This changes for different armies. In World War II, a total war with conscription, anyone up to 40 could be conscripted, and so the armed forces age profile changed significantly. The age factor will impact on what that military force can do. If it involves a lot of marching, someone who is 40 cannot march as far or as fast as someone who is 25, so tactics have to change. Older people may also be more affected by illness and the ability to cope with difficult conditions. Older people are also less reckless. In WWII nearly all RAF bomber crew members were under 25. With a 50% death rate those over 25 were perhaps more aware of their own mortality!

This also works the other way. People who are too young may not yet have the strength or resilience to deal with fighting conditions. This is why most modern armies require their front line troops to be at least 18 years old (some would argue this is too young).

There are other factors of course, but again this book is not about the details of a fighting force, but these matters are included as they may have relevance as we are discussing the various battles in this book.

Psychological factors relating to war

While much of the focus of psychological work has considered the impact of the traumatic experience of war, and the latter part of the chapter will deal with that, it is essential to consider some of the other psychological factors that impact on how a soldier deals with war-related experiences. These factors include comradeship, discipline, training, resilience and leadership. These are in many ways related. For instance, comradeship will increase resilience, as will leadership and discipline. Training and discipline are intimately related. All these factors emerge at different points in the book, often illustrating why a particular battle was successful or not successful.

Before considering these factors, it is worth quoting from Carl von Clausewitz, *On War* (1832). He says:

> War is the province of uncertainty: three fourths of things upon which action in war must be calculated, are hidden more or less in the clouds of great uncertainty. (p. 38)

Comradeship

Most accounts of war written by participants discuss comradeship. In my interviews with World War II veterans, it was a common theme (Hunt & Robbins, 2001b). Veterans described the importance of comradeship, how it was somehow closer than friendship, yet also less close. They described how comradeship develops through living together 24 hours a day, training together, and depending on each other for their lives during battle. Comradeship survived the war, with many stating how they would talk about the war with comrades *down the Legion* but not to people who had not been through similar experiences. There remained an emotional attachment even decades after the war. They also described how comradeship was weaker than friendship. You do not choose your comrades, and it is possible to continue fighting a battle even as your comrades are dying around you.

Comradeship is actively encouraged during training, with individuals learning to function as a team. It is critical to success in battle as soldiers have to implicitly trust one another with their lives. This tends to continue when soldiers become veterans. They will usually have more time for those who have also fought than for civilians. The benefits of this are potentially enormous, with an ex-military *family* always there to care.

Training

Accounts of different wars often show that good training is critical to success in battle. The first aim of training is to develop the coherent team that can work well together. The second is that carrying out tasks repeatedly eventually leads to a conditioned response to orders. This is critical to success in battle, because it is not normal to stand up and walk into machine gun fire or a hail of arrows. The natural response is to run away. Training conditioned responses to various actions ensures that the soldiers will not run away, but will do as ordered. Training should also prepare soldiers for the conditions in which they will find themselves in war and how to respond to unexpected events. Training involves learning how to use equipment. The British Army has always had a good reputation for missile drill. In the Hundred Years War, archers were trained weekly from a young age in the use of the longbow. Effective training required years of practice, developing the appropriate muscles, shooting straight and shooting quickly. It is why we won battles such as Crecy and Agincourt. In the days of muskets, a good infantryman could fire up to four shots a minute, usually in well-disciplined volley fire, which effectively destroyed French columns in the Peninsular War. At the outset of World War I, the Germans thought they were facing machine guns at Mons, when it was really rifle fire. The British infantrymen learned to fire up to 15 rounds a minute. A company of around 100 men would be firing up to 15,000 rounds a minute, the equivalent of three times the rate of the Vickers machine gun if continuously fired. The coverage of the rifle fire could also be greater than that of three Vickers guns.

The other aspect of training that is regularly mentioned in accounts of battle is whether the troops have been sufficiently trained. Poor training is often given as a main cause of why a battle is lost or why a battle is won. At times when there is a need for many soldiers very quickly, an army may expand quickly but there may not be sufficient time to adequately train the troops. Over time this has increased in importance. While the English archers in the Hundred Years War trained for years to be able to shoot the longbow, most soldiers received very little training. Even in the times of the Napoleonic Wars soldiers might receive little training other than how to fire their musket before being sent into battle. Soldiers in the past tended to learn as they went along. With the advent of the twentieth century this was no longer possible. Soldiers needed a greater range of skills before being put into the fight. Everything from training across a range of small arms to discipline and tactics takes time. This is not a problem for a professional army, but it still remains a problem for many of the armies who fight across the world.

Discipline

Discipline is closely linked to training and is developed through training. It is also associated with the conditioned responses already discussed. The key aspect here though is the factors surrounding ill-discipline, when a soldier or soldiers break the rules. What are the punishments? Generally speaking, across history up to fairly recent times, the punishments for disobeyed orders have been very harsh. It was always argued that this was necessary because of the prime importance of obeying orders without question. A failure to obey orders can lead to the loss of a battle, the loss of troops, and so forth. In the British Army, up to the twentieth century, a soldier could be hanged for a range of offences. Until the 1880s, flogging was one form of punishment for offences that didn't warrant hanging. Until the twentieth century there was Field Punishment No. 1 and No. 2, which involved being tied to a gun carriage wheel for a number of hours a day. Soldiers can also be sent to prison for various offences. The problem is that there are not always prisons available on operations, which is why other punishments have been important through the ages. The other difficulty regarding punishment is that an army does not want to lose troops to punishment as that leads to a reduction in strength, which is why there have been field punishments that enable the soldiers to continue with duties. Yet at the same time the punishments are sufficient to – hopefully – put the soldier off committing the crime again or serve as examples to prevent other soldiers from committing it in the first place.

The central role of discipline is to enable troops to continue to act efficiently even under fire. It is a natural urge to run away when threatened with a gun; it is discipline that keeps the soldier in the line. Discipline emerges through practice, whether with drill or tactically. It is continuous practice, repeating the same actions over and over again until they are automatic, until the soldier will repeat the behaviour while under fire or under other threat from enemy forces.

Leadership

In the chapter on the Crimean War, there are several examples of how bad leadership can create problems for the troops. In history, there are many other examples. Leadership at all levels, from non-commissioned officer (NCO) through to generals and politicians, is important. The decisions need to be effective (though not necessarily right), and they have to lead towards victory in some way. The troops need to believe in their leaders. At platoon level the Sergeant tends to be the one who knows the troops best and is liaison between them and the platoon commander, the lieutenant. In World War I the casualty rate for junior officers was higher than that for other ranks as it was expected that they would go over the top in front of their men. There are many accounts through history of ranks up to colonel leading the men into battle. At the higher ranks, the generals and field marshals, there is no expectation that they will be in the heat of the battle, but there is an expectation that they will look after the interests of the men and of the tactics of war. The Crimea is a good example of how that failed both at the commissary level, failing to provide sufficient suitable equipment and food for the men, and at the tactical level, not following through the victory at Alma with an immediate attack on a lightly defended Sevastopol. The Russian generals were no better, issuing conflicting orders at the Battle of Inkerman, ensuring defeat. Dixon's (1976) *On the Psychology of Military Incompetence* examines military inefficiency from the Crimean War onwards, with a large part devoted to bad leadership. Dixon notes that if the troops' main role is the delivering of energy, the main role of the generals is to communicate information. This information must be correct, and it must be transmitted through an effective means. It is difficult to get information correct (note von Clausewitz's comment earlier), and in the past it was often difficult to communicate it as there was a reliance on runners and horsemen. Even in World War II there was a reliance on wire transmission, and around the front line wires were regularly broken, so some of the problems that have been associated with generals lie more in the problems of communication. As we shall see in the chapter on the Crimean War, transmission of information was crucial in sending the Light Brigade charging in the wrong direction, but that was also linked to Raglan's pride and anger at the Russian taking of the British guns and the frustration among the Light Brigade – commanders included – who had not yet been involved in battle.

Resilience

Without resilience, no one would fight in a battle. The strains that soldiers are put under during battle, and often in the days and weeks before, in marching and preparation, are immense. When we think about how so many soldiers do break down as a result of battle, we should perhaps be more surprised that so many do not break down. Most people can continue to fight in a war for weeks, months or years, though it may be argued that there is a U-shaped curve for combat. Initially there are quite a few breakdowns (this is among the troops who cannot put up with any fighting), then for a relatively long period there are very few breakdowns, then the number starts to rise again as soldiers reach their fatigue point, the point at which they cannot continue to fight. This analysis is arguable regarding the length of time people can fight for, the type of fighting, the type of training and preparation, leadership, and so on, but there is a fundamental argument that no matter how resilient someone is, there is always a breaking point.

The soldiers who had fought in the 8th Army with Montgomery in North Africa, and then through the invasions and advances through Sicily and then Italy, were brought home to the UK so that Montgomery could use them again for the Normandy invasion, as he thought they were the best, most experienced troops. Among the men themselves there was a common theme that they had had enough, or that it was someone else's turn. They were fatigued by being in combat so long. They were good soldiers, but even good soldiers have limits.

The best analogy regarding resilience is the tree that bends in the wind. A resilient tree will return to the upright position after the wind stops; but the stressed tree will continue to lean over. Eventually it will be pulled out by its roots, so it is perhaps best not to expose it to too much wind.

Traumatic stress

A lot has been written about traumatic stress and the problems faced by people in war. It is not the place of this book to repeat that information in detail, but it is important to provide a general outline. In modern psychology, post-traumatic stress disorder (PTSD) is considered to be an accurate account of war trauma, but it is not. PTSD provides an outline of many of the key problems (symptoms, diagnostic criteria, and so on), but it does not provide a full account. Hopefully we will see some of what PTSD is missing in this chapter and in the accounts of battle later in the book.

The section provides a concise account of how traumatic stress has been represented in literature, history and elsewhere – including psychology and psychiatry – to show what has been known for a long time. It will also illustrate some of the limitations of PTSD and the need to develop a fuller understanding of the impact of battle. There are numerous accounts of the history of traumatic stress, particularly in relation to war, so this section will be brief, with recommendations to find further information elsewhere (including my previous book, *Memory, War and Trauma*).

A brief history of the psychological impact of battle

The further back in time we go, the more difficult it is to interpret the information we have from battles. Accounts of the psychological impact of battle are relatively rare, and where they do exist they are often ambiguous and short. It is only in modern times that the experiences of the ordinary soldier have become important. Earlier accounts largely – but not solely – focus on key individuals, the generals and politicians involved.

Many of the early accounts relate to myths that may or may not have some element of truth. In the Bible there is a recognition that soldiers may be fearful in battle and that this fear may be transmitted to other soldiers, effectively damaging morale; "Is anyone afraid or fainthearted? Let him go home so that his fellow soldiers will not become disheartened too." (Deuteronomy, 20, 8) The same section shows that the soldiers need external support to help them overcome their fears: "Today you are going into battle against your enemies. Do not be fainthearted or afraid; do not panic or be terrified by them. For the Lord your God is the one who goes with you to fight for you against your enemies to give you victory." (Deuteronomy, 20, 3–4)

The *Epic of Gilgamesh* has a fairly explicit account of what we now see as PTSD. This is perhaps the oldest epic known to mankind (Crocq & Crocq, 2000). In the *Epic*, Gilgamesh loses his friend Enkidu and then experiences fear and nightmares; "Why am I so disturbed…? Why are my muscles trembling? Enkidu my friend, I have had a third dream, this dream surpasses the first two in terror." (Davis, 2014; p. 36) This was originally written by the Mesopotamians around 2100 BCE.

Another early account is of veteran soldiers' dreams – again in Mesopotamia – in 1300–609 BCE (Abdul-Hamid & Hacker Hughes, 2015). These Assyrian texts indicate that soldiers described seeing and hearing ghosts of people they had killed in battle. This is similar to descriptions by modern-day soldiers who have been involved in close combat.

A few hundred years later, in Homer's *Iliad*, written around 800 BCE, Achilles is traumatised by the behaviour of his general and the loss of his friend. Much of the book describes his subsequent actions. The hypothesis that Achilles was traumatised was first proposed by Shay (1991, 1994). Achilles is one of the greatest generals under the overall commander, Agamemnon. His character is undermined by two key factors. First, Agamemnon takes away the woman Achilles has won in battle. This leads to Achilles retiring to his tent, refusing to take part in further battles, and saying that he will be taking his ships and men away from the army – effectively taking his ball home because he is sulking. Second, while he remains in his tent there is a further battle and his friend, mentor (and perhaps lover?) Patroclus is killed in battle. Prior to this action they had protected each other on the battlefield, so Achilles is devastated by the loss, blames himself, feels guilty, and goes into a rage. He returns to the battle, killing Hector, the son of the King of Troy, Priam, and then abuses the body by dragging it around the walls of Troy three times.

The story does not end with Homer's version of events. According to Aeschylus, when Agamemnon (Achilles' general and nemesis in the *Iliad*) returns home he is bereft and broken from 10 years of war away from his home and family. He experiences:

> Why so thick around me now strophe 1 float the fear-storm-clouds that won't depart? Why this armed guard on the doorstep of my heart, this distant doom-chant throb that pounds my brow? How is it that I can't spit out the sour-breath aftertaste of uneasy dream, re-enthrone the simple trust in whatever seems that this darkness felt inside has made me doubt?
>
> *(Aeshchylus, Agamemnon, lines 976–983)*

Sophocles describes how Ajax the Great, after Troy, is driven mad. He goes on a killing spree and then commits suicide:

> In he came, driving lashed together/Bulls, and shepherd dogs, and fleecy prey. Some he beheaded, the wrenched-back throats of some He slit, or cleft their chines; others he bound And tortured, as though men they were, not beasts. [...] Soon he rushed back within the tent, where slowly and hardly to his reason he returned. And gazing round on the room filled with havoc, He struck his head and cried out; then amidst The wrecks of slaughtered sheep a wreck he fell, And sat clutching his hair with tight-clenched nails. [...]now prostrate beneath so great a woe, Not tasting food nor drink, he sits among the sword-slain beasts, motionless where he sank.
>
> *(Socrates, 440 BCE, Ajax)*

Shay, focusing on the *Iliad*, compares the experiences of Achilles and those around him with the experiences of the U.S. troops in the Vietnam War, arguing that while the construct of PTSD describes some of the symptoms experienced by traumatised troops, Homer's *Iliad* goes further. He shows a whole new set of symptoms that diagnostic and statistical manual of mental disorders (DSM) fails to describe (APA, 2013), from pathological grief felt at the loss of Patroclus to running amok or the berserker state (as Achilles does when and after he kills Hector) to the survivor guilt felt by many soldiers whose comrades have been killed.

The analysis of the *Iliad* by Shay is a very good example of how we can draw on literature to help us understand the impact of war. The *Iliad* goes beyond a simplistic individualistic explanation and focuses on the social factors that affect how people behave in war. It is also a good example of how there are universals regarding the impact of war. People's emotions and relationships do not change a great deal across time and culture. Exploring ancient literature can provide significant benefits to modern understanding. Indeed, Shay argued that psychiatrists and others dealing with war veterans should study the *Iliad* to help them get into the minds of traumatised soldiers.

A few hundred years later, Herodotus described an Athenian soldier, Epizelus, who had an hysterical reaction at the Battle of Marathon in 490 BCE as a result of his battle experiences. He was suddenly struck with blindness, though he had not been physically wounded. This blindness continued for the whole of his life. According to Herodotus, Epizelus described seeing a gigantic warrior with a huge beard looming over him, but the giant killed the man at his side (Herodotus, translated by Rawlinson, 1910/1992). This story has similarities to the descriptions by Freud and others from the late nineteenth century through the First World War, where traumatised individuals experienced an hysterical reaction, often a paralysis of arms or legs (see e.g., Horowitz, 2005).

Froissart, the main chronicler of the Hundred Years War between England and France, said that Pierre de Beam could not sleep near his wife and children because he regularly got up at night, took hold of his sword and appeared to fight his enemies (see Crocq & Crocq, 2000).

Several of Shakespeare's plays deal with trauma and the impact of war. This will be discussed in more detail in a later chapter, but one example – keeping the theme of nightmares and sleep – is in *Romeo and Juliet*, Act 1, Scene 4, where Mercurio provides an account of someone's nightmares about battle, and awaking "frighted, swears a prayer or two, and sleeps again."

Around half a century later Samuel Pepys described in his diaries how the great fire of London had an impact on him, causing him to have distressful dreams. Pepys basically described elements of PTSD and the ways he coped with his problems (Daly, 1983). He is demonstrating implicit learning – or fear conditioning:

> 7 Sept 1666: Still hath sleeping and waking had such a fear of fire in my heart, that I took little rest. 28 Feb 1667: I did within these six days see smoke still remaining of the late fire in the City; and it is strange to think how to this very day I cannot sleep a-night without great terrors of fire; and this very night I could not sleep till almost 2 in the morning through thoughts of fire.

There are accounts of trauma among French soldiers in the eighteenth century. This was termed nostalgia. Bentley (2005) said that a French surgeon at the time proposed nostalgia as having three stages: (1) heightened excitement and imagination, (2) period of fever and prominent gastro-intestinal symptoms, and (3) frustration and depression. It was said to occur when men lost all hope of returning home safely, becoming listless, solitary and taciturn, eventually becoming indifferent to everything around them. They would not get better through medication, persuasion or threats of punishment, but the number of soldiers experiencing such problems reduced significantly when France started limiting military service to a fixed number of years. By Napoleonic times it was thought that curing nostalgia was a matter of having sufficient rest, changing daily tasks, having some mode of meaningful instruction, and providing warlike music to uplift their spirits (Jones, 2006).

Most of the previously discussed accounts have focused on the negative aspects of war – what we would now call trauma; but it can be seen that it is not all about describing trauma. There are examples where the reporter is proud of his behaviour, demonstrating heroics and a lack of fear. On the negative side it is not all about trauma, sometimes it is what we might call burnout, simply fighting for too long. This was experienced by many troops during the World Wars.

Perhaps the first school of military psychiatry was set up in Russia shortly after the Crimean War in 1859. The instigator was Ivan Mikhailovich Balinskii, generally known as the father of Russian psychiatry (Wanke, 2005). Balinskii was more concerned about the general incidence of psychiatric problems in the Russian army than psychological trauma resulting from war experience, but it was a start. The notion of nostalgia was still used in the Crimean War, but there is little information about the number of troops suffering from it, nor how they were treated. I shall explore this further in Chapter 10.

During the U.S. Civil War, the term *nostalgia* was still applied. It was estimated that around three in 1000 soldiers in the North suffered from the disorder. The U.S. Surgeon General suggested that the minimum age of a soldier should be increased to 20 to solve the problem, but this made little difference (Jones, 2006). Around 5200 cases of nostalgia were recorded during the U.S. Civil War, along with 2600 cases of insanity; but there were also 160,000 cases of constipation, which may be linked in some or many cases to trauma, or to fear of expected battle – or some other psychological factors relating to war.

Another interpretation of the problem during the same war was that soldiers were suffering from a disorder entitled *soldier's heart*, which was a response to their war experiences (Da Costa, 1871). Da Costa suggested the soldiers were having problems similar to heart disease, but there were no physiological abnormalities. Da Costa studied 300 soldiers, noting that the syndrome developed after a bout of fever or diarrhoea. The soldier generally had problems with a high pulse rate when bending or stooping. A period of rest at a hospital was followed by a return to active duty. The problem then became one of difficulty keeping up with his comrades, being dizzy or out of breath. As the psychological nature of trauma was not yet recognised, *soldiers' heart* may be a physical manifestation of the problem. This is classic burnout. A soldier can only put up with so much. A person in any line of work can only put up with so much. It is very different to traumatic stress. The soldier with burnout is simply too tired to carry on. The experience of trauma can be irrelevant to the soldier who has spent weeks or months living uncomfortably in holes in the ground, or spent weeks marching from one site to another, living on insufficient food.

This idea of a physical problem rather than a psychological one was something that would be debated over the next half century or so, with one side arguing that only men with physical weaknesses would break down in battle; there was little consideration to the idea that someone might break down in battle because they were frightened or traumatised, that the cause was psychological rather than physical. The realisation of the importance of psychology began around the turn of the century and was more or less accepted by the end of the First World War – at least by most authors.

For most of history, the idea that someone would be frightened in battle was considered shameful, so it is not surprising that psychological trauma was often put down to a pre-existing physical weakness.

Psychiatrists first went to war to support troops in the Russo-Japanese War (Wanke, 2005), which took place 1904–1905. Traumatised soldiers were treated both near the front lines and when they returned home from the war (Richards, 1910). Richards also noted that those who were sent home generally did not return to active duty. When this was noticed by the soldiers the number of psychiatric casualties increased enormously. This would again be noted during the Second World War, when U.S. psychiatric casualties were returned home with the physically wounded after action in North Africa, rarely to return to combat.

The conflict where we learned a lot about the psychological effects of war was the First World War, where psychiatrists on all sides were trying to establish the nature of soldiers' responses to battle. In terms of war trauma or shell shock there are many excellent accounts of what we learned in the First World War (e.g., Leese, 2002; Shepherd, 2002; Barham, 2004; Grogan, 2014) but here I will present a brief outline.

The term *shell shock* was introduced by Myers (1915), describing three cases of soldiers psychologically affected by their experiences. These were disparate, and as further cases were investigated it became clear that there was a range of problems experienced, not a single disorder. Several people attempted to establish the cause of these problems. Mott (1919) thought it was a form of concussion caused by the blast of a shell (literally shell shock). Long after the war, Myers (1940) thought there was a psychological cause, as there was little evidence for many shell shock victims to be near exploding shells when they experienced their symptoms. He thought of it as a conversion disorder experienced by soldiers who were unable to cope with combat. Shell shock was a form of dissociation, with the splitting of the traumatic memory from consciousness. Jones, Vermaas, McCartney et al. (2003) noted that though shell shock had some features in common with post-traumatic stress disorder (PTSD), such as startle reaction, distressing recollections, difficulty concentrating and nightmares, it was not the same disorder by another name.

There has been much discussion about the relationship between the disorders in WWI and later defined disorders such as PTSD. There are undoubtedly similar symptoms across all these trauma-related disorders, as shown by Jones et al. These are likely to be the universal characteristics of any trauma-related response. It is the other symptoms that are more problematic. In World War I many soldiers had a hysterical reaction to their experiences. Mott (1919) argued that officers and other ranks had different reactions to combat stress, claiming that officers were more likely to experience pure shell shock (whatever that might be) and other ranks were more likely to show hysterical paralysis, usually of the legs. There are a number of videos available on YouTube that show these cases in hospital in Devon. The symptoms range from an inability to walk to disjointed walking. If other ranks were more likely to display these symptoms while officers displayed more classic PTSD-type symptoms, then we do need to ask why.

The answer may not relate to the psychological make-up of the different ranks, nor the higher level of education received by most officers – particularly as in the later years of the war many officers had risen through the ranks and had not received anything beyond a primary education. It may be related to general intelligence; indeed, PTSD may have a negative correlation with IQ. However, this probably is not sufficient to explain the variety of disorders experienced during World War I and how the problems have become more focused in later years, i.e., most people are now diagnosed with PTSD rather than other trauma-related problems, though that is perhaps because it is virtually the only option, unless other DSM diagnostic categories are used such as anxiety, depression or substance abuse.

We should look to social and cultural factors to explain the wide range of disorders, and how there were perhaps class-related differences. Before World War I the classic stereotypes were strongly held about personal moral responsibility for health, both mental and physical. Throughout the war that emphasis remained, with medical personnel emphasising the importance of a man displaying a personal commitment and the will power to recover (Reid, 2010). There were programmes indicating the links between mental health and physical fitness. "All great military leaders from Napoleon to Kitchener have been men of great nerve force and a compelling personality… The neurasthenic on the other hand is literally foredoomed to failure." (*The Times*, March 1915, cited in Reid, 2010, p. 15) There was an understanding that the upper classes were more able to display such will power, while the working classes were less able. This is of course a misconception, but there are elements of truth, as working people were often undernourished and unfit as a result of the way society failed to look after those less well off. Undernourished people are intrinsically unhealthy, both physically and mentally, so it is not surprising that some may be susceptible to mental fatigue in times of war.

At this point there were also few cultural references to psychological trauma. The works of Freud were known by a few – again the educated classes were more likely to be aware of him – and mental breakdown in war was an expression of the unknown for most people, who had never experienced anything like battle. If we categorise the reactions to a traumatic event as either universal or cultural, then we need to establish what those universals are, and research findings are ambiguous. Jones et al. (2003) found, as we have seen, some common features between World War I symptoms and PTSD, but it is not clear that they are universal. They also tested one particular symptom, namely flashbacks, among groups of UK servicemen from 1854 on and found that they were more common in veterans of the 1991 Gulf War and were absent from veterans of the Boer War and World Wars I and II.

The only symptom that appears to be relatively universal are nightmares and sleeping problems. These are described in accounts throughout history, including descriptions by authors from Homer to Shakespeare and Dickens.

If people do not have a cultural model for psychological trauma then they are going to present with a wide range of symptoms, perhaps partly reflecting their own experiences, thoughts and feelings. The hysterical paralysis symptom makes sense if a soldier perceives, perhaps unconsciously, that if they are physically disabled, they cannot go back to war. This also makes sense morally, as being traumatised is seen as morally reprehensible. A similar argument can be made relating to how many soldiers found themselves unable to speak. People who write or tell about war will often say that it is unspeakable, indescribable. All these soldiers are doing is demonstrating this through a physical disability.

Throughout the war there was a clash of classes, with those diagnosed with neurasthenia seen in a more positive light than those with physical hysteria – and of course officers were more likely to be diagnosed with neurasthenia (though originally it was seen as a working class disorder), as it was inappropriate to accuse them of malingering or suggest that they had low intelligence or a poor education.

Out of the millions of men who fought we have accounts of thousands who experienced war trauma, leaving an almost total lack of understanding of the vast majority of men who fought through the war. There are numerous accounts from people who were not (apparently) traumatised, but again they are a drop in the ocean. We simply know very little about most participants. Medical records, beyond the recognised individuals with war trauma, tell us very little. We still need to explore the records post-war to determine whether we can find out anything else about war-related impact on health, though it will be difficult at this point to prove that something on a medical record (usually rather sparse information) relates to a wartime experience or consequence of such an experience.

Presumably, most soldiers got through the war with relatively few ill-effects, or they were affected in ways in which they (or their families and friends) could handle. What we do not know is how many took the effects of the war into their post-war lives, perhaps through the way they were with others, with their wives and children, or their workmates. There is evidence that the impact of war can pass through generations, but most of this research has been conducted in relation to survivors of the Nazi genocide (e.g., Danieli, 1998) rather than on the impact of the ordinary soldier on others. If we look at the newspapers from the 1920s, there is ample evidence that ex-soldiers who were brought to court often – rightly or wrongly – used shell shock as a defence. There is also evidence of an increase in the suicide rate among ex-soldiers as compared to other groups, but relatively little else that we can use now to interpret what was happening in the 1920s.

On the positive side, we have little information or evidence relating to the positive side of fighting in the war. Soldiers learned discipline, which would be of benefit in later civilian life, perhaps for many increasing their chances of success in life. There could be similar positive effects relating to the people met in war, or the places where a person travelled. It was the first opportunity many people had to get away from their home town or village, from the job they were expected to do, and so many would take the opportunity to do something different. The problem is, much of this is speculation, as the evidence is weak.

As World War II approached, the men of the generation who fought in World War I were now the fathers of those who would fight in the next war. We know little of their views, or the views of mothers who may have lost a husband and might now be in danger of losing a son.

This phenomenon has been expressed in terms of masculinity because for most people it was the men who went to fight. Nevertheless, in increasing numbers, through both World War I and World War II, women were actively involved. In many countries the women took over the jobs the men had been doing. In some they fought alongside male soldiers. In many they were the victims of attack by the opposing forces, whether from air or land. Many British women in World War I became voluntary nurses, often caring for the wounded in range of enemy artillery shells. In World War II they manned (sic) the anti-aircraft guns around the country.

With regard to dealing with war trauma, by World War II most of what had been learned in World War I had been largely forgotten. There were very few psychiatrists in the British Army, nor were there many in either France or Germany, the key protagonists at the outset. Germany would go through the war with very little recognition of war trauma, and many sufferers were shot for cowardice. The French were out of the war very quickly, and so the subject hardly has relevance, apart from the notion that one of the reasons the French were defeated so quickly in 1940 was that they – as a country – remained traumatised by the destruction and death associated with World War I. In a societal or cultural sense, they could not go through the experience of the trenches again. While the British had similar experiences of the trenches, they were not on British soil and, in 1940, there were relatively few British troops in France, so they were unable to stop the German attack in May 1940 without assistance.

A large part of the British forces ended up being evacuated from Dunkirk. It was in the aftermath of this that the troops were spotted by a British psychiatrist, William Sargant, as they marched away from the ships. He noticed that many displayed signs of traumatic stress, and realised that the British Army was in need of psychological assistance in order to treat those mentally affected by their experiences (Sargant & Slater, 1944). Over time, the military psychiatric service was built up in Britain and was largely effective during the war. Unlike World War I, no British soldier was (officially) shot for cowardice when the problem may have been war trauma.

Constructing post-traumatic stress disorder

This brief history of trauma ends by showing how psychologists and psychiatrists developed the construct of PTSD from research into war experience – particularly the experiences of the U.S. troops in the Vietnam War, and how that construct has developed over the years and been extended to cover not only war trauma, but other forms of traumatic experiences such as rape or sexual abuse, disaster, and unexpected death.

While military psychology does focus on psychological aspects of battle, improving the efficiency of soldiers and trying to reduce the impact of trauma, other aspects of the consequences of war experience are largely forgotten. The benefits of soldiering, those aspects mentioned previously in relation to World War I, the meeting of different people, the discipline, the learning skills, and so on, has been largely ignored by psychologists and others, while the focus is ever-increasingly on PTSD.

Deconstructing PTSD

We have already seen there are problems with PTSD as a construct relating to war trauma, and these will arise repeatedly through the book. The construct does not equate to war trauma. One problem is the debate over the first criterion, Criterion A, which describes the traumatic event. It is highly unusual to have a mental health condition defined by an external event. What is particularly difficult is that this external event and its impact are not well-described in PTSD. There is no definitive list of what can constitute a traumatic event. What is traumatic for one person is not traumatic for another. The criterion describes the event as focusing on death or the threat of death, but it takes no account of individual perceptions of what the threat of death might actually mean, and how someone (perhaps someone who is nervous) may be more likely to perceive a threat of death than another (APA, *DSM-V*, 2013). There are serious problems of comorbidity, with many people diagnosed with PTSD also receiving other diagnoses such as depression or substance abuse (Foa, 2009). Many experiences relating to trauma are not well-described in PTSD, such as the feelings of survivor guilt when others have died, the hatred felt for an enemy, or the fatigue of constant battle or constant alertness in case of battle.

This highlights the need to have a more detailed and complex construct of psychological trauma, taking into account not only the personal, but also the social and the cultural; along with individual differences (i.e., providing a justification for the book).

4

MEMORIALISATION, REMEMBRANCE AND COMMEMORATION

Memory and history

People have always remembered battles and wars. They are important to individuals and they are important to society. They transform both. For many societies in the past, the knowledge – the narrative – would be handed down orally and gradually shifted, changed and eventually forgotten or turned into myth over the generations. Battles are often key experiences of people's lives, so it is important for societies to remember them, to commemorate them, certainly during the person's lifetime. How much this matters once the participants are dead is another matter.

In the past, remembrance was largely an elite practice, with the masses, those who actually fought, having little involvement. In the West it wasn't until the nineteenth century that this started to change. Throughout most of history, soldiers who died in battle were buried in mass graves at the site of battle or left for the animals. Officers might be lucky to have an individual burial. For instance, when General Crauford was killed at the siege of Ciudad Rodrigo in 1812 he was buried under the wall where a breach had been made and a plaque bearing his name was placed there. At the Battle of the Alma in the Crimean War, there is still a memorial site, which contains the graves of the first British officers killed in Crimea, complete with carved commemorative plaques indicating their names. There is no such memorial for the ordinary soldiers who are buried there.

For Europeans, it was the First World War that led to the introduction of individual graves for all the soldiers and gravestones carved with their names.

While memorialisation, remembrance and commemoration will be considered in the light of specific battles in the book (particularly Waterloo and Ypres), this chapter provides a general discussion of the importance of memory regarding war and the relationship between memory and history. This has implications for the role of commemoration in the contemporary world and the role it plays in societies, with particular consideration of the problems associated with commemoration in the United Kingdom beginning with World War I. A note on terminology: By *remembrance* we are referring to how a society (not an individual) remembers war, usually – but not always – a specific war. By *memorialisation* we are referring to the objects created to help people remember, whether these are the familiar war memorials of World War I, the Allied and German cemeteries of the same war in Northern France and Belgium (and across the world) or the growing number of memorials on the Internet. By *commemoration* we are referring to the events that take place in relation to remembrance (often at the site of a memorial).

The importance of memorialisation of the World Wars continues in the UK. It is only relatively recently (2001) that the National Memorial Arboretum (NMA) was opened in Staffordshire to commemorate – mostly – the world wars. It may seem a little odd to open a large-scale new memorial site to wars that took place a long time ago, with even the Second World War almost out of living memory, but the visitor figures (the second most visited tourist attraction in Staffordshire after Alton Towers a few years ago) indicate it serves some sort of need.

A series of inter-disciplinary seminars, organised by the Chief Executive, Charlie Bagot-Jewitt, historian Maggie Andrews and myself were conducted at the NMA to try and address some key questions regarding remembrance, such as: Is the phenomenon a modern Western approach to understanding war or is it universal among human culture? How does remembrance relate to core human emotions? What role do events at memorial sites play in society and for individuals? Whether we answered any of these questions successfully is up for debate, but the seminars did generate wide-ranging publications on the topic, in the form of a book, *Lest We Forget* (Andrews, Bagot-Jewitt & Hunt, 2011a) and a special issue of the *Journal of War and Cultural Studies* (Andrews, Bagot-Jewitt & Hunt, 2011b).

A chapter that I contributed to *Lest We Forget* (Hunt, 2011) focused on memorialising the Spanish Civil War, specifically the area around the Ebro – the 1938 battle is discussed later in the book – and the changing sense of memorialisation in the area. Memorialisation is difficult after a civil war, as it is usually the victors who are able to construct commemorative monuments to the war and its participants, and they generally focus on the victorious side. This was the case after the Spanish Civil War. The biggest monument to the war is the mausoleum for General Franco in Valle de los Caidos ('Valley of the Fallen') north of El Escorial in the Sierra de Guadarrama near Madrid. The monument covers 13.6 km^2 in the mountains at nearly 1000 m. It consists of a basilica, a guest house and a towering 150 m high cross erected on a granite outcropping over the basilica esplanade. It is visible from miles away. It took nearly 20 years to build, a lot of the labour being Republican prisoners. Although forced labour was banned, Franco allowed convicts (including many Republican prisoners convicted of fighting against the state) to choose voluntary work at the site, redeeming two days of the conviction for each day worked. Incredibly, the law was in force until 1995, 20 years after Franco's death. At one point the redemption scheme was *improved* to six days with the possibility of the convict's family benefiting from the housing and schooling scheme provided in the valley for other workers.

Franco's grave, along with that of the founder of the Falange movement, Jose Antonia Primo de Rivera, is deep inside the Basilica, underground. The basilica itself is larger than St Peter's basilica in Rome. There are around 40,000 people who died in the civil war buried in the valley itself – Fascists rather than a representative group across all sides, which puts the lie to Franco's idea that the site would be one of reconciliation.

The site is strongly contested. It is run by Patrimonio Nacional, a Spanish government heritage agency, though inside it does appear to be guarded by Falangists to ensure that no one desecrates Franco's grave. It was closed briefly in 2009 by the socialist government, who claimed safety issues. Indeed, when I visited some years before that, much of the building appeared to be in a very bad state of affairs. There were strong complaints against the closure, and it reopened in 2012. Jauma Bosch, a Catalan politician complained that it was very similar to a Nazi concentration camp and should not be used as a site of pilgrimage for neo-Fascists; although since 2007, the Historical Memory Law in Spain has meant that pro-Franco political rallies are banned from the valley. It also suggested that it should be re-designated as a monument to democracy, and to contain a memory centre regarding the war, but it is unlikely to function as this given its association with Franco and the Fascists. As I write (late 2018) the decision has been made to remove Franco's body and that of Primo de Rivera from the basilica to a place of their families' choosing. Attempting to turn the place into a national memorial site is likely to be very difficult given its past and the way it was built. It is further complicated by the basilica being a church, and so any changes would require the Catholic church's permission.

Spain remains problematic regarding memorialising the civil war in other ways. It is only since around the 1990s that they have started to put up memorials to the Republicans who were killed. The Ebro is a good example. The International Brigadiers placed a memorial in the mountains near Gandesa that the Fascists never found through the Franco years. Other monuments to the battle were always Fascist, celebrating their victory. It is only in the last 20 years or so that an interpretation centre has opened in Corbera del Ebro, along with a series of monuments around the battlefield, indicating what happened in various places. There is a route to travel via these monuments (see Chapter 13). The ruins of Corbera del Ebro, abandoned after the war when the new town was built lower down on the hill, has also received a number of plaques, including displays in the ruined church. Fascists might argue that the monumentalisation and memorialisation has now gone the other way, focusing on the Republic, and they are at least to some extent right, because the country as a whole is anti-Fascist, but that demonstrates the difficulty of being fair with memorials. They always depict something of one side or the other, rather than a balance between all participating forces.

A good example of that is the Armistice Day events in the UK. The service at the Cenotaph in London and those throughout the country focus very much on British (and Empire/Commonwealth) losses. Even a century after World War I we are apparently unable to commemorate the losses of all sides in that arguably pointless war, fought for the benefit of politicians' and monarchs' egos. Perhaps that is one reason why there are so many anti-Europeans in the UK. They cannot see that we ought, as a European entity, be commemorating the losses on all sides. Why is a British young man to be remembered more than a German young man? Neither are responsible for the war, and we are all Europeans. Those who are responsible for the war get statues in prominent places, when perhaps those are the ones we should be condemning.

Commemoration changes – or should change – over the years. After World War I, the British ceremonies were very large-scale, with many veterans, families, widows and others attending. It was considered important that monarchs and politicians took part. Then came World War II, and for a time the ceremonies became less popular, growing in interest again as the World War I veterans got old and the Second World War veterans entered middle age. By the 1990s, interest was waning, as would be expected when most of the veterans were dead or in old age. The ceremony would probably have died a natural death within a few years of the last of the World War II veterans dying. It is, after all, a very old fashioned service, one more suited to the days of empire rather than the twenty-first century. It came back in the early twenty-first century, when the UK was involved in very unpopular wars in Iraq and Afghanistan. The government saw the Remembrance Day service as a means of getting the public back on side with the armed forces, and it worked very well. Add in the factor of the centenary of World War I and the services are again popular – and unchanged from the days of empire.

The ceremony was designed by middle class white British males for middle class white British males who were militaristic, royalist and Christian. Whatever the benefits or otherwise of multiculturalism (and there are both), the ceremony looks very odd in modern Britain. It is very Christian and very conservative.

No one now remembers anyone who died in World War I, but we continue with the service as though we do. The words are explicit: "At the going down of the sun and in the morning we shall remember them." Really? No, we shall not, because they were dead before we were born. We can read names on gravestones, or on the website of the Commonwealth Graves Commission. We can carry out historical research into members of a family or a community that died. That is all interesting work; but it is not remembering them. We have no emotional connection even with members of our own family who died during that war.

2 up 2 down

We have emotional connections with relatively few of our relatives. We usually remember our grandparents and our parents; we have concern for them or fond memories of when they were alive. We are the same with our children and grandchildren. With some significant exceptions we best know those people who are two generations removed from us (hence 2 up 2 down). We are concerned for the well-being of our children and our children's children, but we are not particularly concerned about those that will be born after them (if it were otherwise, perhaps we would look after the planet a little better), unless we are lucky enough to become great grandparents. We are the same with past generations. The reality is that we are concerned about those who we know or knew; but we don't have emotional attachments to people we did not know. I had family who fought in World War I. At least one died. I am interested in his experiences and who he was, but I have no emotional attachment so I would not cry at his grave (if he had one; he has no known grave – he was blown up somewhere around Sanctuary Wood).

This is why 2 up 2 down is a good explanation for the emotional attachments we have with family. It is the generations we generally know. We could also add in 2 across (though it is getting a little like a crossword), meaning that we are emotionally attached to siblings, and also to cousins (if we know them), but not really beyond that, because we tend not to know them. We even call them *distant* cousins. Particular individuals can argue that there are more distant relatives they are attached to, and if they know them that may be the case, but it does not invalidate the general theory that our emotional connections are generally no more than two removed in any direction.

2 up 2 down is one reason why there is a problem with the commemorative procedures that take place in November each year. By using the term *remembering* we are pretending to know people we do not know. We pretend to remember them, but we do not remember them. This is not an argument against remembrance, but against the fake remembrance and fake remembrance service we use in the UK.

One societally recognised piece of evidence relates to the purchase of a grave. We tend to buy or rent a grave plot for a period of around 60 years. After that, the site reverts to the control of the authorities. It works differently around the world, but it is a general principle. After 60 years, there are very few people left who remember the person who died. After 60 years, the person who does remember them must have been both young and remembering an old person. In Spain and other countries many cemeteries are graves in clusters above the ground. The body is sealed in a concrete box and remains there until the cemetery is full. The remains are then removed to a nearby boneyard, and the space is available for the next corpse. Again, the system works because the remains are not removed until those who remembered the person are usually dead.

The logical extension to the 2 up 2 down proposal is to consider whether we should remove the World War I cemeteries across the world. If no one remembers the people in the graves then perhaps they should revert back to the farmers. It is a logical argument that applies to other graves, so why not war graves? There would be a massive outcry if this happened, but that is not because we remember the dead, it is because we have built a culture of remembrance around the dead of World War I – even to the extent that we focus on them rather than the far larger number of people who died in World War II. But of course in the UK fewer died in World War II – and we are not concerned with remembering the dead of other countries.

The narrative of remembrance, at least in the UK, is a static narrative. It is not allowed to evolve and develop because to change it would – to many people – be in some way disrespectful. This is an unusual narrative. Normally things change and develop as society and people change and develop. Our cars look very different to how they were 20 years ago. Our furnishings have fundamentally changed. Some changes are cosmetic, relating to fashion, others are technological. We have learned better ways of making things. Why do we have this unusual fixed narrative regarding remembrance that no one can or dare change?

If one problem with the Armistice Day remembrance service is that we are attempting to remember people we do not remember, another problem is the relevance of the ceremony itself. The service has changed little from the first service that took place after World War I. It is a service based on militarism, the British Empire, monarchy and the Christian god. How relevant is this in a country that is not militaristic, does not have an empire, has a monarchy that exists to fill the pages of *Hello* magazine and – perhaps most importantly – is a culture characterised by secularism and multiculturalism? If the remembrance service is to be retained – and there is good justification for some sort of event to commemorate those who died in more recent wars who have surviving family and friends – then it needs radical updating to account for the disparate views held by modern day Britons.

Memory and history

Remembrance and commemoration lose much of their meaning once the participants and their immediate families are dead, and so it is time to move on. Everyone who took part in World War I is now dead. There is no one alive who remembers somebody who died in World War I. The war is now history, the psychological element has lost its personal touch and it could be argued that continuing to *remember* in this way is an unhealthy obsession by society. Indeed, it could be argued that *remembrance* of something we do not remember is a kind of cultural disorder, a fixation on the past in – at least in this case – an unchanging manner that works to the detriment of modern society and to the detriment of those who are remembering members of their families who have died in more recent conflicts. We should perhaps focus more on the history and heritage of World War I. The memory of that war has become history.

If you want to remember Tommy Atkins, you don't need a rock in a field to do so. There are records galore across the Internet and in libraries.

Remember the living

On a final note, the obsession with *remembering* the dead of a war that is forgotten can mean that we forget to remember those still living who have been affected by war, those wounded physically and psychologically by their experiences. Add in those who were not wounded but who have difficulties living in civil society, perhaps because they cannot adapt to civilian life, and there are massive unmet needs. These people still live in society; so instead of the continual fixation on the long dead, we should take more time to consider the needs of the living and those who died in living memory.

5

THE LANDSCAPE OF BATTLE

After the Battle of Sedgemoor in 1685, King James II, whose armies defeated the rebels but who was not himself present at the battle, visited the battlefield in order to better understand the terrain over which it was fought. From this, and from the accounts of participants, he produced an account of the battle, even though he had not fought at it, that was undoubtedly improved because he had visited the battle site.

A great general will always take care to ensure that he fights where he chooses, when he chooses and with whom he chooses. The landscape is critical in this. One of the most famous examples of this working effectively was Wellington's decision at Waterloo to control the higher ground and to order the infantry to lie down in the dead ground behind the top of the ridge south of the village of Waterloo so that the French would not see them and so would not be prepared for them. Napoleon had little idea about the extent of the allied forces facing him, though he had just fought battles with both the English and the Prussians, which weakened him. He thought he was facing fewer troops than he expected, and that made him overconfident. Wellington's tactic was also perhaps why Wellington was never defeated by the French throughout the Peninsular campaign – to which I will return in a later chapter.

If we are to understand the role landscape plays in battle then we need to think a little about military tenets, about the thoughts that go into any battle. Most of the book focuses on the individual, on individual units, and on how command decisions were made on the battlefield, but there are some general ideas that apply across most or all battlefield situations.

The U.S. Army has a series of tenets and principles of war (*Army Field Manual*, 2001). These are useful when trying to understand battle. There are five tenets: (1) Initiative – the ability to determine the terms of battle, (2) Agility – the ability to react faster than the enemy, (3) Depth – the extension of operations in time, space, resources and purpose, (4) Synchronisation – the ability to focus resources at the right time and place, (5) Versatility – the ability to meet diverse challenges, change focus, and move between missions and forces effectively. From these tenets emerge nine principles of war: (1) Direct every operation towards a clearly defined, decisive and attainable objective, (2) Offensive operations are the means by which a force seizes and holds the initiative while retaining freedom of action and achieving decisive results, (3) Mass the effects of overwhelming power at the decisive time and place, (4) Judiciously employ forces, (5) Place the enemy at a disadvantage, (6) seek unity of command, (7) Do not permit the enemy to gain the advantage, (8) Strike the enemy in a manner for which they are unprepared, (9) Prepare clear, uncomplicated plans and concise orders.

It is helpful to think of these tenets and principles when exploring a battlefield and thinking about how well they were applied by each side.

We could go much further and start thinking about military strategy, but that is beyond the scope of this book. There is one further area of military thinking that is important in relation to terrain, and this is known as OCOKA (Collins, 1998). This acronym stands for Observation and fields of fire, Cover and concealment, Obstacles, Key terrain, and Avenues of approach. If you are going to walk a battlefield and begin to use the landscape to understand that battlefield, then OCOKA is very important to understand (Scott & McFeaters, 2011). Key terrain refers to a locality that affords an advantage to the side which controls it (e.g., a hill). Observation is about what can be seen from a given point. Generals always want good observation points, such as Raglan at the Sapoune Heights in Crimea, or Wellington on the ridge at Waterloo or on his hillock at Salamanca. Cover and concealment is protection from both enemy fire and observation. Obstacles can refer to man-made or natural obstacles, things that delay or divert movement. Finally, avenues of approach are features that allow an attacking force to reach the enemy.

These factors all help interpret the battlefield. Inevitably, battlefields are fought over by people, and people make mistakes. There are also two sides, so the decisions made by one side affect the decision making of the other. The previously mentioned rules are ideals. They are rarely fully kept to because battles are fought by two sides each trying to out-manoeuvre the other and by fallible people. Landscape is not an objective factor, but a subjective one, the perceptions of which affect decision making and ultimately the outcome of a battle.

Landscape is not in itself enough. In order to understand past battles we need to link the landscape with historical interpretation and with accounts written by participants and witnesses.

If someone wants to understand a battle, they will do so better by visiting the battlefield if possible. There are many reasons to do so, from examining the area in terms of military terrain and all that entails, to the experience of walking where people fought, drawing together the historical, psychological, cultural, geographical, psychogeographical and other reasons that help us understand battle. If one has not experienced war, one cannot gain such experience through going to a battlefield, but the understanding will be greater than if one does not visit.

Imagination

There is often a sense of wonder at a battlefield site that you have previously researched, perhaps an *aha* moment of realising that actually looking at the battlefield provides a far more profound view than simply perusing a map at home. On the battlefield itself you can work out whether, how and when the opposing troops could see each other, how a particular observation point served the commander well or badly, where the dead ground is, and a host of other factors that can only be partly seen through maps, drawings and photographs. The effects differ according to whether we are looking at a modern battlefield, which is often much larger than an ancient battlefield, and may still contain the detritus of battles, from bunkers and concrete emplacements, to tanks and guns – not forgetting memorials. Older battlefields are often just fields, many looking very different to how they did at the time of the battle. It requires extra effort to determine what happened on the day of the fighting, not only because there are few if any remains, but because we have far fewer details of older battles than we do of battles of the last couple of centuries. Sometimes we need to rely more on the imagination, envisioning what might have happened. This is where we move beyond history and memory to myth, to realising that the novelist might have a more psychologically useful (even if not strictly accurate) perspective of what happened than the historian. It is up to us as individuals to determine whether we need some sense of truth of what happened, or whether the narrative of the partial imagination provides an acceptable alternative. We can also see the battle from the perspective of those who fought in it. Accounts vary, with some providing detailed information of the landscape and others providing few such details. Furthermore, there are cases when we are not sure where the battlefield is, or we may be wrong about it, as in the case of the Battle of Bosworth.

For those who have not experienced war it takes an imaginative leap to put yourself in the position of the people who fought in the battle. Whether you are reading first-hand accounts, historical analyses, or historical fiction, you are bringing together your historical knowledge about the events of the battle, so you know something of the dispositions and movements of the contenders. Your knowledge helps provide a bird's eye view of the battle, the commanders' stratagems, how these played out and the final consequences. For a fuller understanding you need an understanding of the socio-cultural circumstances of the time, what life was like for people living then; not just the warriors, but the people generally. What did they eat? How did they live? What were relationships like between the different classes? Were the soldiers full-time troops or did they join up or were forced to join up for a particular period, campaign or battle? How well trained were they? The archers of the Hundred Years War practiced archery every week from when they were children at the local butts. That doesn't mean they were good soldiers, just that they were good archers. Shooting an arrow into a fixed target is not the same as shooting an arrow into the armour of a French knight. In World War II, Marshall found that relatively few U.S. troops fired at the enemy. This was later improved by using human-shaped targets.

The circumstances leading up to battle are important. For instance, Harold's troops before the battle with William in 1066 were very tired after fighting against Tostvig at Stamford Bridge and then marching all the way to the south coast to meet William's army. No wonder the Saxons lost. It was difficult in a similar way for the French troops who fought at the Battle of Sedan in 1870. They had marched backwards and forwards for weeks before being attacked in the cauldron (*Kessel* in German, a concept favoured particularly in World War II, and British police in the modern day!) of Sedan. They were too tired and hungry to fight well, and their morale was low after so much marching.

Then there is the weaponry involved. Did the soldiers have long range weapons, which usually implies a larger battlefield? In Normandy in 1944, the Allied battleships off the coast fired their heavy guns inland to Caen and beyond, sometimes 20 miles. Modern ordnance can be fired from drones piloted from the safety of another continent. Archers could shoot a couple of hundred metres. Spears can only be thrown a few 10s of metres. Missiles determine the size of a battlefield in as important a way as the number of troops involved on each side. In pitched battles involving several 10s of thousands of troops, such as some of the battles of the Napoleonic wars, a battlefield could be one or two square miles. For battles involving hundreds of thousands – sometimes millions – of troops, the battlefield can encompass whole regions, such as Moscow, Stalingrad or Normandy.

While weaponry changes, people do not. They have always been frightened, excited and bored by war. Being at the site of the battle with at least some of the above information enables a better understanding.

The landscape

Landscape plays a critical role in our lives. We like to look at and experience mountains, hills, meadows, rivers, and so on. There is a fundamental pleasure derived from such sights. This is why so many painters and photographers provide those of us who cannot always get out into the landscape with pictures to hang on our walls. The landscape is relaxing. To walk in the landscape, to *get away from it all* is something many of us crave and do.

The landscape is not just the countryside. We observe landscape in towns and cities. Architecture is part of the landscape, as are roads and railways. There is a complex blend of individual elements that make up any landscape.

Archaeologists play a key role in understanding the landscape. By identifying remains on and under the battlefield, by exploring the surface remains, they provide a great deal of information about a particular battle, not only about who was where, but sometimes also about troop movements and activities during the battle itself (e.g., from the positioning of arrowheads in the ground or the location of trenches or bunkers). But this is all relatively new. It is only in the last few years that advances in technology have provided new tools, enabling archaeologists to challenge previous ideas and expand the field of conflict archaeology. Scott & McFeaters (2011) argue that it is only now that we are reaping the benefits of these new tools, methods and theoretical approaches to scientifically study conflict sites. These studies are likely to have profound effects on our understanding of battlefields, particularly older battlefields where we rely on often unreliable accounts written at the time or later. The archaeological record is not meant to supplant what we know from historical and oral sources, but to provide an independent line of research that challenges or supports what we already know.

Walking in the landscape

There are myriad benefits of walking in the landscape. There is evidence from psychological work that walking in the landscape provides significant benefits such as reducing depression and relieving anxiety. People have always – at least since the industrial revolution which took many of us away from the countryside – used the countryside and walking in it as means of getting away from the strains of work.

The benefits of walking

Ample research suggests there are benefits to walking, but here we are not concerned with the health benefits of going for a walk, though walking is of course a healthful activity. There is a growing number of researchers who propose that walking interviews are beneficial, not only for a person's health, but also for the kinds of information that can be generated from the interview, with qualitatively better and more information generated depending at least to some extent on the landscape through which the walk takes place (Evans & Jones, 2011; D'Errico & Hunt, 2019). This demonstrates that the landscape that we are in has an immediate impact on the ways in which we think and speak. If this is the case for the walking interview, it is likely to be the case for the experience of walking a battlefield, where the landscape provides the backdrop to our prior understanding of the battle and the people who took part in the battle.

These benefits can work in different ways, according to the situation. However much we read about a particular battle, visiting the battlefield will always provide us with a clearer picture of what took place there. Not only do we have our maps and our accounts, but we observe the landscape. It is all very well walking the scene with a veteran, but most of us cannot do that. One of the purposes of this book is to enable the reader to walk the battlefield as though they were with a knowledgeable veteran.

Landscape and memory

Numerous people have written about the relationship between landscape and memory (e.g., Lowenthal, 1975; Schama, 2004), often from a humanities perspective. In the nineteenth century John Ruskin painted many landscapes, but through his writings he always provided landscapes with a deeper meaning, usually about the phenomenon of man, and how men can be educated, how they live, how they think and react to events. This is what I am trying to put across here; the complexity of understanding that is needed regarding war and battle, and the importance not only of the psychology of war and detailed historical accounts, but the need to understand the landscape of the battlefield.

Landscape is one of the important things learned at military training schools around the world. Any officer in a war situation has to understand the landscape and how it can benefit them and their troops and disadvantage the enemy. This was true at Agincourt in 1415 when Henry V positioned his archers so that they had a clear line of sight of the enemy who was forced to charge through a narrow space between two woods; and it was true in 1944 when Montgomery was trying to clear the plain to the south of Caen to enable his tanks to speed along the plain to Falaise and help cut off the retreating Germans. Landscape is as important as the soldiers and their weapons. Understanding a past battle requires a study of the landscape of that battlefield.

The sights of battle

There are many things that aid understanding when you are planning to visit a battlefield – or when you are trying to understand the battle without visiting the battlefield. The evidence relating to what happened and where on a battlefield comes from many sources. There may be photographs of the site (at least from the mid-nineteenth century, for example the photos of the Crimean War or the U.S. Civil War), or there may be paintings or drawings (though these often lack accuracy because artists may want to give a certain impression). Witness the portraits of the British cavalry charging at Waterloo, or the charge of the Light Brigade in Crimea, both portraying heroic men on their fine mounts. There are accounts written by careful historians who, drawing on their historical sources (which again may or may not be accurate), have put together a picture of what happened on the day of the battle. This is possible even with battles from hundreds of years ago. Little pieces of evidence add up to a clearer picture. There may be accounts by people who took part in the battle. These are sometimes the most and the least reliable accounts. I have listened to accounts of battle and sometimes been amazed about what people know – the movements of troops or tanks several miles away, the casualty figures, and so on, when they were a simple soldier. These memories are not always accurate. They may be confabulated. A person's memories can get mixed up with what they've read or seen about the battle. Sometimes these latter elements become part of the memory, so their narratives may be partially personal – and perhaps accurate, though memories fade – and partially constructed from other sources.

The landscape: Detritus

Depending on the battle there may be evidence of trenches, gun emplacements or other fortifications, sometimes the guns themselves. These give a clear sense of the battle, but such relics are just that, they give little sense of the scale of a battle. A tank perched on a plinth says little about the experience of defenders seeing several hundred tanks advancing across a plain towards them with air support.

This is where memorials can help, as they claim to provide an exact location for an event in the battle – though care should be taken because again they are not necessarily accurate and may rely on a participant's fading memory or an historian's error.

The landscape: Natural features

Battles are fought in different kinds of terrain. Until the last 200 years, most battles were pitched, i.e., fought in an open field between two armies with infantry, cavalry and artillery (depending on the time period). These *fields* could be flat, hilly, wooded, with a clear view of the enemy or an obscured view. There could be water features or rocky areas. These all provide useful clues regarding the battle, and details will be given in the appropriate chapters. The Battle of Balaklava and the charge of the Light Brigade provides a good example of the need to see the battlefield, rather than just read about it (see Chapter 9). Lord Raglan, the commander, was positioned at the top of the Sapoune Heights, from where there is a magnificent view of the whole battlefield, from Balaklava Bay to the Causeway Heights and to the Valley of Death. It is probably the best view a commander could have of his own and the enemy dispositions. His only excuse for failure of observation would be the smoke of the guns obscuring his vision. These heights were also the site of major confrontations between the Russians and the Germans in the 1940s – the area is still strewn with weaponry, trenches and concrete fortifications from that time.

The site of the Thin Red Line is clear on the approach to Balaklava (it is now a vineyard). When one sees the Causeway Heights it is clear how ownership of them by the British was essential to the safety of Balaklava itself. As for the Valley of Death (now also mainly laid out with vineyards), standing in the middle of the valley it is easy to see how the Russian guns to both flanks and in front caused havoc among the Light Brigade.

More recent battles have sometimes been on a much larger scale than Balaklava. For instance, it is impossible to walk around the sites of the Battle of Normandy in a single day – or a single holiday – as the battlefield extended for many tens of miles in different directions. One needs to be selective about where to visit, for example, a memorial, the remains of gun emplacements, the place where a family member fought, a particular beach or air landing site, and so on.

Simple errors

As noted elsewhere with regard to the positioning of memorials, it is not always easy to determine what happened where on a battlefield. You can make an educated guess using the landscape, the detritus and the knowledge you have from historians and others, but most are prone to human error (except perhaps a breach in the wall of a castle or town that had been besieged, or where old trenches are extant). Sometimes the site of the battle itself may not be known. For example, it was long thought that the Battle of Bosworth was fought at Ambion Hill in Leicestershire, but recent evidence demonstrates it was fought a mile to the south west. Battlefield archaeology helped establish the site of this battle and has enhanced our understanding of many battles across the ages. The context of place, of landscape, is essential to the narrative of battle.

Battle sites: Psychology

An historian is interested in the facts of history and in historical interpretation. In the end, I am a psychologist interested in how we can understand battle and the experience of battle psychologically. What I am trying to establish is the nature of our response to battle experience and what it means to us as individuals and as a collective. If we think a battle took place in a particular field but it actually took place in the next field, do we as psychologists really care? We do at the level of trying to get historical accuracy and to understand the landscape, but as psychologists it is often less important. Nevertheless, seeing and walking around sites of battle enables people to have a deeper understanding of the perspective of the participants.

Landscape and identity

The landscape is tied up with identity. Identity is formed and reformed at many levels (Hogg, 2006), from the person, through the socio-cultural, and through the landscapes in which we live. When we move from landscape to landscape we become different people. Many people who live in the landscape of a city crave the landscape of the countryside, using the countryside as a place for a restful break or a place to relax. Our behaviour is thus determined not only by personality and the social world, but by the landscape we inhabit. Take this a step further and we can see how landscapes will inevitably affect our understanding of what is holding our interest at a given time – in our example battlefields.

Terrain in battle

Throughout history, soldiers have understood the importance of terrain. There are many accounts of the use of terrain (e.g., Doyle & Bennett, 2002), but all emphasise the importance of the landscape and how it inevitably affects the outcome of battle, with all battles being controlled or influenced by the terrain over which they are fought. Doyle & Bennett's edited book provides excellent examples of the importance of terrain from medieval warfare through to World War II. They acknowledge the growing importance among the academic community of the landscape of battle, bringing together a range of people from different disciplines to develop a better understanding of the impact of terrain.

Mitchell & Gavish (1980) argued that the terrain is the most significant factor regarding the outcome of a battle. The medieval army that held the hill had the advantage. The English army at Crecy in 1346 had this advantage and held on to it, letting the French and their allies attack up the hill. At Hastings in 1066 Harold had this advantage but relinquished it by attacking down the hill. The high ground remains key to battlefield operations. Not only has the enemy got to advance uphill, but the commander with the high ground has the better vantage point. He can see the enemy positions, whereas the commander on the low ground lacks such vision. A good example of this was the situation at Ypres through most of World War I, where the Germans held the high ground around the Ypres salient and could observe (and thus direct the guns onto) the British and allied troops in the salient. The Germans could also move their own troops more freely, largely unobserved by the British.

Battlefield commanders know about particular terrain in two ways, from intelligence and information gathered before the war (extant maps, local knowledge, etc.), and from intelligence gained during the preparation for battle (observation from above, reconnaissance, etc.). We can, by walking the battlefield, replicate this information.

Landscape archaeology, conflict archaeology

Since at least the nineteenth century, it has been recognised that the landscape of a battle often has a significant impact on the events of a battle, at every level from strategy (where, how and why should the battles take place?) to operational and tactical (how do we deal with the current battle situation?) (Keegan, 1978). If we want to understand a battle, we need to have an understanding of the landscape (Carman, 2013). Doyle & Bennett (1997) discussed this in detail in relation to the Western Front around Ypres and the Somme, with detailed descriptions of the different kinds of terrain. The Somme has rolling chalkland that drains well, and Ypres is on a clay plain that drains badly. The results of drainage significantly impacted on how the battles were conducted. For instance, at the Somme, the two sides could dig deeper dugouts and the trenches tended to be drier, causing fewer problems with trench foot and other health problems. Drainage differences are still found. Extant craters around the Somme are mainly dry whereas those around Ypres are flooded.

There is a huge difference between our understanding of battles from the nineteenth century onwards compared with those that took place before, largely because of the detailed mapping of the world that has taken place since the nineteenth century (Delano-Smith & Kain, 1999). The landscapes of English battles was first considered with care by Burne (1950/2005) in the 1950s, and this careful approach to landscape has continued with many authors of accounts of battle, not only because of the maps, but also because of the freedom to travel in the areas where battles took place, drawing battlefield maps and taking photographs. For instance, later in the book I discuss Sevastopol and Balaklava. Before the fall of the Soviet Union not only was it not possible to travel to Balaklava, it wasn't even on the maps because it had a top secret underground nuclear submarine base (thankfully, it is now a museum open to all), which also contains another museum about the Crimean War.

As mentioned earlier, another problem faced by people who want to explore older battlefields is that in many cases, the landscape has changed significantly since the battle took place. On many occasions, we cannot walk the battlefield because we do not know where it is with any accuracy. For instance, it is only recently that the actual site of the Battle of Bosworth has been discovered. Before that, it was thought to be situated two miles to the north east (Foard & Curry, 2013). I remember going to the interpretation site after this finding was initially reported and commenting on it. The person behind the desk vehemently denied they had the wrong site, but they were proved wrong. It is modern techniques of landscape archaeology, such as aerial mapping and metal detectors, that are enabling geographers, historians and others to determine with greater accuracy the site of a battle and, just as importantly, some of the actions of the participants of the battle, to which I will come shortly.

Foard & Curry (2013) argue that studying the historic terrain of a battlefield supported by the documentary record and the archaeological evidence can provide two genuine benefits for the study of battlefields: (1) using the topographical evidence to place the events within the landscape, and (2) examining the impact of the historical terrain on the events of the battle. Basically, we can find out what happened and where, and how the battle progressed due to the terrain over which it was fought. This is an important point. When we walk the battlefields we need both sorts of information. We can learn what happened at key timepoints during the battle and where these events took place, and – perhaps more importantly – we can see how the terrain had an impact on the battle.

This is particularly important from a psychological perspective. The more we can learn about individual and group behaviour on the battlefield, the better will be our understanding of the battle. We are starting to develop this understanding (Scott & McFeaters, 2011) by learning how human actions in battle are constrained and patterned by the technology of war and the sociocultural context. The archaeological record will provide little unless it is supplemented by historical and psychological data.

All forms of data become less reliable the further we go back in time. One of the problems is that many battles become shrouded in myth, so it becomes ever more difficult to establish the truth. Sometimes we don't even know whether particular battles actually occurred. While we think that Achilles fought against Hector at Troy, we only believe this because Homer says so – and Homer is not a reliable source. Nevertheless, archaeological digs at the site of Troy did establish that a war took place at the site at a time compatible with that described by Homer. As this is 2800 years ago the archaeological record will never provide enough detail to accurately establish the authenticity of Homer. In more recent times, say the last 1000 years, we have a better idea of where battles took place, but many are still disputed, largely because the descriptions of the battles by participants and others are usually vague about detailing the actual place. This is why accurate maps are important. If a good map is extant when the battle took place, then we are much more likely to pinpoint the site accurately. Before the nineteenth century there were few good maps.

Is landscape really important?

There is a dispute about the importance of the landscape in battle. While many argue it is critically important across a range of battlefield situations, others argue that it rarely has importance, at least not to the extent of affecting the outcome of a battle (Ehlen & Whisonant, 2008). There may be many who dispute this, perhaps the soldiers at Passchendaele who were unable to climb the ridge due to the mud, or the cavalry of the Light Brigade as they faced guns to the right of them, guns to the left of them, and guns ahead of them. The type of landscape is inevitably going to affect a battle. The Allied tanks in Normandy had a difficult time fighting in the bocage because it was all sunken lanes and small fields with banked hedgerows that provided excellent cover for the German defenders. It was better once they had broken through south of Caen and were on the flat plain to Falaise. The biggest tank battles of the war were fought on the plains of Ukraine, were there are few natural obstacles.

Nevertheless, Ehlen & Whisonant (2008), though they argue that terrain usually has a limited effect on the outcome of a battle, acknowledge that the terrain at Antietam – or Sharpsburg – was a critical factor. It is worth exploring this a little as I believe it shows that terrain is likely to have an effect on the outcome of many battles rather than only a few as they argue.

Ehlen & Whisonant describe in some detail the landscape around the Antietam battlefield, and how General Lee used the various mountain ranges to protect his troops as he advanced into enemy territory. There were several mountain ranges running roughly north-south, and the rivers in the area often had steep banks sometimes several metres high. The mountains served two purposes: screening Lee's forces and forcing the enemy to cross the mountains east-west. All Lee needed to do was protect the passes, which he did in the battles of Harper's Ferry and South Mountain, and his main force could proceed northwards into Maryland.

The Battle of Antietam was the bloodiest day in U.S. history, with more than 23,000 troops killed, wounded or missing. It ended in a draw that was a tactical defeat for Lee, who had to retreat back to Virginia. In terms of landscape, the battle was fought on two areas. To the north and west it was Conococheague limestone, undulating grasslands with limited shallow cover except for outcrops and a sunken lane. To the south it was Elbrook, a combination of dolomite and limestone with shale.

The first stage of the battle was fought in the limestone area, with the right flank of the Union army attacking through the cornfield area. There were enormous casualties in this area as there is limited cover. The limestone outcroppings were small and while they provided cover for individuals in fixed positions, they were not useful for anything larger such as artillery. This was unlike the outcrops at the battle of Fuentes d'Onoro in the Peninsular War, where the British troops, especially the skirmishers, hid behind the outcrops and effectively disrupted the cavalry charges of the French. The cornfield area at Antietam was effectively a series of fields with Dunker Church to the rear of the Confederate lines. Later the fighting spread to the sunken road, the middle area of the battlefield. This undulating area meant that the advancing Union soldiers would disappear for a while and then reappear much closer to the Confederate positions. Again there were many casualties in this area. The final part of the battle took place in the afternoon around what became known as Burnside's Bridge, mainly due to General Burnside's incompetence and insistence of continually attacking across this bridge. The key problem was that on the opposite bank of the bridge the road went up a very steep hill and the Confederates were well dug in at the top. The Union soldiers coming across the bridge in packed groups were excellent targets and were driven back each time they attacked.

Ehlen & Whisonant do a good job of describing the importance of the landscape, showing that where there is less cover the casualties are higher. They also describe key elements of the battlefield that had an impact, including the sunken lane in the central part of the battlefield, Antietam Creek and the steep slope leading up from Burnside's Bridge. There were obstacles on the battlefield such as fences and walls, woods in the northern and central areas, small quarries in the south. There were also small outcrops scattered around, mainly in the northern limestone area. Ehlen & Whisonant draw a helpful distinction between open terrain, which is mostly free of topographic obstacles and dissected terrain, which is characterised by steep slopes, hills, ridges, ravines and valleys. The difference can perhaps be illustrated by comparing the plains of Holland and the hills of the Ardennes.

The description of the terrain is very good, along with the discussion about the impact such terrain has on the battlefield. Their argument that terrain does not usually have such an impact perhaps refers to most battles that took place in the USA, whether Revolutionary, Civil or Indian Wars, because it is certain that many European battles were dramatically affected by landscape. The Battle of Crecy was won by the English partly because they dominated the hill and the French had to scramble upwards. Agincourt was partly won because the French knights were filtered through a relatively narrow gap between two woods.

Opposed to this is the argument that dissected terrain should create difficulties for an army. That wasn't the case for the Germans in the Ardennes in 1940 and 1944.

Landscapes and memorialisation

Memorialisation at sites of battle and elsewhere is discussed in another chapter but needs a brief mention here. Battlefield landscapes vary according to the number and type of memorials that are present. The battlefields of the Western Front and that of Waterloo proliferate with memorials that have been constructed at various times from soon after the battle and continuing to the present day. The later chapter will discuss why this phenomenon continues long after a battle is fought. Here we mention different kinds of memorials, the ones that are part of the landscape, the remnants of fortifications, trenches, shell holes, ruined houses and villages, which exist not because someone has built them after a battle, but because they are the remnants of the battle itself that no one has bothered to remove. Sometimes they are left deliberately, to create a memorial, such as the village of Orador sur Glane, destroyed by the Germans in June 1944 as an act of revenge. The population was massacred. Often memorials are there because no one has removed them, and over time they become informal in themselves, such as the mine craters at Beaumont Hamel and Lochnagar on the Somme, the ruined villages at Verdun or Chemin des Dames, or the concrete remains of the Atlantic Wall. Often, at some later point, the authorities decide that these mounds of earth, brick, stone or concrete are to be classified as memorials. As discussed in more detail in a later chapter, these remains or memorials are often contested, rejected by some, accepted by others, but become an important part of the social construction of the battlefield memory.

Contestation

While landscapes of battle are solid and in many ways factual, much is open to contestation, to the development of different forms of social or cultural memory of battle. Even where there is broad agreement about the location of a battle (often a source of great debate as we see for Bosworth or many other medieval battles for which records are limited and archaeological evidence sparse) there is often disagreement about many other factors. The data relating to a battle, whether that is an aspect of the landscape or the words of a participant, must involve the person accepting, rejecting or ignoring the data, depending on its perceived reliability and usefulness. As we are walking the battlefield, we are interpreting the data we have. We will sometimes get it wrong and will sometimes have to use our imagination to fill in the missing details, but an assessment of the data in light of what we understand is important. That is not to say that we should reject information provided on information boards or in museums. We should just keep in mind that these are one interpretation, and even if we accept their accuracy they only provide partial information.

The disagreements may arise due to the varied sources of information about a battle. Collective memory is developed collectively, that is, by different people and sources, and we know that people like to disagree (Halbwachs & Coser, 1992; Barash, 2016). There are often competing interest groups (people who want to put one version forward rather than another), and there are always groups who are left out of the collective memory (often the losers of the battle or the elements of the victorious army that the victorious army cares not to remember). Collective memories are developed from sources including professional historians and archaeologists, participants in the battle and their relatives, people local to the battle site, politicians of various shades, and others. Each group may disagree about facets of the battle, and it may be the loudest, the ones who come across most in the media, who represent the *truth* of what happened to the general populace.

The versions of the past in general are communicated through different institutions such as schools, amusements, art and literature, government ceremonies, families and friends, and landscape features that are considered historical (Shackel, 2003), so our collective memories (in general and in relation to battles) rely not only on professional sources, but also on a range of other sources that may or may not be accurate (though of course historical and archaeological sources are not always reliable either).

The process of developing the landscape as a source of memory of the battle is the development of heritage, with all its problems of definition. Heritage serves to create a useable past, one that serves our present needs (Shackel, 2003). The problem with heritage is that it is often created to serve the needs of specific groups in society (e.g., the Government), rather than provide an accurate representation of the past. Given that we live in a society that craves the past, this is inherently dangerous, as heritage suggests authenticity, so if heritage holds a representation of the past that is inaccurate or serves against a section of the populace, then it is potentially problematic. This will be discussed further in the memorialisation chapter, but the important point for this chapter is that the person walking the battlefield has sufficient knowledge to overturn the heritage aspect of the battlefield if necessary and look at it with clearer more objective eyes, focusing on what happened rather than any single interpretation of events. Taking a psychological perspective to this can be helpful, as this not only discusses the experiences of the individual soldiers, but also helps to understand the meaning of memory and perception and to see through biased heritage stories.

Contestation takes many forms. Memories of the Spanish Civil War still create problems for Spanish archaeologists and others who wish to study the war. A Spanish law that dictates sites under 100 years old are not protected means that Civil War sites are not protected from looters or developers. Archaeologists who want to study the battle sites of the war face problems from local people and authorities who would prefer such sites to be untouched. This is particularly the case for the mass graves that exist all around the country. The Spanish are reluctant to excavate conflicting memories (Gonzalez-Ruibal, 2007). The remains of the war are often socially invisible, though they are frequently well-preserved as the front lines were in places that are away from population centres and on land that is not intensively farmed.

A key reason for the Spanish reluctance to discuss the Civil War has been the transition to democracy, where it has been the case that the crimes of the Civil War and the subsequent Francoist oppression would be ignored in order for democracy to succeed. In more recent years this has changed, and the Historical Memory Law (Blakeley, 2008; Espinosa Maestre, 2013), passed in 2007, recognises the victims on both sides of the war and their descendants, and formally condemns the Francoist regime. While the law is controversial, with those on the right saying it should not have been passed and those on the left saying it does not go far enough, it has enabled archaeologists and others to start more detailed studies of Civil War sites, including digging up mass graves and attempting to identify the bodies, the discovery and documentation of military architecture and the excavation of battlefields.

The Spanish Civil War will be discussed in another chapter. The reason for including it here is that landscape not only has links to memory and history, but also politics. It is problematic if archaeologists and others cannot get on and do their jobs because of politics.

Finally

Some argue that battlefield archaeology can provide a deep understanding of the role of the individual on the battlefield (Scott & McFeaters, 2011). This is a fine aim, but it will largely be limited – even at the most productive sites – to some understanding of the movement of groups and possibly some individuals. In order to have a better understanding, we are still going to rely on history and psychology, the former for bringing together the accounts written about the battle and the latter for having an understanding of how people react in battle.

6

THE HUNDRED YEARS WAR

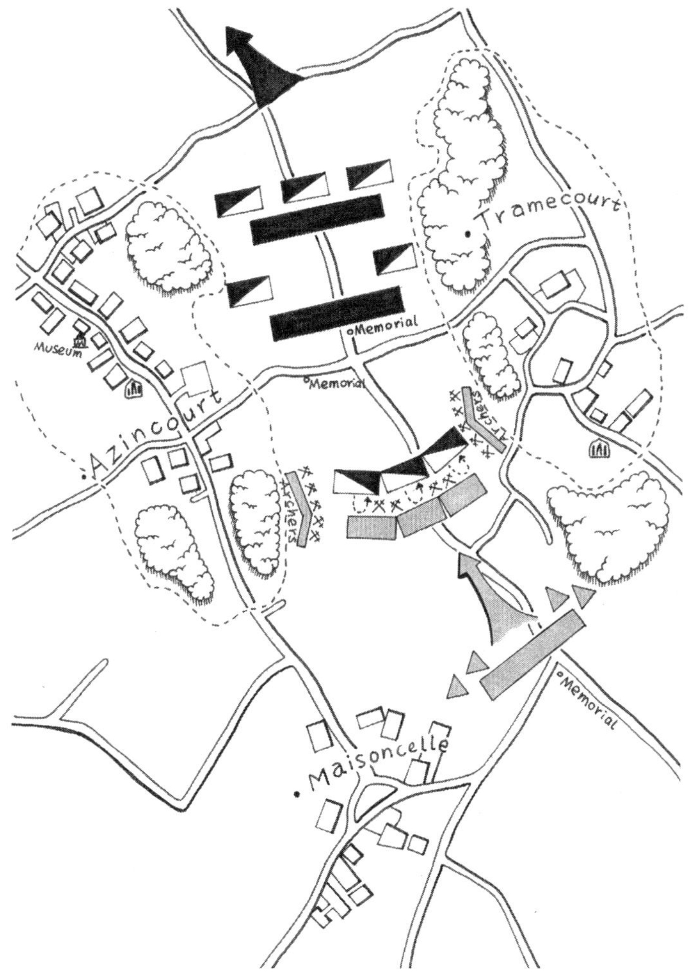

AGINCOURT. The map shows the estimated positions of the English and French troops at the outset of the battle. The previous night the English had camped around Maisoncelle. The trees formed a funnel through which one side or the other had to advance. The English drew the French forward. When they advanced the English archers to the flanks of the English troops devastated the advancing French. So many were killed that they piled up and restricted the movements of further troops. The English ran out of arrows and resorted to killing the wounded French with their daggers. According to some authors the area has not changed much. The funnel can still be seen. The memorials provide further information. Details of the memorial to the east of Maisoncelle can be seen on pp. 26–27.

This chapter briefly examines the late medieval and early modern period; in particular the period which became known as the Hundred Years War between the English and the French. The evidence for any psychological impact of this war is very limited, virtually non-existent. Languages change significantly over time. The English language has evolved from the languages spoken by the Saxons, Angles and others who came to the British Isles from the fifth to the sixth centuries. Along the way it picked up a lot of words and syntax from the Scandinavian languages and from French. For the purposes of the present book, at the time of the Hundred Years War the main language of many people in England was a form of Chaucerian Middle English, with many (not necessarily mutually intelligible) variants around the country. By this time English was also the dominant language of the ruling classes, after several centuries of the rulers speaking French. There are two key sources in this chapter, one English but writing a long time after the war and writing for entertainment – Shakespeare. The second is French, an older form of French, written by Froissart in his detailed account of the Hundred Years War.

The Hundred Years War

The Hundred Years War between England and France was not a single conflict, nor did it last 100 years. It lasted 116 years and was several conflicts, ending with England being ejected from most of what we now know as France, apart from Calais. We know very little about the ordinary soldiers of these wars, though the wars were chronicled in detail at the time of the wars by Froissart (1978) in *Contemporary Chronicles of the Hundred Years War.* Froissart details the key people and events of most of this period, including the killing of soldiers and civilians in battle and elsewhere, but there are few details of the impact these events had on anyone, other than minor details about the more senior personages. Contemporary accounts provide limited evidence for the psychological impact of war on soldiers or civilians.

Froissart focused on the importance of honour in battle and on how war can appear like a tournament: "Many gallant deeds of arms were performed, many knights and squires on each side were unhorsed and pushed back into the saddle." (Whittington, 2016, p. 27) In more practical terms, Froissart noted the growing importance of the English archer, first at Crecy in 1346, then at Poitiers in 1356, where he notes: "the English archers were an inestimable advantage to their comrades, and struck terror into the hearts of the French, for the rain of arrows was so continuous and so thick that the French did not know where to turn to avoid them, with the result that the English kept gaining ground," and then again at Agincourt in 1415. The French had major difficulties in dealing with this weapon. "Most of the knights and all of their horses were driven back among the vanguard for fear of the English archers." (Whittington, 2016, p. 28) The sheer terror of seeing hundreds of arrows flying through the air at the same time, with the rush of air, must have been for the French similar to that experienced by the

Germans facing the Russian rocket launcher in World War II, the Katyusha, which the Germans labelled Stalin's organ because the array of rocket launchers looked like a pipe organ and the howling sound was terrifying to the soldiers. Noise has always been used as a weapon to terrify the enemy, preferably attached to a lethal weapon, whether English arrows, Russian rocket launchers, or the German Stuka with its siren wailing as it divebombed the enemy.

Froissart's chronicles show how actual war-related events were described very differently than they are today. They were generally quite factual, with little consideration of the individual unless commended for issues of honour (apart from high ranking individuals) and contained little on fear or other emotions. We do not know why this is. What we do know is that people were probably not very different. They would experience fear and horror in battle. They would rely on comrades to stay in the fight. They would have memories of their wars for the rest of their lives. In order to understand the lack of psychological content we have to look at why accounts were written. They were usually for the consumption of kings and their barons, the people who wanted to know that their troops fought well without fear, that they had strong armies and that they were great leaders. All texts are biased. What we have to understand is how and why. Few people were interested in hearing about the trauma of war; that would probably be saved for the ballads and the oral stories passed down through the generations of ordinary soldiers and their descendants. Written ballads were quite rare at this time. We will see a change by the time we get to the seventeenth century and the British civil wars.

In order to begin to understand the psychological impact of war in this period we need to turn to storytellers. As we have seen in an earlier chapter, this started many years ago with the Greeks and has continued through history. The greatest storyteller in English, Shakespeare, did have some things to say about the experience of war that goes beyond simple description or questions of honour.

Shakespeare

Shakespeare, writing at the end of the sixteenth and early seventeenth centuries, focused on individuals, on their personalities, thoughts, emotions and behaviour. Many of his historical plays are set during the various wars of the previous centuries, and he does describe the impact of war on some of the key characters. While these are fictional accounts, they do demonstrate the universality of the reactions to war, with the descriptions being very close to how we describe trauma in modern terms. While the language is quite different, it is closely related to modern English. This main cause for concern is the translation from early modern English to modern English. As in all translations, there are differences between what the translation says, and what the original author meant. That does not detract from the general accuracy of the translation, but we have to recognise that a word in the year 1600 does not necessarily mean the same as that word in the year 2000. Of course, this is a difficulty that does not just relate to a time span of 400 years. Similar difficulties with interpretation can exist between two speakers of the same language in the present day. When I say, "I am stressed," that is not necessarily the same as when you say you are stressed. I might have a much lower threshold for stress, in which case I am more likely to experience stress than you are in a similar situation. *Stressed* to you might mean *very stressed* to me. Alternative interpretations of the same words are still with us, and we as psychologists attempt to remove ambiguity.

Shakespeare talked about battle and the psychology of battle in several of his plays. For instance, in *Henry V*, Act IV, Scene 1, he notes that "there are few die well that die in battle," which contradicts much of what is often said about death in battle. The classic line, particularly to a wife or other relation, is that the individual died cleanly and without feeling a thing, when in reality people often die slowly in a great deal of pain. In Act IV, Scene 3, Shakespeare has Henry saying: "He which hath no stomach to this fight, Let him depart; his passport shall be made." Those who are too frightened to fight a battle are not only a danger to themselves, they may infect others with their fear and damage the performance of the army as a whole. This recognised that people are fearful, and sometimes too fearful. Shakespeare has Henry saying this at the end of the sixteenth century (though supposedly in 1415), yet men in the civilian armies of the two World Wars were not allowed the luxury of leaving if they were too frightened to fight, indeed, many of them were court-martialled, and large numbers, particularly Russians and Germans, were executed. In many wars, soldiers have been temporarily taken out of the front line because their fear might infect others; but they are usually expected to return to their unit after a period of rest. Even the Einsatzgruppen, the troops who followed the German invasion of Russia to kill Jews, homosexuals, Roma, intellectuals, and so on, allowed men not to take part in the shooting of people if they could not cope with it.

One of the best examples of psychological trauma in Shakespeare is in *Henry IV*, Part 1. When Hotspur (Henry Percy) is back from war his wife, Lady Percy, describes the symptoms (Act 2, Scene 3, 48–66). Shay (1994) offered a modern translation, where "oh my good lord, why are you thus alone" is 'social withdrawal and isolation'; "For what offence have I this fortnight been a banished woman from my Harry's bed?" becomes 'random, unwarranted rage at family, sexual dysfunction, no capacity for intimacy'; "Why hast thou lost the fresh blood in thy cheeks" becomes 'peripheral vasoconstriction, autonomic hyper-activity'; "In thy faint slumbers I by thee have watched" becomes 'fragmented, vigilant sleep'; and after describing battle in detail which becomes traumatic dreams and reliving combat, finishes with "beads of sweat have stood upon thy brow like bubbles in a late-disturbed stream…" which becomes 'night sweats, autonomic hyperactivity.'

Visiting early battlefields

As argued elsewhere, visiting battlefields can help develop our understanding of the psychology of battle, and the details of particular battles, though inevitably our constructions relating to battles that occurred centuries ago are very limited both in terms of exactly where and how the battles took place and the effects on the people involved. The problem is the lack of contemporaneous detailed accounts of the type produced in more recent times and the lack of accurate maps dating back more than a century or two. Ordnance Survey fundamentally changed our understanding of place in the UK in a similar way to national railways standardising our concept of time. We now expect maps to be accurate in ways never thought about in earlier centuries.

A good example of how we can get the site of the battlefield very wrong is that of Bosworth (1485). For many years it was thought that it took place near the foot of Ambion Hill near Market Bosworth, and that is where the heritage centre was built. More recent archaeological research by the Battlefields Trust suggests that it took place two miles southwest of the hill (Battlefields Trust, 2009).

The key battlefields of the Hundred Years – War, Crecy (1346), Poitiers (1356), Agincourt (1415) and Castillon (1453) – vary in their accuracy regarding location. The location of the battlefield of Crecy is reasonably certain, situated close to the village of Crecy, with the English positioned along a high ridge and a windmill situated in the centre, which formed a good lookout position. The French and their Allies had to attack up the hill, which disadvantaged them because the English had many longbowmen who simply had to shoot down the hill. Different elements of the French army attacked in turn. The French had Swiss crossbowmen, whose bows took longer to load with a much shorter range than the English longbow. This meant that for most of the battle the English could inflict severe damage on the French without coming into direct contact with them. The French eventually got annoyed with the crossbowmen because of their ineffectiveness and ran them down with their horses, killing many. On only one occasion did the French cavalry threaten the English line, which was commanded by King Edward's son, Edward, the Black Prince, who was only 16 at the time. The King refused to send help, saying that the Prince would have to prove himself worthy – which he did, by beating the French and holding the line. This was virtually the only dangerous time for the English army. The site of the windmill, roughly the position of the King, now has a useful lookout position, from where the whole of the battlefield can be seen. It is obvious why the English, though outnumbered (the French army had perhaps 30,000 men, compared to the English 14,000 – though these numbers are not known with any accuracy), easily beat the French because of the steepness of the hill and the power of the longbowmen – the machine gunners of their time. The overall casualties for the two sides are unknown, though the best estimates suggest perhaps 100–300 English killed, and perhaps 4,000–5,000 French killed (though contemporary sources suggested around 30,000 French were killed).

The Battle of Poitiers took place just to the southwest of Poitiers near the modern village of Nouaillé-Maupertuis. The site is marked by monuments and information boards describing the battle. Never take such monuments and information boards as accurate. Like any story they are telling one interpretation of events, based on the evidence available at the time and the viewpoint of the writers. While there is evidence that the battle was fought around here, the actual site is less clear than Crecy. This was another English victory. The English were led by the Black Prince, and were again outnumbered by the French, with roughly 6000 English and 11,000 French. Again, the longbow played an important role, with around 2000 English archers. At the start of the battle the English removed their baggage train from the site, prompting an attack by the French cavalry, who were cut down by arrows and by the infantry. The English then used their longbows against the massed French infantry, eventually causing two of their three divisions to retreat. The third, under King John, advanced at the same time as the English cavalry and infantry. The French were destroyed, and King John was captured. It is Froissart who provides us with most of the details, though with such a paucity of sources we cannot know how reliable the account is. The battle site itself, assuming it is accurate, shows how the English did not have an ideal position, being at the bottom of the hill around a river. The French attacked downhill, but again were beaten in large part by the longbowmen. As at the Battle of Crecy, there were very few English casualties, but around 2500 French dead and perhaps 2000 captured.

Agincourt and Henry V

Henry V was by all accounts a brave soldier. As a teenager he had fought for his father at the Battle of Shrewsbury (1403), where he was badly wounded. He was hit in the face by an arrow and was lucky to survive. He continued to lead his men in the battle after he was wounded, and must have been a terrifying sight, but this does indicate extreme courage and ability to withstand pain. Afterwards, he was treated by a top physician, Bradshaw, who described the wound and the medical procedures in detail. It was difficult to treat. The arrow went in downwards below the eye for several inches. After removing the arrow shaft the arrowhead remained inside the bone of the skull for several inches. Bradshaw cut through Henry's face to the wound then, using tongs at the same angle as the arrow had gone in, placed a screw in the arrowhead and gradually wiggled it around and got it out. As there were no anaesthetics, that must have been very painful. It took days to clean the wound, pack it and wait for it to heal. The packing was applied and regularly changed, gradually being put in less distance each time.

While we see profile portraits of Henry with an undamaged face, his soldiers on the French campaign must have seen some terrible battle scars and be prepared to follow him with some confidence. This, along with his behaviour on campaign, does suggest someone with good leadership qualities, essential in a field commander.

The Agincourt campaign began with landing in Normandy and successfully besieging Harfleur, now a suburb of Le Havre, but then the main port on the

Seine. Henry's speech at Harfleur, as suggested by Shakespeare, demonstrates the importance of how a man should be different in peace and war:

> Once more unto the breach, dear friends, once more,
> Or close the wall up with our English dead.
> In peace there's nothing so becomes a man
> As modest stillness and humility:
> But when the blast of war blows in our ears,
> Then imitate the action of the tiger...;

Of course, Henry did not say these words, but we have little to go on regarding what he did say, if anything. There are several characteristics of his speech as per Shakespeare that fit Henry being an effective field commander – so he might have said something similar. Effectively there is a choice. We can win or lose. We need to storm the breach made by mining under the walls (the original form of undermining), perhaps with the help of artillery, and either succeed or die. We must not retreat. That is clearly telling the men bravery is required, and they already know he will be with them, not behind them. Henry points out that in peacetime men should behave accordingly, not be aggressive or violent, but once war is declared then intense action is required. This reads similarly to the typical stories from the World Wars, when people would argue that the English are a peace-loving nation, but if they get angry watch out.

The Shakespearean Henry goes further,

> Stiffen up the sinews, summon up the blood
> Disguise fair nature with hard-favoured rage ...
> Hold hard the breath, and bend up every spirit
> To his full heart. On, on you noblest English ...

Again, recognising that the men are peaceful people who need to bring out their warrior self, with rage and spirit, Henry is attempting to ready the men for the fight, even referring to their parentage:

> Dishonour not your mothers; now attest
> That those whom you call'd fathers did beget you.

One major difficulty for the English after the successful siege at Harfleur, that is before Agincourt was fought, was large numbers of troops having dysentery. Many died and thousands were sent home. There was one medical and logistical success story that came out of this. The Marshall of the Army, John Mowbray, was responsible for discipline and the basic regulation of the troops. He realised that the dysentery was caused by the poor quality of the drinking water and so arranged for ale, cider and wine to be sent from England. This, along with sending troops home and getting replacements, was a huge logistical task for the early fifteenth century, but it worked. The army was resupplied (provisioning armies is often very difficult and will be returned to later), some reinforcements arrived, but it was not sufficient to continue towards Paris, an initial objective. Instead, Henry headed north towards Calais, which was part of the English realm. On the way they found their path blocked by a larger French army near the village of Azincourt.

Shakespeare again has Henry preparing the men for the fight. After sleeping overnight not far from the French army, Shakespeare has Henry making another speech, this time it included information about the quality of the men who should fight. Henry showed an unusual difference regarding the way soldiers are normally treated. It is rare that a general will allow a soldier to leave if he does not want to fight, but this is what Henry does on the morning of the Battle of Agincourt:

> … he which hath no stomach to this fight
> Let him depart; his passport shall be made
> And crowns for convoy put in his purse'
> We would not die in that man's company
> That fears his fellowship to die with us.

This is an early example of showing how comrades should never let each other down and that they should always be prepared to die for one another.

Henry also comments on how the veterans of war will be proud of their story. Again, this is before Agincourt:

> This day is called the feast of Crispian:
> He that outlives this day, and comes safe home,
> Will stand a tip-toe when the day is named,\And rouse him at the name of
>   Crispian.
> He that shall live this day, and see old age,
> Will yearly on the vigil feast his neighbours,
> And say 'Tomorrow is Saint Crispian:'
> Then he will strip his sleeve and show his scars.
> And say 'These wounds I had on Crispin's Day'…

It is common for veterans to be proud of their battle experiences and wish to share them with others. Many of us grew up with veterans of the two World Wars often ready to talk about their experiences; though some, a proportion of whom were traumatised, rarely or never spoke of their experiences, except perhaps to their comrades. When we talk of soldiers and veterans being a *Band of Brothers* that is a direct line from Shakespeare's *Henry V* before the Battle of Agincourt.

Shakespeare does have particular tones in his narratives of war. They are generally heroic, reflecting back on how the England (usually England) of old was a superior place, with heroic warriors as kings and princes. They are very pro-English. Perhaps this is because he was writing *Henry V* (and the two *Henry IVs*) in the last years of the sixteenth century, when Elizabeth I was coming to the end of her reign and the country was still struggling with its history and its future. It was a time of secret agents, enemies within, the threats from Catholicism, and so forth, and the people in the country were looking for stability and strength – bear in mind that the country fell apart only 40 years later in the Civil Wars.

The battle of Agincourt

The Battle of Agincourt (1415) took place near the small village known in French as Azincourt. The site is disputed as there is limited archaeological or written evidence, but most agree that it was fought across a relatively flat field between two woods, which now – it is claimed – looks similar to how it did then. There were around 6000–9000 English under Henry V fighting against anywhere from 12,000–36,000 French under several leaders, including Charles D'Albret, Jean Le Maingre, and Charles D'Orleans, with much of the French aristocracy in the army. It was a slaughter of the French by the English – again largely the longbowmen. The woods on either side of the battlefield forced the advancing French to funnel together to try and get through. It was here that most of the slaughter took place. After a period of waiting, with the French trying to persuade the English to advance, the French knights advanced on horseback in full armour, with many of the key aristocrats at or near the front. They engaged the English men at arms, but were themselves attacked by the longbowmen, with many being killed. One contemporary source described the bodies slowly building a wall that the French found difficult to climb over. They advanced through mud, and with the heavy armour many would be too tired to fight the English. When the French in their heavy armour fell to the ground, either knocked down or because their horses were shot from under them, it was relatively easy for the English troops to either kill or capture them.

At one point there were many, possibly several thousand, French prisoners, held at the rear of the line. The only (limited) success the French had during the day was an attack on the English baggage train, which led to the English King Henry V ordering the killing of the prisoners in case they were freed and returned to the fight. Fortunately for the prisoners, it appears that relatively few were actually killed, perhaps partly because the English soldiers were not happy to kill in cold blood, and partly because the French soon retreated, defeated. It is not clear how many casualties there were, but again there were far more French casualties (perhaps 5,000–10,000 dead) than English (around 100 dead). There were – fortunately for them – many prisoners who were transported back to England to be later ransomed. The remaining French had abandoned the field, leaving it clear for the English to get to Calais and home to England.

It is possible to walk or drive around the battlefield, though it may be better to drive around as the roads are dangerous for walking, and the actual battlefield is mostly agricultural so cannot usually be walked on. A good starting point is the small museum in Azincourt itself. Then head southwest towards Maisoncelle. The battle took place across the fields to the left. Maisoncelle is where Henry V supposedly slept the night before the battle and where the English army may have camped. Turn left on the D107E2 and you will be travelling in the footsteps of the main English army on the left as it lined up at the start of the battle, with the baggage train and prisoners somewhere to the right. At the junction with the D104 you will turn left, but at the corner is a memorial to the battle, with a description of the battle (in French and English) that is a French interpretation. I will return to this shortly. There is also a map indicating possible battle positions. From here drive ENE on the D104. Just beyond the junction with the D71, on the right, is a recent French monument indicating the possible mass grave of the soldiers (most likely French, but probably a mix of French and English). Return to the D71 and turn right. After a few metres stop at the memorials on the left. You are in front of the probable original French lines looking towards the English. From here return to Azincourt.

I presented the French interpretation at the memorial in full in the first chapter. It might be worth looking again to see something of the difficulty of interpretation, the impossibility of presenting either an objective or an accurate account of something that took place so long ago where we have imperfect records.

Historians have long wondered how the relatively small English army defeated the larger French army. For one thing, the French army may not have been as large as some have speculated. Curry (2000) argues that the English army may have consisted of as many as 9000 troops (usually 8000 is given as a maximum), and the French may have had as few as 12,000. She suggests that the notion of a small army defeating a much larger one may just be propaganda. Second, the English army – as at Crecy – had archers equipped with longbows. They had a good range (far longer than a crossbow), could cut through most armour, and a volley from a large group of archers could stop an advancing army instantly. Third, from various accounts it appears that Henry V was a good leader of men. He inspired them by his actions and by being involved himself in the fighting. Jones (2005) notes that during battle he was in the centre of the line, wearing his crown, indicating to the enemy that he was the leader – and making himself a target. He would create a sense of unity among the men in his army. Unlike the French army, Henry had peasants in his army. The archers were all from the peasantry; indeed, the French were horrified by how badly the archers were dressed (Jones, 2005, p. 22).

Many of the comments regarding Henry V were made by people who would want to be seen positively by the king. We have to be careful in interpreting what people said 600 years ago – and how Shakespeare interpreted his speech and behaviour. The notion of providing historical truth was not a concept widely recognised at the time. Instead the intention was to put the English, and particularly the nobility, across in a positive manner and tell a good story. This creates another difficulty with trying to understand battlefield behaviour in the distant past.

Castillon

The Battle of Castillon was the final battle of the Hundred Years War. It was a significant defeat for the English and led to the loss of Aquitaine. The English were commanded by John Talbot, Earl of Shrewsbury (whose family we will meet later in relation to Wingfield Manor). In 1451, the French had taken Bordeaux, but the people of Bordeaux considered themselves subject to the English crown and so requested an army to retake the city. Talbot turned up with about 3000 troops. Talbot was in his 60 s – possibly his 70 s – at this point, with a reputation as an effective military leader. He quickly retook the city. The French armies headed for Bordeaux, as did the 3000 English reinforcements. The French camp was situated to the east of the town of Castillon, which itself is to the east of Bordeaux, and the English went out to meet them. Initially they managed to chase off some French archers, but Talbot was impetuous and attacked the main French force, which was significantly larger than his army. He ordered his men to attack dismounted, and so Talbot was the only one who attacked on horseback. The French army had around 300 guns, both handguns and artillery pieces. When Talbot realised the strength and arms of this force it is said that he was aware he had made a mistake but carried on attacking anyway. The English were routed. Both Talbot and his son were killed. The French then retook Bordeaux and the Hundred Years War was effectively over.

There is a monument to Talbot just to the east of Castillon (now called Castillon-la-Bataille) near the river – the road is called Route du Monument Talbot – and a much larger monument to the French village on the D936 again to the east of Castillon. From here, which is around the central position of the French army, there is a clear view of the battlefield down to the Dordogne. Looking to the west, towards Castillon, the area where the English advanced can be seen. The advantage of the French is obvious from the lie of the land. The French had the high ground and far superior numbers. Talbot should not have attacked.

The Hundred Years War in retrospect: What can it tell psychologists?

The Hundred Years War, while it was a very important period of time in the history of Western Europe, in the development of armies and tactics, weaponry and supply, and also in the development of the nation state, with England and France becoming more secure as nations by the end of the war, tells us relatively little about the experience of the ordinary soldier in war. As you go through the chapters you will see that the closer we get to the present day, the more we can glean from the accounts that are used.

There is little that Froissart can tell us about how war was experienced by the ordinary solder. Froissart, like other writers of his time, was more interested in the kings and barons, the high ranking people and interpreting their experiences, than he was with the foot soldier. Drawing on Shakespeare is also problematic, as it is not only fiction, it is fiction of a time and place, that of the closing of the first Elizabethan era, when he needed to demonstrate the strength of English leaders, their heroism and courage. Truth was probably far from Shakespeare's mind, but that does not detract from his accounts of the psychology of war, which do, at least, demonstrate the universality of war trauma, the fear and horror, the nightmares and traumatic memories that accompany war. In the end, a study of this period can add just a little to our understanding, so it is time to move forward to the genuinely modern era, that of the British Civil Wars of the mid-seventeenth century.

7

THE BRITISH CIVIL WARS

Wingfield Manor

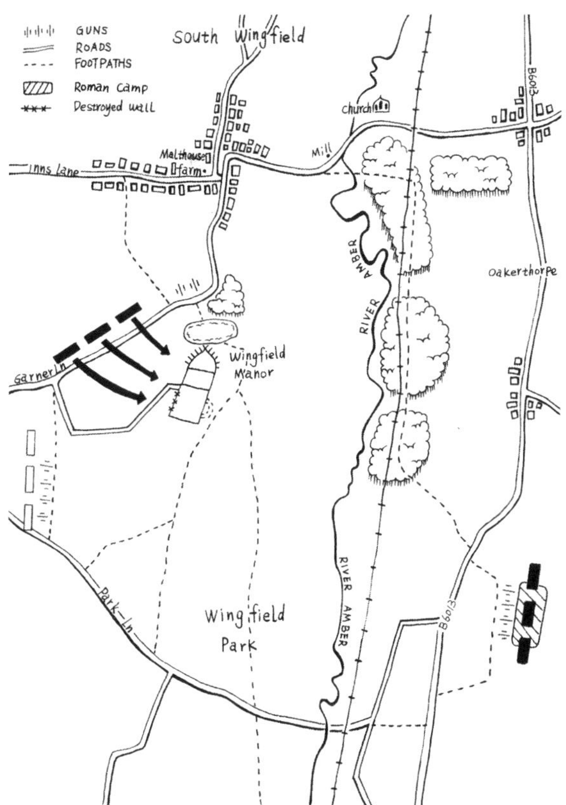

THE SIEGE OF WINGFIELD MANOR. There is little remaining evidence of the siege of Wingfield Manor (1644). The manor itself is ruined, partly because it was damaged in the siege and partly because it was later dismantled. Using an OS map, it is worth walking from the centre of South Wingfield at the crossroads where a farm that held Royalist prisoners still stands, down past the mill and across the river, and up to the initial positions of the large guns. From here the range was too great, and they only managed to damage a half-moon battery (seen attached to the south west of the manor). The guns were then moved via Park Lane to the position at Manor Top at the west of the map. From here the key wall of the manor was destroyed and the Parliamentarian troops advanced from a ditch at Garner Lane to take the manor. The Royalist commander was shot in the face as he tried to march out of the gate (still to be seen by the half-moon battery) with his soldiers.

But though, Oh England! Cans't not hear the Voice in thy own inventions; The trampling of Horses, the noise of the drums, the Clashing of Swords, the noise of the Hammers... And the many projects in your heads, your great gains, and sometimes great losses, the distractions in your families and among your friends

Covel (1659), pp. 3–4

The British Civil Wars of the mid-seventeenth century set the scene for the political future of the later United Kingdom and for the political future of many nations, particularly with regard to how to go about creating a revolution. The French and the people of the USA learned a lot from the British revolution that ultimately failed.

These wars were fought between 1642 and 1651, though there were several minor conflicts in the build up to the main outbreak of war in August 1642. Proportionally more lives were lost in this war than the UK lost in either World War I or World War II. People not only died in battle, but civilians were killed by troops or disease, and people starved through famine caused by the failure to collect crops. Any civil war is destructive, probably more so than most wars between countries. Most, including those being fought today, devastate the countryside and the towns and kill or injure many people; others starve or succumb to disease. The effects of these wars are felt long afterwards. In the 1640s, England had a particularly narcissistic and brutal king, Charles I, whose ego was such that he thought he was God's representative on Earth (a little like his namesake and descendant, the future Charles III). Parliament did not agree and after years of negotiation realised that Charles could not be negotiated with. Charles, too, realised that Parliament would not do as he said, so he raised his standard in Nottingham in August 1642. The two sides quickly created their armies, and the next four years saw many battles and many people dead through battle, starvation and disease. The period was one of the worst in English history (and little better for the rest of the British Isles). Calling up large armies required people to leave their farms, which led to crops not being sown, cared for or harvested. Stored food was often taken by passing soldiers and often not paid for. Many thousands starved to death as a result of this. A combination of being hungry and many people travelling around the country – mainly soldiers but also civilians – led to increase in disease, and with little in the way of medical treatment for most diseases many people died. Some of the major battles (e.g., at Edgehill, Marston Moor and Naseby) saw thousands killed via musket shot, artillery and sword. Those that survived these battles with sometimes terrible wounds often died in the days and weeks afterwards, as surgery was very basic. Most people who needed an amputation died, often of shock. There was little in the way of hygiene, so many wounded prisoners succumbed to infection. Levels of crime rose, as those responsible for keeping law and order (generally the lord of the manor and his people) were off fighting. Henry Foster (1643) who fought at Newbury explained that with the difficult conditions, the long marches, living in the open and little food led to: "a great distraction among our soldiers, everyone standing upon his guard and fearing his fellow souldier to bee his enemy"(6). In other words, paranoia and delusions were rife among the troops, though it is rare to find examples of descriptions of stress as we understand it. It is mostly implied through descriptions such as seeing the dead and wounded – of course we need to be careful when interpreting writings from this time. As shown later in the chapter, there is a developing conceptualisation of psychological trauma during the seventeenth century. In terms of memory, John Evelyn (1661) wrote about how some accounts of the wars by people writing much later "uncover the buried memory of the evils past." Apart from the actual phrasing, this is very similar to how we regard traumatic memories today, with memories being buried and later re-emerging into consciousness and impacting on the individual.

The wars were fought over a dispute between king and Parliament, over Charles' flirtations with Catholicism, they were fought to try and obtain more power for the people – at least the upper middle classes – they were the first wars arguably fought for republican, democratic and modern ideas – at least in the latter stages. In 1646, after the first victory, there were many people such as the Levellers and the Diggers, who thought that ordinary people should have the same rights as the rich and powerful. These ideas were ahead of their time and were not seen again until the U.S. Revolutionary Wars and the French revolution more than 100 years later.

Besieging the manor

The focus here is on the main siege of Wingfield Manor, a little known battle, but illustrative of the kinds of fighting that took place all across the country during the main civil war, away from the large-scale pitched battles involving thousands of participants on each side. There were two sieges at Wingfield Manor. The first was where the Royalists ejected the Parliamentarians, but this was little more than a skirmish. The main siege, where the Parliamentarians ejected the Royalists, took place in the summer of 1644, with a short break when many of the Parliamentary troops went to fight at the Battle of Marston Moor. After the war, Wingfield Manor was further destroyed so that it could not be used again as a fortress, though actually, it never had been a fortress. It was built in the middle years of the fifteenth century for Lord Cromwell, who was effectively the Chancellor of the Exchequer and managed to enrich himself. It was built as a classic manor house and would be the model for Hampden Court, built some decades later. There were no fortifications as such, except those that could be quickly built. There had been a Norman Castle on the site and the remains of the moat were used for defence. A series of trenches were constructed, with gun positions, around the sides of the manor. There was also a half-moon battery outside the main gate. The manor had been owned for many years by the Talbots, the Earls of Shrewsbury (one of whom had lost the last battle of the

Hundred Years War, Castillon, as described in the previous chapter), who were also the keepers of Mary, Queen of Scots, who on occasion had been imprisoned at Wingfield Manor. By the time of the civil wars the manor had moved into the hands of the Earl of Pembroke, a Parliamentary supporter.

While there is relatively little written about these sieges of the manor, there is a lot written about the civil war, about the numerous sieges and battles, and we can use this information to build a picture of life during the war for the participants and for the civilians caught up in it.

Wingfield Manor is in the centre of Derbyshire. It lies just west of the main north-south road between Derby and Sheffield (both held by Parliamentary forces for most of the war), and on a key route crossing the southern part of the Peak District between Alfreton and Ashbourne (again both held mainly by Parliament). The significance of the east-west Peak District route is that it is the most northerly route south of the Pennines that would usually stay open for traffic in the winter snows. Derby was garrisoned by Colonel John Gell, whose forces were strong enough to defeat the Royalist Northumberland at Hopton Heath early in the war, and who kept most of Derbyshire for Parliament for much of the war.

Wingfield Manor was initially held by Parliament under Pembroke, who left to join the Parliamentary government in London. In 1643 it was taken by the Royalists after a short siege, which had very little impact. The Parliamentary forces were not strong enough to hold the manor for any length of time and soon surrendered. There were few known casualties. The problems started for Parliament when the Royalist garrison regularly raided local villages for supplies and generally caused a nuisance in an area with general support for Parliament. So, Colonel Gell (a lead mine owner and friend of many of the local Royalist commanders, as was common during the war) decided to take it back. In June 1644 the siege began, but it was quickly suspended when many of the Parliamentary troops had to go to Yorkshire to take part in the Battle of Marston Moor – which itself led to the defeat of the Royalist forces in the North.

On their return the siege began in earnest. Gell's siege guns lacked power, so several large 32 pounders were borrowed from Sheffield. These were placed on a hill to the east by a Roman camp. Unfortunately, they were placed too far away – around 1400 yards – and only managed to destroy a half-moon battery outside the main entrance to the manor.

The guns were moved to the opposite, west side of the manor, and the bombardment began again. This time the curtain wall was quickly destroyed, and the Royalists surrendered. As was usual, the men (not the officers) were allowed to leave instead of being made prisoner. The commander of the Royalists, Colonel Danby, attempted to leave dressed as a common soldier. A deserter now with Parliament recognised him and shot him in the face as he tried to leave through the gates of the manor.

The manor then stayed in Parliamentary hands until the end of the war, when Parliament ordered its destruction so that it could never again be defensible.

With some exceptions (a house rebuilt in the great hall for the astronomer Immanuel Halton, now ruined, and a farmhouse, still occupied in the centre range of the manor) it has been a ruin ever since.

The story of the siege of Wingfield Manor is an ordinary one, repeated throughout the country on a smaller and larger scale. It is a largely unknown battle, but strategically important for the local area, being near those main east-west and north-south roads. It was not a large-scale battle, and the casualties were not great, but it is a reminder that such battles were going on even in the small villages and towns around the country, that nearly all local people would have been affected. There would be local men fighting on both sides. Sometimes brothers would be on opposite sides. All these things had to be contended with once the war was over. Social splits within a community are very difficult to heal, as the miners' strike in the 1980s showed us.

Walking the manor

Unlike most of the battlefields described in this book, this chapter provides a detailed walk. Wingfield Manor is managed by English Heritage, and at the time of writing it is only open for the first Saturday of the month in the summer months, and then only for guided tours. The manor itself is worth seeing if possible, as a visit quickly shows that it is not a fortified building. It is a large manor house. Part of it is still a working farm and is not accessible. The building has two courtyards. Off the north courtyard, the area of the main visit, there are the remains of kitchens, living quarters and the great hall, all roofless. There is also a tower that can be climbed from where the positions of the Parliamentary troops and guns can be seen. The south courtyard is the farmyard. The only thing to be seen on a tour is the great barn.

To walk the battlefield, set off from the marketplace in South Wingfield. On the market place there is an old stone farmhouse (look at the shop; it is to your left), which was used to lock up Royalist prisoners in the Civil War. This is a private house. There is still graffiti on the cellar wall that purportedly comes from this time. Head up Inns Lane. Shortly after the end of the houses there is a footpath to the left. Take this. In the first field there is a good general view of the manor. Go straight down, heading roughly towards the manor, until you reach the road. Turn left up the hill and turn right before the corner down a tarmacked bridleway. Again, there is a good view of the manor, showing how it was protected on three sides by a steep hill. At the top of this hill there were small artillery pieces used against the manor, and there is extant damage caused by these guns on the nearest walls of the manor. At the bottom of the hill you will cross what was a mill pond at the time of the war. The route veers left and then right up the hill. At a junction of three paths, the field to the right (which is not a right of way) has the remains of trenches used in the defence of the manor. The remains can still be traced. At the top of the hill, on the northern side, are the remains of the moat of what was probably a Norman castle before the manor was built. Continue up the hill toward the old entrance to the manor. After the surrender of the Royalists this is where the commander, Danby, disguised himself as a common soldier, but as already noted, he was recognised by a deserter and shot. Face away from the manor. Immediately in front are the remains of a half-moon battery that protected the entrance. On top of the hill across the valley is the site of a Roman camp. It was here that four 32-pounder guns were set up by Parliament to attack the manor. Their success was limited. They only succeeded in destroying the half-moon battery and so needed to be moved to the opposite side of the manor. With an OS map you can extend the walk to that point if you wish.

Continue the walk up the hill past the manor. Where the path splits, veer right across two further fields and exit on the narrow lane. This is the route the cannon took to their new positions. Take the next footpath on the right and go several hundred metres until you have passed a small copse to the right. This is where the guns were repositioned. It was from here that the renewed bombardment led to the destruction of the main curtain wall of the south courtyard and the quick surrender of the Royalist troops. The wall facing this side also shows damage caused by cannonballs. There is a particularly good example which shows the direction of the cannon, with one side of the indentation jagged, and one crushed smooth, just before the entrance into the kitchen of the manor.

You can either walk back to the village by the road or cross the road, head left and then enter another footpath. There is another path heading down the hill which joins the first one taken. Ideally, this walk could coincide with a visit to the manor, in which case walking down the road leads to the main entrance. Just below the entrance to the manor is part of the road which at the time was a ditch. It was here the Parliamentary forces were positioned as the cannon destroyed the curtain wall. The soldiers then ran across the fields and into the manor. It is not known how many casualties there were, but it is likely that the numbers on both sides were small.

After a civil war

Civil wars often have the biggest impact on a population, as they can affect virtually everyone, not only as war comes to towns and villages, affects food supplies, and takes away men and women to fight, but it also leads to break ups within families, as some take one side and some the other. It was not uncommon for brothers to be fighting on opposite sides. The impact is not just during the war years, but in the aftermath. Families may be permanently split, the country is a physical mess, the economy is in ruins, and the political system has to be rebuilt. In seventeenth-century England, it was years before there was political stability after the wars were over. Officially, the fighting stopped after the battle of Worcester in 1651, but the remaining years of the republic were largely chaotic, followed by the decadence of the restoration King Charles II. This king, on getting to the throne, behaved abominably, spending money on lavish parties, whoring around with many mistresses, ignoring the plight of the poor. Perhaps this behaviour is a reaction to his own traumatic experiences during the war, where he was involved in several battles as a young man, and in the end barely escaped with his life.

It was only after the so-called *Glorious Revolution* of 1688, when William of Orange became king and removed the Catholic James, that the constitution began to settle down and the country began to move on from the war, at which point the participants were getting quite old. It might be argued that the country really moved on with the development of democratic ideals, with the critical point in 1720, when the UK (as it was after the union with Scotland) had its first Prime Minister.

Wars leave thousands of veterans and civilians suffering and homeless. It is estimated that in the Civil War 11,000 houses were destroyed. Around 55,000 people were made homeless, and perhaps 100,000 died of disease. There were those who were wounded or maimed who could not look after themselves. The country itself was effectively bankrupt, and there were insufficient food stocks to feed everyone.

The psychological consequences of the war

The memories of war trouble many of the veterans, who may find it difficult to take up normal life again. It is difficult to reconstruct the psychological impact of war from a distance of many hundreds of years. As already discussed, we speak a different language, with different words that mean different things to what they used to mean. We have a set of words relating to the psychological consequences of war that did not exist or were used differently in the seventeenth century. We can try by using the texts that were created in that period. Erin Peters (2016) has attempted to do so in a paper entitled "Trauma narratives of the English Civil War." Peters describes an event from a battle described in verse in 1660, where a soldier thought he was killed and asked to be buried. A surgeon checked him and found no wound.

> 'They bid him rise, and fight, for nought him ail'd,
> But all their words with him nothing prevail'd … (p. 79)

This is similar to the account of the Athenian in Herodotus, who was found on the battlefield without any visible wounds, but was profoundly psychologically damaged by his battle experience, perhaps an hysterical response in both cases.

Many historians will agree that the Civil War must have been very traumatic, perhaps the most traumatic experience the English have had (Hutton, 2004), but most of the evidence is conjecture. The assumption is that because we know the wars were terrible – with many killed and wounded, with starvation through crops not being gathered, with murders by renegade troops, and so on – they must be traumatic, but this does not necessarily follow. Perhaps people responded differently then; perhaps people did not generally have such psychological responses. We need more than an historian's non-psychological interpretation. We need to base our conjectures on what people said and try to interpret what they mean.

Peters (2016) provides another good example, this time from Major George Wither, a Parliamentarian who recorded his *field musings* during the war:

> What Ghosts are they that haunt,
> The Chambers of my breast!'
> And, when I sleep, or comfort want,
> Will give my heart no rest?
> Me thinks the sound of grones,
> Are ever in mine eare:
> Deep-graves, Deaths-heads, and Charnell bones
> Before me, still appeare.
> And, when asleep I fall,
> In hope to finde some ease,
> My dreames, to me, are worst of all.
> And fright me more than these. (pp. 82–83)

Peters is right to suggest this is a post-combat condition that includes several PTSD symptoms such as intrusive thoughts, nightmares, flashbacks and anxiety. It is possible that Shakespeare, writing half a century earlier, had brought the psychological impact of war to the minds of the people writing about it in relation to the Civil War.

Wither (1661) makes a similar point:

> The trumpet sounding, all my thoughts did scatter,
> And gave me, since that houre, but little rest. (p. 84)

This demonstrates that psychological problems relating to war can be incapacitating. According to Peters, the author may be attempting to narrate the troubled past as a way of dealing with the trauma. This may be true. If we draw on our modern assumptions, people who are traumatised may be able to deal with their problems through narration, through telling the story in detail, highlighting critical thoughts, feelings and behaviours. It may also be taking it a little far, in that we have no idea whether Major Withers managed to deal with his problems through his poetry writing. This may be a danger of using assumptions about modern behaviour to understand past behaviour – or it may be a sensible assumption that people do not fundamentally change.

The distinction between individual and collective trauma was not always clear in the Civil Wars; there is a significant overlap between the two. Edmund Pierce (1660) wrote: "Was there ever upon earth any state and society of men, who in so few years have endured such, and so many bitter pangs.... And we, poor hachney'd. spuirr'd and galled people... be we in a dream all this while?" (4–6). Of course, at the time of the Civil War, Europe was suffering through the 30 Years War (1618–1648), which was perhaps the most destructive war in terms of how it affected civilians until the 30 Years War of the twentieth century, 1914–1945.

It was after the restoration of 1660 that much of this work was written. As with so many wars, there is a period of time before veterans start writing about their experiences. This was added to by the impact of the restoration, which led to many Royalists getting their property returned, while those who had signed the document to execute Charles I were arrested, imprisoned, and often executed. The writings post-restoration were also to some extent politicised by the writer's desire to support or attack the restoration. It has been argued that the need to justify the exclusion of dissenters from religious and political life lay at the heart of public memories of the wars until 1715 – the time at which most survivors would be dead. This is another factor largely ignored – how a war can impact on a society for the next 50 years or more while participants are still alive and active.

The restoration led to the re-emergence of memories of the war, along with a growing interest in and awareness of the damage war can do to the mind. This recognition of collective trauma through trauma narratives written and published in the early years of the restoration showed that a psychological impairment of the whole nation is recognised through the writings of a range of individuals. In a sense it is recognising that the master narrative of the nation is suffering the same psychological wounds (on top of physical injury and wounding) as the traumatised individual veteran or civilian. As the seventeenth century progressed, while many people continued to be executed, the method of execution became less brutal. There was a reduction in the number of people being hanged, drawn and quartered, basically disembowelled and chopped up. Perhaps this was a result of the experience of war, and the need to be less brutal.

This chapter has shown that while our terminology relating to psychological trauma is relatively recent, we can identify evidence of the psychological impact of war in the writings of the seventeenth century. While we need to be careful in how we interpret this evidence – using modern language and assuming the responses were the same as they are now is a dangerous road to take – we can tentatively claim that at least some of the psychological response to witnessing and taking part in violent events has changed little in three and a half centuries. What we must be aware of is that life was very different in the seventeenth century. It was harder, people died frequently and at a younger age, starvation was common in the winter, there was little access to medicine and health care. This may have made people stronger when it came to facing traumatic situations such as war, but in the end the responses, on the basis of the evidence presented, suggest the general response to traumatic events was similar to the present day.

Stoyle (2003) has claimed that there is still much work to be done regarding the *mental scars* of the Civil War. It is not only that we know little about the immediate impact of the war, but we know very little about how these traumatic experiences and times were integrated into the cultural narratives of the country. Those who study history do tend to split it into particular eras, sometimes without considering the impact, particularly the psychological impact, of one era on another. The survivors of the Civil War, the majority of the soldiers, would be the ones running the country in the 1660s and 1670s. People who were too young to fight but who might have been seriously affected by their experiences would be running the country in the 1680s and 1690s. Perhaps they were the ones who were driven to try and improve the democratic standards in the country because they did not want to see another civil war.

In 1661, just after the Restoration, Wither wrote about the war:

> My pen I re-assum'd, and (full of matter)
> Sate down to write: But ere I ought exprest,
> The trumpet sounding, all my thoughts did scatter,
> And gave me, since that houre, but little rest.
> Destructive times, distractive muzings yeeld,
> Expect not therefore method now of me,
> But such as fits Minerva in the Field,
> Where Interruptions and Confusions be …. (pp. 2–3)

It is as though he thinks it is time to write about the war, but that when he tries he is still unable to express himself clearly. He has not processed his traumatic memories of the war into an organised narrative. Perhaps it is still too soon for him.

This chapter has highlighted how we can find evidence of the seventeenth century Civil War all around us. They affected communities all over the country. While we may know a lot about the major battles such as Edgehill (the first major – and indecisive – battle of the war), Marston Moor (where the Royalists lost the North of England) and Naseby (where the New Model Army effectively destroyed the remains of the Royalist army), all over the country there are the sites of smaller battles, skirmishes and sieges and, just like Wingfield Manor, it is worth finding out the stories of these often lost locally important events.

It is also clear that people were writing about the trauma of the civil wars, the psychological impact of the wars on those who took part. The language is sometimes surprisingly modern, and not difficult to interpret. As with most wars, a lot of the writing took place some years after the fighting ended, when people were still significantly affected by their experiences. In this case, much of the writing was done after the restoration, over a decade after most of the fighting.

8

CIUDAD RODRIGO AND SALAMANCA

The Peninsular War

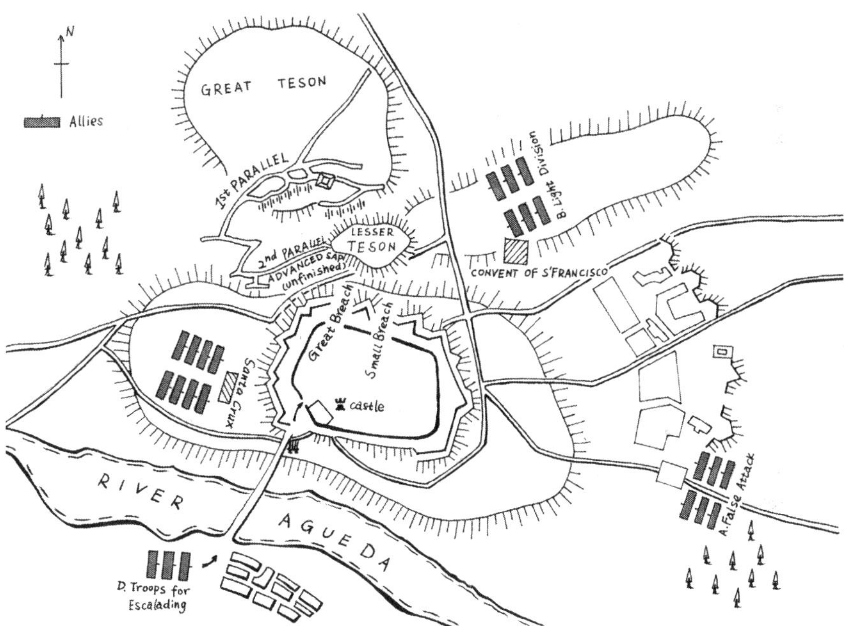

CIUDAD RODRIGO. The siege of Ciudad Rodrigo was a classic siege. The parallels for the siege guns were dug into the Greater and Lesser Tesons, and bombarded the town, creating the Great and Small Breaches. The former is still visible today. There are unfortunately houses built over the Lesser Teson, but you can walk up the Greater Teson and observe the town. The walls are largely complete, as are the surrounding fortifications.

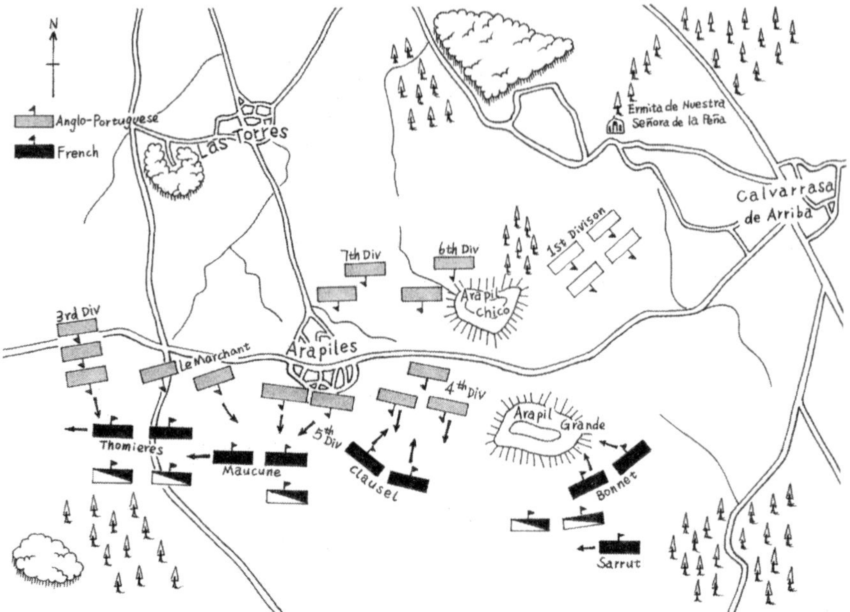

BATTLE OF SALAMANCA. This area is still largely as it would have been at the time of the battle, large open spaces (probably more fences than in 1812) with the distinct small hills of the Arapiles. From the top of Arapil Grande there is a good view of the whole battlefield and it was for a time used as an observation post for the French commanders, until it was taken by the Allies. There are markers places around the battlefield, and a trail that can be obtained from the Internet or from the tourist office in Salamanca. The battlefield can be walked in a day.

The Peninsular War was fought between the British and the French in Spain and Portugal. France and Spain had invaded Portugal in 1807 and then France took over Spain in 1808 as a result of the Spanish rebelling against de facto French rule in Madrid. Napoleon installed his brother Joseph on the Spanish throne. Throughout the subsequent war the Spanish and Portuguese were both nominally allied to Britain, and on occasion fought in the same battles. The British troops were led by Arthur Wellesley, who gained his dukedom in this war, and so became Wellington. It was actually his brother who chose the name Wellington as Wellesley was fighting in the Peninsular War. Fortunately, Wellesley was happy with the title.

There were many skirmishes and battles during this complex and extended war, which lasted from 1808 to 1814, when the British Army crossed the Pyrenees into France, but the focus here is on two of them, the Battle of Salamanca (July 1812), a large-scale set piece battle fought to the south of Salamanca; and the siege of Ciudad Rodrigo earlier in the same year (January 1812), which is a good illustration of siege warfare.

The siege of Ciudad Rodrigo

Ciudad Rodrigo is near the Portuguese border, on the River Agueda. It is also on the road from Portugal to Salamanca and Madrid, so was an important strategic point for both armies: the French to attack Portugal, and the Allies to strike from Portugal towards Madrid and northern Spain. The town was – and is – fortified, but the fortifications were old fashioned and ineffective. An old Moorish castle overlooking the river provided little defence against nineteenth century artillery, and the main walls of the town, surrounded by a deep dry moat, were supposedly protected by the glacis (a long shallow bank which was meant to deflect shot away from the main walls), but the glacis was at some points three metres lower than the walls, enabling direct fire on the walls. Normally the top of the glacis is at the same height as the town walls to protect them from cannon fire. This was the town's downfall, as the British artillery quickly forced two breaches.

The British attacked from the direction of Portugal (you can still drive along the old dirt track used by the British Army and get straight through to Portugal), quickly taking the outlying forts of Santa Cruz and San Francisco – both of which are now buried among the expanding town; and the French redoubt on the Grand Teson, a hill a few hundred metres to the west overlooking the town. It was from here that the siege began. The British dug traverses and three parallels for the artillery to focus its fire on two points of the wall, one corner near the main church, and the other near the northern entrance. In siege warfare it is critical to concentrate the fire on localised points to weaken the walls and – hopefully – make them collapse. There is still some evidence of the British earthworks on the Grand Teson, though the hill is on private land. Unfortunately, the view enjoyed by the British observers at the top of the hill is partly obscured by modern buildings which are at the foot of the hill.

The larger breach is still evident in the wall and is a good example of a breach. The rubble has been cleared and the wall partly rebuilt, but the site is obvious. The lesser breach has been rebuilt and there is no trace of it, apart from a marker indicating where General Crauford, who was the commander of the Light Division, is buried inside the breach itself.

The siege began on 8 January 1812 and had to be hurried because of the fear that the town might be relieved by advancing French armies. It was garrisoned by 2000 Frenchmen under General Barrie and had strong defences, with walls, dry moat and glacis, all reasonably modern, though unable to protect against accurate cannon fire. The weakness of the town was the proximity of two hills, the Greater Teson and the Lesser Teson, which are very close, and the site chosen for the Allied artillery.

The conditions for the troops were terrible in that winter, with troops creating shelter by "[digging] a large hole in the snow. In the centre, we kept a good fire, round which we sat the men on duty.... Often we would sink [through the snow] nto some hole or burrow... . We were on duty every other night, our clothes worn thin and wrecked by the fatigues of the former campaign." (Wheeler, quoted in Esdaile, 2009, p. 202)

The cold was remarked on by many of the participants: "The weather was so severe and the cold so intense that the army could not encamp … the frost was so excessive that we were almost completely benumbed, and nothing but hardworking, I believe, kept us from perishing from the cold; indeed, it was said, some Portuguese soldiers actually died from its effects." (Donaldson, 1841, p. 149)

On the first night the French Reynaud Redoubt, situated on the Greater Teson, was captured, and so the siege trenches (parallels) could be started, the first on the Greater Teson and the second on the Lesser Teson. These were constructed by the troops under fire from the French, so it was a dangerous business. Immediately after they were constructed the cannon were brought up to attack the town's walls. Unfortunately for the French the walls, after the 1810 siege, had been reconstructed with poor quality mortar, so they started crumbling almost immediately. By the 18th of January, a fourth battery had been placed in the first parallel. This fired on a tower situated where the main road now enters the town. The tower collapsed forward, providing a path for the attackers. By the 19th, the two breaches were ready, though they were steeper than they should have been.

The attack occurred in the evening of the 19th of January. A diversionary attack across the river against the castle took place. This succeeded in capturing two guns placed outside the castle which would have provided enfilade fire on the main breach. The main breach was then attacked. The forlorn hope was required to cross the glacis, drop into the dry moat and climb up the broken walls – under heavy fire – and on reaching the top they had a 5 m drop onto strong defences made of sharp swords, metal, wood, and anything that would hurt the attackers while the defenders fired on them with everything they had, from muskets to grapeshot. As the attackers broke through, the French detonated a large mine, which killed many of the troops, but the rest fought through into the town.

Edward Costello was in the forlorn hope at Ciudad Rodrigo: "As we neared the breach, canister, grape, round-shot and shell, with fire-balls to show our ground, come pouring … around us, with a regular hailstorm of bullets….up we mounted to attack the breach. The fire kept up was most deadly, and our men, for some minutes, as they appeared in small bodies, were swept away. However, they still persevered, and gradually formed a lodgement … I had got up with the first, and was struggling with a crowd of our fellows to push over the splintered and broken wall." (p. 203) The men got through the breach and entered the town, "pell-mell …. Among the first I saw … was my oen captain, Uniacke, rushing along with a few men to the right of the breach …. This was the last time he was doomed to be our head: a few moments afterwards the French sprang a mine, by which the whole party were killed or maimed." (Costello, quoted in Esdaille, p. 203) In this same account, Costello describes the wounding of General Crauford after he had given orders to lead the way. There is some confusion here as Crauford was at the lesser breach, while the incidents described previously occurred at the main breach. This suggests Costello's account is not fully accurate, but perhaps partially built on memories of events and tales retold by others. His account was published in 1841, nearly 30 years after the events, and suggests we need to be careful in assigning truth to personal accounts.

John Douglas described the experience of being part of the forlorn hope. This was at Badajoz, shortly after Ciudad Rodrigo, but the similarities are strong: "Yet death in all its terrors was unable to quench the courage of the British soldier. Amodst the storm of bullets and missiles of death which were hurled on them, they stood braving the tempest which no human power could quell." (p. 37) He then describes the aftermath of the siege, with the soldiers let loose in the streets: "To attempt anything in the hope of a description of the scene that was going on would be a task not easily performed, and even could it be delineated no one (unless an eyewitness) would credit the tale." (p. 38) This recognition that there are things that are too horrific to be believable or to be described is common to the experience of war, with no words able to relate the horrors, but Douglas does provide some examples, though less graphic than might now be written: "The excesses committed were horrible .... An office of the 30th Regiment lost his life in attempting to save a young woman from violation .... In the streets the scene was at times laughable; here a fine fire blazing, while every tot was in requisition. Up comes a soldier with his bayonet fixed and as much bacon and salt fish on it as he could skewer.... the drunken rascals could not let a swallow fly past without a dozen balls being fired after it." (pp. 38–39) Much of the detail of the rapes, murder and pillaging is missing from this description, presumably not seen as suitable for a civilian reader. As John Mills wrote in a letter to his mother: "The scene such as it was when I saw it, stripped of half its horrors, was beyond all imagination... one continued mass of friends and foes lying dead – caps, clothes, arms, cannon balls, ammunition, beds, chairs, wearing apparel, legs, etc, filled the streets. Those who saw this scene on the morning after describe it as dreadful beyond expression." (quoted in Richards, 2002, p. 133)

Douglas also describes being ordered to the main breach after the battle was over: "Such a sense of destruction as was here presented to the view baffles description. The very rungs (or steps of the ladders) by which the troops descended into the ditch were literally shot to atoms with musket balls, while underneath the dead and dying lay in heaps; some calling for a drink for God's sake while their drunken comrades were selling their booty without taking the least notice." (p. 39) Care for the wounded in 1812 was generally very poor. If a soldier was wounded, there was a good chance he would die. The medical services were limited, with the surgeon and his assistants generally trying to prevent gangrene by sawing off limbs. Those who experienced amputation still had a high chance of dying from blood loss or shock. Follow up treatment was limited. The attitude of the authorities to the ordinary soldier was dismissive. While alive and fit for duty he had some worth. If wounded or ill he was of little value. The respect for human life was very different in the early nineteenth century. The soldier was still expected to keep his upper lip stiff. Major George

Napier had to have his arm amputated after Ciudad Rodrigo. The operation took at least 20 minutes due to blunt instruments. "I must confess that I did not bear the amputation of my arm as well as I ought to have done, I made noise enough when the knife cut through my skin and flesh. It is no joke I assure you …. I then thanked [the surgeon] for his kindness, having sworn at him like a trooper while he was at it … and proceeded to find some place to lie down and rest." (quoted in Richards, 2002, p. 133)

There are other accounts of the sacking of Ciudad Rodrigo: "Our troops, as soon as the breach was gained, more eager for plunder than their duty, broke and ran in defiance of their officers … and committed shameful excesses disgraceful to the whole army. [There was] not a soul that was not rifled, and the dead were scarcely cold when they were inhumanly stripped… No intentional murders were committed, though some men were so drunk that they fired promiscuously in the streets and killed many of their comrades." (Swabey, quoted in Esdaile, 2009, p. 205)

It is rare for a participant to admit to taking part in what we now see as atrocities but were at the time the right of the soldier to rampage in a city after a successful siege. John Mills was no different: "The scene of rapine I am told beggared all description. The town was on fire in many places, every house was ransacked; in short, for the whole of the night it was given up to pillage." (quoted in Richards, p. 132)

Inside the town the troops plundered, raped and killed, though this was mostly under control by the following morning. The behaviour of the troops after a successful siege was part of the rules of warfare. If a besieged town surrendered quickly, the besieging army would protect the civilian population, but if the town held out in the hope that a relieving force might attack the besieging army then on the successful completion of the siege the troops were allowed to attack the population at will. One of the worst examples of this during the Peninsular War was at the siege of Badajoz shortly after Ciudad Rodrigo, another Spanish town on the border with Portugal further south. The Allied soldiers suffered around 4800 deaths during the intense fighting when the breaches were being stormed. They were so enraged that they went on the rampage, killing perhaps 4000 Spanish civilians, along with mass rapes and thieving. It took three days to bring order to the town. When officers tried to control their men, they were threatened with death. Only a few years ago on the 200th anniversary of the siege one of the regiments involved attempted to set up a memorial to those who had fought there but the Badajoz people refused them permission due to their behaviour after the siege. Memories can be long.

Ciudad Rodrigo: The tour

This tour relates to the January 1812 siege, where Wellington's troops overcame the French garrison in short order. This is a walking tour which can be done in an hour or two, depending on the time spent exploring. Start from the northern entrance to the town where the lesser breach was made. Just inside the walls is the plaque to General Crauford, who was buried here after he was killed on the glacis outside as the Light Brigade attacked the breach. Go through the entrance and look back at the citadel, noting the walls that were rebuilt after the siege. Note the structure of the defences: from the outside, a glacis that gets steeper near the main breach, then an outer ditch 3 m deep with a 6 m climb to the faussebrai with its covered walkway, then another ditch 7 m wide with a 10 m climb to the parapet of the main wall. Just beyond is a ravelin, that would enable enfilade fire on troops attempting the breach. We will come back to the defences, but Donaldson (1841) indicated how they climbed down into the ditch: "each section was provided with a pick-axe and rope, we advanced rank entire under a heavy fire from the garrison, to the brink of the trench, where planting the one end of the pick-axe firmly in the ground, we threw the noose of the rope over the other, and then descended by it into the ditch." (p. 151)

Head down Avenue Yurramadi and then left along Avenue Espana to the St. Francisco convent. This was fortified by the French and taken by the British before the main assault. The Light Brigade waited behind here before attacking the lesser breach, as this was the nearest cover. Facing the convent, turn left (west) down avenue Portugal, and where it forks take the upper road. Note the citadel, the cathedral tower damage caused by the guns and the site of the main breach to the right of the cathedral tower. Turn right up Calle Bailen. You are now climbing the Lesser Teson where the 2nd parallel was sited – there were no buildings here of course. It was from here that the site of the lesser breach was cannoned. Go over the hill. In front is the Greater Teson, the site of the first parallel. At the end of the road turn right, and then left up a footpath to the left of the sports complex. Cross the railway line – it is in use so be careful – and climb the Greater Teson. From the top you can see across the buildings on the Lesser Teson and across to the citadel, and with a little imagination you can see how the guns were sited to bombard the main breach. Beyond the top of the hill the remains of the French Reynaud redoubt can be seen, but this is on private land. This redoubt was built after the first siege to protect the citadel, but it was quickly taken by the Allied force. To the right as you are looking towards the citadel there is a depression in the field (private on my last visit though open before) which is presumably part of the first parallel, though there is no evidence for this apart from its position.

Return down the hill and turn right. Go along to where the road starts to go downhill and then turn left. Go down the steps at the end of the road, observing the size of the citadel's defences as you are taking the same route as the soldiers attacking the main breach. Cross the road and climb to the top of the glacis. It is steep, but a little easier than it was for the forlorn hope attacking the breach under fire. From the top there is a good view of the site of the main breach, which was repaired by the British after the siege, and the difficulties the troops would have had climbing down into the first ditch, up and over the faussebrai, down into the inner ditch and up the rubble left by the breach. At the top the French had put all sorts of makeshift defences, along with cannon and muskets, and then a mine they exploded as the British troops got through the breach.

Explore the area. Turn left and walk along the top of the glacis, observing the damage to the inner wall caused by stray shot, and the clearer view of the damage to the cathedral. Go past the ravelin and to the road where you started the tour. Turn right and then immediately right up the steps to the faussebrai and the covered walkway (only covered in the sense of providing a wall to protect the defenders. Again, as you walk this route you get an impression of the formidable defences. You can climb down and into either ditch and up into the ravelin, but continue along the covered way to the main breach. Again, there is a good view of it, and you can see the height the men had to climb to get into the citadel. Continue along until the next entrance, taking time to observe the cannon and the position of the Tesons.

Just after the entrance there is the castle, which is now a Parador – well worth visiting. A secondary attack here destroyed two cannon that were placed in the castle gardens, endangering any men who came along this route.

Go through the entrance and immediately turn right to climb the steps to the main terreplein, where the defenders could see and attack the British. Here there were emplaced cannon to counter the Allied cannon and disrupt troop movements. From here you can also see that there is a drop down to the level of the town itself, sometimes as much as 5 m. Head to the position of the main breach and take the perspective of the defenders and also the attackers. From here there is a clear view of the Tesons where the British prepared for the assault, and it is a good position to fire down on the men assaulting the defenders. There are various plaques commemorating both the 1810 and the 1812 sieges.

The tour ends here, but it is worth exploring the walls further along to the site of the lesser breach and beyond to get a better view of the town's defences. It is also worth exploring the streets, which are much as they were in 1812 when the soldiers went on the rampage. The main square, where many of the French surrendered, has numerous cafes and restaurants for refreshment. It was here that Donaldson (1841) reported that 18 deserters were also found, who were then tried and shot.

Salamanca: The battle

The Battle of Salamanca took place on 22 July 1812, after the Allied armies had invaded Spain from Portugal after the successful sieges of the frontier towns of Ciudad Rodrigo and Badajoz. There was no real intention to fight at Salamanca, as the two armies had been shadowing each other for some time. For the last few days they had been heading south towards Salamanca, with the French on top of a ridge and the Allies in the valley below. After crossing the Tormes outside Salamanca, the French made to wheel west, with the Allies wheeling inside them, around the edge of Salamanca. The French commander, Marshall Auguste Marmont , thought the Allies were retreating when he saw a dust cloud heading away to the west, so he moved the French forward. Unfortunately for the French he was mistaken. The dust cloud was from the baggage train. Wellington's army was hidden behind a ridge, out of sight of the French. When Wellington saw the French heading west and becoming over-extended, he ordered the attack.

The battle was a significant defeat for the French. The armies were roughly equal, with around 50,000 troops each. A Spanish division was present but took no part in the battle. The British undertook a series of flanking manoeuvres on the French left wing, which led to the collapse of the French forces there. The French commander Marmont and his deputy commander were both wounded early in the battle, inevitably causing some confusion. The battlefield has two distinct hills, the Greater and Lesser Arapiles (named after the nearby village, which was itself within the boundaries of the battle). The French placed artillery on top of the Greater Arapil, which enabled the French to repulse two Allied attacks, one Portuguese attack being directly up the slopes of the Greater Arapil.

The French attempted to counterattack in the centre. This initially had some success but was beaten back by the Allies. This led to the eventual French collapse and retreat towards the bridge at Garcia Hernandez, where there was a skirmish along the line of low hills, with Wellington's King's German Legion, a unit of heavy dragoons, breaking a French square, a highly unusual and difficult feat – so they did it twice for good measure.

Salamanca: The tour

This is a driving tour around the battlefield, which is better driven using a 4 × 4, as a lot of it is off-road, on tracks that may not have changed that much since the battle. While most tracks are passable in an ordinary car, some are not. There are parts that can be walked instead of driven, though the whole route is a good day's walk.

The local authorities have highlighted a set of sites that were critical to the battle, so the route more or less follows these. Further details can be found at the website http://www.sitiohistoricolosarapiles.com/sitiohistorico.php.

Leave Salamanca to the south east on the CL-510 towards Alba de Tormes – which incidentally is where the Spanish division was meant to cut off the French retreat towards Alba de Tormes. Unfortunately, they were not in place at the right time and had not informed Wellington, so the French army got away along this route. The ridge joins the route the French army took before the battle, heading south past Salamanca before wheeling right just after the point we turn off at Calvarassa de Arriba. On entering the town, turn right at the signpost for Ermita de Nuestra Senora de la Pena. This becomes a dirt track. The ermita is 500 m along the track. It was here that some of the first shots of the battle took place between the skirmishers of the French and Allied armies. This is also a good viewpoint for the eastern part of the battle, with the Arapiles ahead, the lesser to the right and the greater to the left. There is an information board.

Take the track below the ermita and follow it until it joins the Los Arapiles road. Turn right, cross the disused railway and park below the Lesser Arapil with the information board. The British occupied the Lesser Arapil with two cannon and infantry, firing on the French who occupied the Greater Arapil on the other side of the road. It was at the latter where Marshall Marmont, commanding the French forces, was wounded, an act which arguably won the battle for the British as he was about to give orders that the French divisions advancing to the west (effectively into the Allied flanking attacks at the start of the battle, which overstretched the French Army) should halt. The order was never given.

From here return to the road and take the next track to the right. Head to the top of the small hill, where information boards can be seen to the left. This was where Wellington spent most of the battle directing his forces. This is one of the best panoramas of the battlefield. The information boards show the various positions of the armies and their movements.

From here continue along the track. La Torro lies below to the right. It was from in front of this village that Le Marchand's heavy cavalry started their charge that disrupted two French divisions. The position is a good one as it enabled the cavalry to be hidden behind the ridge until they began their charge. Head towards La Torro and take the Los Arapiles road to see the information board. Drive to Los Arapiles. Take the road to the right and then almost immediately a track to the left. You are crossing where the French divisions were attacked by the heavy cavalry. The cavalry had to charge uphill to meet the French, but still succeeded in defeating them, demonstrating the power of massed horses. Follow the track to the road, running parallel to the motorway. At the end turn sharp right over the motorway, and then turn left to Miranda. It was around here that Pakenham's division attacked Thomiere's 7th French division, which was marching ahead of the rest of the French army, dispersing the divisions and leading Wellington to decide to attack. Head north on a track to Teso de Aldeatejada, a small hill where Pakenham's division was placed and where Wellington rode to tell Pakenham personally that he should attack.

From here head back to Los Arapiles, where there was severe street fighting involving the Coldstream Guards, and where after the battle the surgeons struggled to keep up with the medical needs of the wounded, particularly the number of men needing amputation. On entering the village from the west, take a track to the right, signposted La Cuquera (though the wooden sign is a good few metres up the track). From here the view to the south indicates the area where the French divisions tried unsuccessfully to defend themselves from the heavy cavalry and from the infantry.

Continue along the track and take the next track on the left, then one on the right. You are cutting across the positions of the French divisions both just before their counterattack that nearly broke the Allied divisions to the west of the Arapiles, and their final position as they tried to provide a rearguard action after the battle was lost.

Continue zigzagging along the tracks until reaching the Greater Arapil (at least one of these tracks is not passable without a 4 × 4 – unless walking). You can either park at the base and walk to the top or (only using a 4 × 4) drive up a track. At the top, though the hill has been defaced with quarries, there is a memorial to the battle. From here there is a clear view of most of the battlefield and it should have given the French an advantage had they controlled their troop movements more effectively (note Marmont's wounding). When the Portuguese attacked the forward slopes of this hill they nearly reached the top but were repulsed as they tried to climb the final rocks.

This is the end of the tour, but in Los Arapiles village there is a museum dedicated to the battle, and it is worth spending time at various sites getting an idea of the small hills, ridges and slopes that would have provided an advantage to one side or the other at various points in the battle. One of the reasons the Allies won is that the French saw a dust cloud towards the west and thought the army was retreating, when actually it was hidden behind the ridge of the Teso de san Miguel, Wellington's viewpoint.

Most of the places on the tour have information boards that provide some information in Spanish and English, though not sufficient to provide a decent overview of the battle. Perhaps the best battlefield guide is the *Osprey* (Fletcher, 2012). In classic *Osprey* style, this provides photographs, maps and drawings indicating the key features of the battle and is extremely useful when visiting the battlefield.

The experience of soldiers in the Peninsular War

There are numerous accounts of the way the troops were treated – usually badly – in the Peninsular War. They were ill-paid, often ill-fed, and were subjected to horrendous punishment for what to the modern mind are relatively minor misdemeanours (see the following section). While the French troops tried to survive by living off the land, which basically meant stealing food from the local people, which of course led to them being hated even more than they were hated for invading Spain and Portugal, the British attempted to provide supplies for their soldiers, bringing in food from Britain and elsewhere, and sending it to the soldiers via ox and mule train. While this was a good idea, the system often failed. For much of the war the British were also fighting the USA, and supplies, particularly from the Americas to Portugal, were sometimes taken by the U.S. fleet. Once the supplies reached Lisbon they were off-loaded and put on mules and ox carts for sending inland to the army. Locals were employed on the task and some would choose to desert with the supplies or to steal part of them. They were also delayed for any number of reasons, and so the troops would often go hungry for days. They were allowed to buy food off the local populace, but this was not always easy. Often there was no money and so promissory notes were used, which many people did not want to accept as there was no real guarantee the money would be forthcoming. Soldiers did sometimes find alternative food.

For instance, after the Battle of Salamanca, Douglas (1997), a Sergeant in the 1st Royal Scots noted: :The only piece of plunder either I or my comrade got happened to be a leg of mutton off a Frenchman's knapsack, which I put in a kettle to boil." (p. 48) Later Douglas describes looking for food in a peasant cottage and finding a sausage hidden up the chimney, it "made an excellent meal, but being highly seasoned, rendered a drink very desirable. Accordingly, a search commenced and succeeded in discovering a cask concealed in the cellar, from which we slaked our thirst." (p. 54) In other words, soldiers of the British Army did plunder the locals, along with the defeated enemy. Another example of the constant search for food occurs in Douglas (1997), after Salamanca: "It would appear that every man was his own butcher, or at least killed his own meat, as the firing was so thick along the hills at the sheep. These in general were not so large as the Leicestershire breed, but their flesh uncommonly well flavoured, at least we hungry soldiers thought so." (p. 48)

There was a recognition that plunder had bad effects, particularly after a siege. Donaldson (1841) describes how the victorious soldiers at Badajoz appeared: It "was like a masquerade, the men going about intoxicated, dressed in the various dresses they had found in the town; French and Spanish officers, priests, friars, and nuns, were promiscuously mixed, cutting as many antics as a mountebank.... Indeed the giving leave to plunder the town, was productive of nothing but bad consequences, and for the interests of humanity, and the army at large, I hope such license may never recur, should we be again unfortunately plunged in war." (p. 162) The Peninsular War was one of the last where armies victorious in a siege were legitimately allowed to plunder a town, though of course it was not the last time it happened.

One common element found in virtually all armies at any period is that of comradeship, the reliance of each man on the others in his unit, and the special feelings between those who shared battles. This is talked about in other chapters (for example, Normandy), but the recognition of comradeship comes through the writings of those who took part in the Peninsular War. While pursuing the French after Salamanca, Douglas (1997) describes meeting a comrade: "I was overtaken by an old schoolfellow of the 27th Regiment, with a hearty shake of the hand. 'Why', said he, 'I was inquiring about you as the Regiment passed, and they told me you were killed yesterday'. 'Well Bob', said I, 'You see it's a lie'. He having a little in the canteen, we drank to bygone days and distant friends." (p. 48)

As noted, soldiers who broke the rules were severely punished. The most serious punishments were hanging or shooting (e.g., murderers or deserters), but the most common was flogging. Many of the veterans writing about the war described the floggings that took place. On many occasions the number of lashes administered would kill the person. Sometimes severe floggings were awarded for minor acts. For instance, Rifleman Harris describes how General Crauford, a leader usually respected by his men and who died at Ciudad Rodrigo, held a drumhead court for two men who allegedly deserted on the retreat to the port of Vigo and awarded 300 lashes on the spot to a rifleman, Dan Howens, for speaking his mind at the hearing (Harris, 1848). Donaldson (1841) describes one officer, in command of the regiment, who introduced flogging for "every trivial offence" (p. 146) There were floggings at most evening parades. He also made the men who had been flogged wear a yellow and black patch on their arm, with holes cut to indicate how many times they had been flogged. Donaldson was quite clear that flogging had very negative psychological effects: "as good men were liable to be punished for the slightest fault, the barrier between them and the hardened ill-doers was broken down, and as they had lost respect in their own eyes, they either became broken-hearted and inefficient soldiers, or grew reckless of every thing, and launched into crime; those who were hardened and unprincipled before, being brought by the prevalence of punishment nearer a level with better men, seemed to glory in misconduct. In fact, all ideas of honour and character were lost, and listless apathy and bad conduct were the prevailing feature of the corps at this time." (p. 146) Donaldson goes on to say that flogging was useless at reclaiming the bad men and damaging to the good. The stigma attached to being flogged was strong and could last years. For many, flogging made no difference, and Donaldson noted two examples, one a deserter and the other a drunk. After receiving several floggings for their behaviour, they still carried on deserting and getting drunk. Donaldson is liberal for his age, noting that drunkenness is something that should be treated medically rather than punished.

We have already seen something of the difficulties faced by the casualties of the war. Many of the participants who wrote about the war described the horrendous casualties. Donaldson (1841) describes the effects of a cavalry charge: "many of them [were] dreadfully wounded by our dragoons, some having their arms hanging by a shred of flesh and skin, and others with hideous gashes in their faces." (p. 168) He then describes other casualties: "A Portuguese cadet who was attached to our regiment, received a shell in the centre of his body, which, bursting at the same instant, literally blew him to pieces. Another poor fellow receiving a grape shot across his belly, his bowels protruded, and he was obliged to apply both his hands to the wound to keep them in; I shall never forget the expression of agony depicted in his countenance." (p. 168) Douglas describes a hospital where: "we had a poor Frenchman with his arm taken out of the socket, and so completely you would really imagine he was born minus that wing. I often thought the French made use of unfair balls during the siege. Such a number of wounds mortified it was pitiable to see the poor fellows when seized with the lockjaw – because there is rarely a remedy." (p. 85) Douglas is suggesting that the French used poisoned musket balls which had the effect of giving the wounded soldiers tetanus, which was then untreatable. Douglas also describes the casualties after Salamanca: "I never saw the British casualties so thick, while we passed on in pursuit, striving to avoid treading on the wounded, who were calling for a little water for God's sake, which was entirely out of our power to give; or in the more feeling accents of comrades they pleaded, 'Don't trample on us'." (p. 47) The other problem casualties at Salamanca faced was the grass and wheat catching fire from the sparks of the muskets. Many on both sides who were unable to move were consumed by these fires. Rifleman Harris describes the effects of being in battle and seeing friends as casualties: "the sight of so much bloodshed around will not suffer the mind to dwell long on any particular casualty, even though it happens to be one's dearest friend. There was no time either to think, for all was action with us rifles at this moment." (Fitchett, 2009, p. 148) These scenes are described across the centuries in battle. When a battle is underway there is rarely time to think or reflect, simply to fight for one's life.

The horrors of this period on the Iberian Peninsula were vividly described in the drawings of Goya, entitled "The Disasters of War," a series of 82 prints that were published in 1863 after the author's death. The prints are in three categories, war, famine and cultural allegories. Many of the plates are ambiguous, and Goya did not provide satisfactory explanations beyond the short title of each. The early plates appear to be opposed to the French invasion and display the French as hulking figures attacking innocent Spanish people, while as the series goes on the representations become more ambiguous, perhaps suggesting that there was guilt in war on both sides. The reason for mentioning it here is that some of the scenes would be familiar to the troops who fought in the war, as perpetrators, victims and as witnesses. Even as witnesses to some of the extreme violence, the impact on the soldiers must have been tremendous.

While there are many detailed accounts of the experience of war, the language used by the participants is very different to the language we use today. To examine the psychological consequences of war using these sources is difficult. No one speaks of psychological trauma, though they do speak of horror, terror and fear. There are descriptions of what we might now call traumatic memory. Donaldson (1841), describing the aftermath of Ciudad Rodrigo, mentions seeing his friend's body. "When I saw him stretched lifeless on the breach, that scene flashed full on my memory," (pp. 152–153) with the idea that the memory was still strong when he wrote the book many years later. There are detailed accounts of battle from which we can interpret the fear that the men must have felt. As in any war it is training and discipline which enable people to continue the fight in the face of overwhelming terror and the urge to run away; yet the accounts we have generally speak in positive tones of the battle. Perhaps this is because those who wrote the books were usually those who had come out of the war psychologically healthy. Perhaps we do not hear from those who were permanently damaged by their experiences, we can only guess at the problems they faced after returning home, though we do know that many ended up in asylums (not unlike soldiers after World War I). It was reported in 1819 that military pensioners were kept in non-military asylums throughout the country.

Other examples of the use of language are found in the writings of Rifleman Harris. In battle he talks of "The French… annoyed us much from that quarter" (p. 17), or "The dreadful turmoil and noise of the engagement." (p. 30) There are interesting terms here. The French were seen as annoying, which presumably is quite an understatement to the modern mind, which is more likely to describe horrific events in full, though it may be that Harris was ensuring that his work would not be censored. It is a similar situation with the word *dreadful*. We now apply this word to rather mediocre situations ("the service in the restaurant was dreadful") whereas in the nineteenth century the word may have had connotations more like how we describe an event as *traumatic*. To a large extent we are guessing when we discuss the changing meaning of words, but we nevertheless need to make the attempt to understand what people are meaning. Harris also used the same word in another situation, "there was a dreadful pause" before executing a fellow soldier; indicating the thoughts that would be going through the minds of the witnesses to the event. While this may not be traumatic, it shows the word is significant. The other important point made by Harris is that those who describe their experiences of battle are limited in their views: "All I can do is tell the things which happened around me, and that, I think, is as much as a private soldier can be expected to do." (pp. 19–20)

Conclusions

In all, around one million British troops participated in the Napoleonic wars, with around 315,000 killed or dying of disease – nearly as many British dying as in World War II. The Peninsular War was the longest part of these wars for the British. It played a significant role in British life for several years, and the veterans of the war often returned maimed, without a job or family, and experienced difficulties in adjusting to civilian life. The Peninsular War saw the participants facing some terrible difficulties, as in all war. This was a large-scale war and was also part of the Spanish War of Independence, that began after the French invaded and conquered the country in 1808, and part of the bigger war against Napoleon. It should also be remembered that Britain was fighting here at the same time as they were fighting against the USA, so resources were stretched, which is why it was sometimes difficult to keep the army on campaign.

The battles were terrible, the fighting savage, the damage that was done to the human body by musket ball, shot and shell, and by sword was horrific. The wounds many faced were effectively untreatable as military medicine was lacking sophistication. There was little that could be given to kill pain apart from strong alcohol, the only thing to ward off gangrene was amputation (which often led to shock, blood loss and death), and any poisoning from cloth taken into the body by a musket ball could easily cause death as wounds were rarely properly cleaned.

The soldiers formed comradely groups as all soldiers do. They generally put up with their lives, though there were many deserters. Discipline was harsh, perhaps too harsh. There was little prospect of the ordinary soldier having an idea of when he might get home, particularly as the war dragged on with apparently little progress. These were very hard times for soldiers. This was also one of the last wars fought on the traditional battlefield, with lines of troops firing muskets at each other from a short range, and cavalry coming along to disrupt the enemy infantry divisions. Salamanca was a very good example of this, with large open fields which were easy for manoeuvres and for cavalry charges, with two small hills that should have been relatively easily defended, but the impact for the French of losing their commander at an early stage demonstrates the importance of leadership. The siege of Ciudad Rodrigo was a classic siege, using tactics that had been passed down from the time of Vauban in the seventeenth century. Weapons were more powerful, but the walls still needed to be breached before the besieging force could defeat the defenders.

Both battlefields are worth a visit, as both provide a situation where, with a little reading, it is relatively easy to imagine the unfolding of events – albeit from the safe vantage point of time.

9

WATERLOO

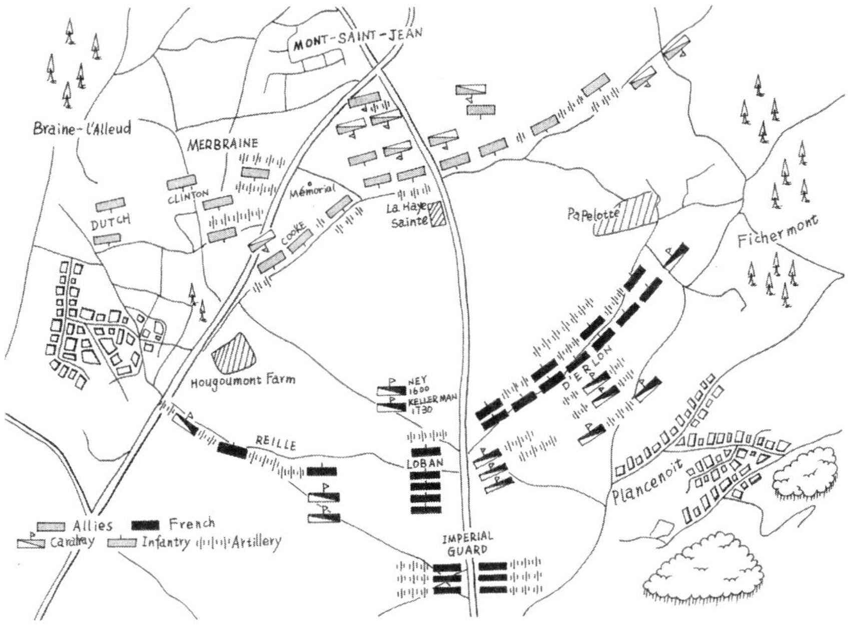

WATERLOO. This is a well-trodden battlefield with perhaps more memorials per square metre than anywhere except some areas of the Western Front. There are clear paths around the battlefield. It is important to walk the ridge to the north of La Haye Sainte and see how the Allies were well hidden behind the ridge, to see the farms of La Haye Sainte (unfortunately not accessible and next to a main road) and Hougoumont Farm (now open as accommodation for the Landmark Trust). Both are similar to how they were at the time of the battle. It is also important to walk the French lines to see how they were at a disadvantage from the start. Wellington chose the site of the battle well. Plancenoit still has the churchyard that was heavily fought over as the Prussians advanced.

This chapter is slightly different from the other battle chapters. While it focuses on the Battle of Waterloo in 1815, there is also a discussion about memorialisation and commemoration, as this was one of the first modern battles to be heavily memorialized, and an exploration of the reasons why we still commemorate this battle after 200 years.

So much has been written about this battle that nothing but a brief outline is required. Someone wishing to explore the battlefield can obtain one of the more detailed accounts – which also applies to the other battles in the book, but Waterloo has had more written than most until we get to the World Wars. Nevertheless, there will be sufficient information here to walk the battlefield and see the main points of interest.

Napoleon was exiled to Elba in 1814 after being defeated by the coalition forces. He escaped on 16 February 1815, arriving on the mainland near Cannes with around 1500 soldiers. This is the start of what became known as the 100 days campaign, culminating at Waterloo. Napoleon marched north, gathering troops as he went. French troops that were sent to stop him joined his army. The initial route that he took from the coast to Grenoble is officially known as the Route Napoleon, and there are various monuments and memorials to Napoleon along the way.

The Allies declared him an outlaw on 13 March, and on 20 March, he arrived in Paris to a triumphant welcome. Five days later the Allies declared war on him and started mobilisation, with Wellington taking command of the Allied forces. Napoleon raised an army of 300,000 men in eight weeks and announced the re-establishment of imperial control in France. During May and the first part of June the Allied armies deployed in Belgium, near the French border. On 15 June, Napoleon's army invaded Belgium near Charleroi, heading north towards Brussels, where he knew the Allied armies were situated, and he also knew that he had to defeat them as quickly as possible before they could gather too many troops from around Europe. The French army arrived between Wellington's force and Blucher's Prussian army. Both commanders were away from their armies at the Duchess of Richmond's ball in Brussels. On 16 June, the Prussians were defeated at Ligny, before they could assemble. Wellington's army arrived too late to help and were themselves only just able to hold on at Quatre Bras, a small village on the main road from Charleroi to Brussels. Wellington's army was forced to fall back to a ridge, Mont St. Jean, just south of the village of Waterloo, 10 miles south of Brussels. The Prussians had retreated to Wavre, to the east of Wellington's men. During the very early morning of 18 June, the French forces deployed opposite the Allies at La Belle Alliance. The Prussians started marching west to help Wellington.

The ensuing battle, which has become one of the most famous battles in history as it finally finished off Napoleon's dreams of ruling Europe, lasted most of the day. It started around 10:30 with a French military review intended to intimidate the Allies. Then the French Grande Batterie opened fire and the first attack against Hougoumont farm on the Allies right flank was mounted. Around 13:30

the main French attacks, against the centre of the Allied line, took place. These were repelled by the British heavy cavalry. The French then attacked the two key farms, Hougoumont and La Haye Sainte, which is on the main Brussels road in the centre of the battlefield. At this point Napoleon believed the British were retreating, but many were lying behind the ridge, waiting for this moment. The British formed up in squares against the French cavalry and held. The French attacks on the farms continued, and while Hougoumont managed to hold on, La Haye Saint fell to the French. This was the most dangerous moment for Wellington, and it was this point that the Prussians started to arrive in force, initially attacking Plancenoit, to the French right rear. Napoleon sent the Imperial Guard to attack Wellington in a last attempt to swing the battle his way, but they were defeated, the Prussians took Plancenoit, both Allied armies advanced across the battlefield and Napoleon's army retreated. At 20:30 Wellington met with Blucher at the Belle Alliance inn (near Napoleon's headquarters during the day) and at 21:00 ordered Blucher to pursue the French. By midnight the French retreat was a rout. Napoleon arrived in Paris on 21 June and abdicated shortly afterwards. The 100 days campaign cost the lives of nearly 100,000 men, wounding and crippling many others, but it decisively finished the Napoleonic Wars, which had lasted since 1793, around 22 years of almost continual warfare between Britain and its allies and France and its allies. It is no wonder that these wars were called the Great War – at least until another Great War took over the mantle a century later.

The men who took part

Several accounts of the battle were written by participants in the years after the war. Kershaw (2014), wrote about the voices from the Waterloo battlefield, drawing on a range of soldiers from all sides and discussing their experiences. The quotations below are taken from this book, the page numbers indicating the page number in Kershaw's book. Waterloo was also one of the first major battles where numerous letters were written by the lower ranks. It is often thought that most people were illiterate in the early years of the nineteenth century, but clearly this is erroneous. It is estimated that the literacy rate at the time was around 60 percent (Glover, 2015).

The British Army at the time of Waterloo was a professional army, but it contained a wide variety of men who joined the army for a range of reasons, not always the best ones. The enclosure acts of the late eighteenth and early nineteenth centuries meant that many agricultural workers lost their jobs, and those who did not want to drift into the towns in the hope of factory work often joined the army. Others with dubious criminal backgrounds also joined; but the most common means was via the recruiting sergeant, who was well paid for each recruit he brought to the regiment.

The rewards for the recruit appeared at first to be significant, particularly when compared with the average agricultural or factory wage. After taking the King's shilling, often under the influence of alcohol, the recruit could – at least theoretically – return it up to the point he was made subject to martial law, which occurred once he had been attested by a Justice of the Peace. After that he was paid a bounty, which varied but could be over £20 – six months' wages for a labourer (Glover, 2015).

One recruiting poster read: "Too much wife?" and "Death or glory boys wanted." Alcohol played a large part in persuading men to join up. Harry Hopkins recruited for the 28th foot:

> There are no men so good soldiers as the man who comes from the plough. We would never take a weaver while they were there. Townsmen require all the means in the power of their officers... to teach them that subordination is the first duty of the profession into which they have entered. (p. 95)

Recruits had to be a certain height and build, and below the age of 35. As the army had been depleted after the surrender of Napoleon in 1814, those sent to Belgium were often barely trained teenagers, supported by some veterans from the Peninsular War and others who had just returned from the war in America, defending Canada against the USA. These veterans returned to the UK, expecting to return home to their families after often years away, but were quickly re-embarked for Belgium.

Once in the army, punishments for misdemeanours depended on rank. Officers would lose their honour. They could be suspended, reprimanded, cashiered or in the end hanged. Sergeants and corporals could lose their rank or be flogged. Ordinary privates could only be flogged or hanged (Kershaw, 2014). The examples given below are from Kershaw (2014) unless otherwise indicated.

Many of those who took part in the battles of the Peninsular War also fought at Waterloo. Edmund Wheatley was one of those. He started the battle in the centre of the Allied line at the top of the ridge. While he was waiting for the battle to start, he was contemplating on what it meant to be a soldier:

> It is an awful situation to be in, to stand with a sharp-edged instrument at one's side, waiting for the signal to drag it out of its peaceful innocent house to snap the thread of existence of those we never saw, never spoke to, never offended. (p. 79)

Donald Mackenzie, also on the ridge was, along with many others, worried about the state of the Allied armies:

> We knew the Prussians had been beaten; we felt no confidence in the Belgian troops with whom we were associated; we knew... that defeat meant complete rout. At the same time we had faith in our general and in ourselves, and were determined that the French would only take our next position with our lives. (p. 82)

This was written after the event, many years after the event, so the narrative is coherent. It is not possible to say how true it was that MacKenzie had these thoughts at the time.

When the battle started there was a lot of movement. The Allies occupied Hougoumont Farm, but as Johann Leonhard noted:

> We had hardly taken up position at the loopholes when masses of French cavalry came out of the wood, apparently all set to capture the farm, but they were too late. (p. 123)

That set the tone for much of the day at Hougoumont, where the defenders struggled to retain the farm, and thus protect the right flank of the Allied army, all day. They only just managed to succeed. At one point around 30–40 Frenchmen broke in and were only killed after savage fighting. Matthew Clay described the scene afterwards:

> On entering the courtyard I saw the doors or rather gates were riddle with shot-holes, and it was also very wet and dirty; in its entrance lay many dead bodies of the enemy; one I particularly noticed which appeared to have been a French officer, but they were scarcely distinguishable, being to all appearance as though they had been very much trodden upon, and covered with mud. (p. 130)

The French started cannon fire at the ridge. Edmund Wheatley, at the centre of the ridge, saw his first casualty:

> The first man who fell was five files on my left. With the utmost distortion of feature he lay on his side shrivelling up every muscle of his body, he twirled his elbow round and round in acute agony, then dropped lifeless. (p. 135)

The bombardment continued on the ridge. William Lawrence:

> A shell from the enemy cut our deputy Sergeant-Major in two, and having passed on to take the head off one of my company of grenadiers named William Hooper, exploded in the rear not more than one yard from me, hurling me at least two yards into the air. (p. 136)

The cannon fire became more intense as the French infantry began their attack. John Kincaid:

> Countless columns began to advance under the cover of [cannon fire]. The scene at that moment was grand and imposing, and we had a few minutes spare for observation. (p. 141)

The French infantry had trouble advancing up the ridge towards the Allies. Pierre-Charles Duthilt was with them:

> The soft and rain sodden earth and tall rye slowed up our progress appreciably. As a result the English gunners had plenty of time in which to work destruction upon us. (p. 149)

Cannonballs caused the majority of wounds. Assistant Surgeon Donald Finlayson noted:

> Most wounds of the limbs are in the lower extremities. There are perhaps 15 or 16 legs taken off for one arm, there are not many bayonet wounds.... One in 7 or 8 may be killed. The rest are wounded. (p. 153)

Unfortunately, many of the wounded would die due to lack of medical knowledge or overwhelming numbers.

The attack on Le Haye Sainte farm was intense, and the French at one point were driven back by the Allied cavalry. They failed to create squares in time, and so many became casualties.

The infantry square played an important part at Waterloo. A good square could keep out enemy cavalry, but it could be threatened by enemy cannon fire, so it was important to know when to form square and when to form ranks. The British were particularly well trained regarding forming squares and not one failed at Waterloo – unlike the French attempts. It is a key matter of timing, not forming square until absolutely necessary, and then forming the square quickly and in good order before the enemy cavalry reach the infantry. Then, when the cavalry has retreated, reforming into line so the threat from cannon fire is reduced is critical. The worst experience of a square for the British was the 27th (Inniskillings) Foot were forced to stand in square near La Haye Sainte because of the threat of French cavalry, but they were in close range of French musket and cannon fire. Out of 750 men, 105 were killed and 373 wounded, the worst casualties taken by a British unit.

At one point a gap appeared in the centre of the Allied line, and it was left to General Picton's battalions to plug it. Picton was an interesting case. Some say he was popular with his men, others that he was universally loathed. He was highly competent, and he was dressed in civilian clothes at Waterloo. He also suffered from some form of combat stress. He had fought through Spain and Portugal with Wellington, and had at one point begged Wellington to let him return home:

> My lord, I must give up.... I am grown so nervous, that when there is any service to be done it works upon my mind.... It is impossible to sleep at nights. I cannot possibly stand it, and I shall be forced to retire. (pp. 166–167)

This is the kind of language we understand in the context of PTSD, but it is language that would not be acceptable from anyone but a senior officer at the time. The battalions plugged the gap, though Picton was killed – the most senior British officer to die in the battle – and the French were forced to retreat by the cavalry, which had been hidden behind the ridge. Infantryman Sergeant Robertson saw:

> [Dragoons] lopping off heads at every stroke, while the French were calling for quarter. We were also among them busy with the bayonet and what the cavalry did not execute we completed. (p. 187)

It was difficult taking prisoners. Charles Ewart was about to kill a Frenchman when his officer, Francis Kinchant said:

> Sergeant Ewart, spare his life and let us take him prisoner. (p. 187)

Ewart's view was that:

> Considering that moment as a period for slaughter and destruction and not the proper time for taking prisoners. (p. 187)

Nevertheless, he did as ordered and told the Frenchman to go to the rear. Moments later he heard a weapon fired, turned around and saw that the Frenchman had killed Kinchant. There was no mercy this time. As he again begged for mercy, Ewart said:

> Ask for the mercy of God for the Devil a bit will ye get at my hands... with one stroke of the sabre severed his head from his body. (p. 187)

This led to another instance of combat trauma. A couple of years later an acquaintance noted that Ewart was still affected by the event, particularly the death of Kinchant, as he was close to him. Some memories of war do not fade away, nor do they necessarily become manageable. We have little ideas regarding the extent of what we now call traumatic stress after these wars.

The slaughter continued with hand to hand fighting. The French infantryman Louis Canler:

> A real carnage then ensued. Everyone saw he was separated from his comrades and fought for his own life. Sabres and bayonets slashed at the quivering flesh for we were too close to each other to use firearms. (p. 189)

Some were saved by the chaos of the battlefield. Jaques Martin was knocked out by a cavalryman, and was concussed:

> I staggered between the cavalry who were remounting around our guns. I looked around me and saw nothing but enemies and without hope, kept

> walking. It was this unbelievable apathy which saved me, although I should have been lost a thousand times. Actually, I survived the fire of our artillery, which was firing at me as well as them, because we were getting up together, how could I escape from them? Three or four times I saw those who were closest turn as if to chase me. I do not know what restrained them, if they thought me too weak, or probably the bullets and balls that flew around drew their attention. (pp. 200–201)

The battle continued through the afternoon, with mass cavalry attacks by both sides, and then La Haye Sainte fell to the French. There was a point at which the French almost broke the Allied lines but, as noted earlier, the Prussians arrived at a critical time. The intensity of the violence throughout the day and across the different parts of the battlefield was, according to Kershaw (2014) bordering on collective mass hysteria, with observers noting that the battlefield was covered with the dead and wounded.

William Gibney was by the main road:

> Nothing could exceed the misery exhibited on this road, which being the high pave, or I might say the stone causeway leading to Brussels, was crowded to excess with our wounded and French prisoners, shot and shell meanwhile pouring into them. The hardest heart must have recoiled from this scene of horror; wounded men being re-wounded, many of whom had previously received the most frightful injuries. (p. 292)

Gibney also noted the walking wounded:

> Here a man with an arm suspended only by a single muscle, another with his head horribly mangled by a sabre cut, or one with half his face shot away, received fresh damage. (p. 293)

Throughout the battle the sheer numbers of wounded overwhelmed the medical services. Amputations took place throughout the day and the following night. Fortunately, improvements had been made to the treatment of limb wounds, and so most amputees survived – as long as they were treated in time. It was recognised that the body's nervous system went into shock when seriously damaged, so it was important to carry out any surgery while the person was still in shock. By now the surgeons had learned to make a more effective amputation than simply cutting straight through the muscle and bone. A pad of muscle was saved so that a prosthetic would be more comfortable. Soldiers with wounds to the torso with damaged organs received little treatment. They were left to die or recover. Flesh wounds were treated, with the surgeon removing any pieces of ball or cloth before quickly sewing up the wound. All treatment was carried out without any anaesthetic, which is why it was important to treat the soldiers while they were still in shock.

The end of the battle was precipitated by the Prussians. The Allies had held the Imperial Guard, but then the Prussians attacked from the Guards' right flank, making it impossible for them to rally and counterattack. The Prussians forced the French to retire.

This demonstrated the importance of morale. Once the French morale was broken by the defeat of Napoleon's elite troops, there was no chance of victory.

Once the battle was over the wounded still needed to be cared for. As noted above, surgery continued through the night. The wounded were then dispersed across available hospitals and requisitioned private houses. Women attended the wounded, ripping up clothing for bandages and providing supplies of food and water.

Veterans of the battle received a pension, but it was not enough to live on. Those who were maimed were the worst off if they could not supplement their income from other work. Many ended up begging or in workhouses. This despite charitable funds being collected for the veterans of the battle. The charitable funds meant that widows and orphans got annuities and grants, but there was not enough for everyone.

Of course, however extraordinary, these are only the stories of those who survived. We know virtually nothing of the experiences of those who died, unless others wrote about them.

Monuments

The first monument at Waterloo was proposed shortly after the battle by the Foreign Secretary, Viscount Castlereagh, who suggested a public monument be erected to commemorate the battle. Now monuments, memorials and guides clog the battlefield. It is not only the battlefield itself that is monumentalised. London has a number of sites: Waterloo station, Waterloo Bridge, the Wellington Arch. Across the country there are monuments to the battle and its participants in churchyards and marketplaces. They are relatively rare, but that is only noticeable because of the ubiquity of First World War memorials. There is also a Waterloo memorial in Brussels which also contains the remains of 17 British soldiers who died in the battle.

The battle was fought over a relatively large area, though it is easily possible to walk most of it in a few hours. The main road from Charleroi to Brussels cuts through the centre of the battlefield, which is not surprising given that the battle was fought to stop Napoleon advancing along the same road. This illustrates how it is not possible (or desirable?) to preserve many battlefields as they were at the time. They are often on key transportation routes or in what are now urban centres. Around Ieper part of the battlefield was lost to a new motorway. People protested but we needed to keep the lorries moving. After World War I Churchill suggested that Ypres itself should be preserved in ruins as a permanent memorial, but what would happen to the population that started arriving back at the end of the war and wanted to rebuild their houses?

At Waterloo the key farms, the strongholds of Hougoumont and La Haye Sainte, are still there. The former was being renovated in preparation for the 200th anniversary the last time I visited. It is now a memorial to the British soldiers who fought at Waterloo – though we could question the need for new memorials of historically distant battles where no one remembers any of the participants. La Haye Sainte is a private working farm situated on the busy Brussels road. Both farms are recognisable from contemporary pictures.

Other contemporary sights are still there. La Belle Alliance, the heart of the French army, is still there also on the main road), complete with a small, life-sized statue of the emperor, though he didn't use the buildings as an HQ. It was also here where Wellington met Blucher and ordered him to pursue the retreating French. At Plancenoit, the church yard defended by the French is still more or less the same as it was, though the church has since been rebuilt. Most of the battlefield is still fields; there has been no urban sprawl over most of it, partly thanks to the Belgians deciding in 1914 that the site should be protected. The law was passed before the start of the First World War, but no centenary events took place due to the war.

There are well-marked paths to follow, with information boards at key points, so following the paths does provide a means of understanding the battle from the ground. The ridge of Mont St. Jean is obvious (though it is somewhat reduced, the ground being used for the Lion Mound), showing how Wellington chose the ideal place for the battle. His troops, hidden behind the ridge, gave the French an impression of a much smaller army. Unfortunately, the ridge is now virtually covered with buildings, restaurants, a museum, shops selling tacky gifts, and so forth. The goods sold, mainly about Napoleon, do seem to suggest that it was the French who won the battle! Both the tacky gift shops and the lack of a memorial to Wellington and the British troops may indicate there are contested memories about the battlefield – though the victory for the Allies was total. History has strange ways of commemorating a battle. There is little tangible evidence that Britain was on the winning side (Stamp, 2010).

The battlefield is, along with Normandy and the World War I battlefields, one of the most popular for tourists. The litter of memorials and buildings are only there because of the battle and those tourists. The biggest monument, the one most people interested in such things will recognise, is the Lion Mound. This monstrosity rises high above the ground and has a statue of a lion on top. It was built in memory of the Prince William of Orange, who was wounded in the battle (not even killed and he gets a memorial!). William was an aide-de-camp to Wellington from the Peninsular War. Opinion is divided regarding William. He was loved by his fellow Dutch but disliked by British soldiers. He was given command of 1st Corps during the Quatre Bras and Waterloo, but three times ordered troops to advance in line rather than square – making them vulnerable to the French cavalry. At Waterloo one battalion was overrun because of this order. He was wounded in the shoulder near the end of the battle but survived. He later got married to a Russian princess but was blackmailed for 'shameful and unnatural lusts' – probably related to homosexual behaviour. He acceded to the Dutch throne in 1840. Wellington was not impressed with the Lion Mound, which was completed in 1826, claiming it had ruined his battlefield – he was probably right; it is a pompous monstrosity (though the statement might have been put in Wellington's mouth by Victor Hugo). It is 43 metres high with a circumference of 520 metres, containing 390,000 cubic metres of earth. It is topped by a 28-ton lion, cast in iron.

After the battle, as was usual, locals and soldiers searched for valuables among the dead and wounded. It was commonplace for a wounded soldier to be killed off by one of these looters, and then the body robbed, perhaps mutilated to take off a ring, even the clothing being taken as long as it was not too badly damaged. Within a few days most valuables had been pilfered, though the Belgians started policing the area to try and stop the thieves. It did not take long for battlefield tourists to start visiting the area. Glover (2015) describes the Morning Post of 23 August 1815 as containing an advert to take people on a tour of the battlefield and to see relics of battle. By November there was a Waterloo museum in London staffed by veterans.

It is not so well-known that the other form of stealing from battlefields at this time was that of bones. Bonemeal had been discovered to be a very effective fertiliser due to the calcium in bones (Byrne, 2013) and so people scoured battlefields looking for the bones of men and horses. This wasn't confined to Waterloo, but across Europe. It was similar for teeth. Waterloo teeth became very popular as false teeth, with full sets taken from dead soldiers being worth a lot of money. Recycling is not a modern phenomenon.

The British have long been fascinated by the detritus of war, displayed prominently and with appropriate explanations. Pearce (2005), examining the relationship between war and visual culture noted that there was a shift in the meaning of material culture around the beginning of the nineteenth century which enabled the objects from Waterloo to bring the past to life. It is argued that this had a significant role in the creation of British culture in the nineteenth century. This growing emphasis on war and the souvenirs of war has continued to this day.

Throughout the battlefield there are stone memorials and metal plaques commemorating some aspect of the battle, a unit, or a person. There are information boards everywhere, explaining what happened. These are also memorials. Waterloo is the first overhyped battle, and has remained so, even after the destruction of World War I where so many more people took part. Waterloo is the first – but not the only – battle theme park.

Dark tourism

Dark tourism, or thanotourism, has always been popular, as for example in the case previously discussed of people being offered trips to the Waterloo battlefield only two months after the battle. People have always been interested in death and the many forms it can take, like museums of war, battlefields, museums of torture, sites where mass murder or individual murders took place, sites of the Holocaust, even visiting cemeteries, and so on. The focus in this book is partly thanotourism for the armchair war tourist, or a guide to visiting actual battlefields. This is not to say there is something wrong with dark tourism, but we should recognise that it exists and try to understand why it exists.

People have visited places associated with death ever since they were able to travel. It is the heritage everyone shares and has been an element of tourism longer than any other form of heritage (Seaton, 1996). Sites associated with war dead have become ever more popular, and the need for information and museums regarding these sites has grown (Sharpley & Stone, 2009). They are perhaps the largest single category of tourist attractions in the world (Smith, 1998). They serve a range of purposes, from the morbid curiosity of some to a means of defining and strengthening social values and patriotism (Chronis, 2005). Chronis was writing about the bloodiest battle in the U.S. Civil War, that of Gettysburg. Sites can also be used to censor and control contested accounts. Carr (2010) examines tensions regarding the Channel Islands in World War II, arguing that the wartime narratives are fragmented, that contested bunker sites are directly analogous to other countries that were occupied by the Germans rather than a British Churchillian paradigm. The claim is that people in the Channel Islands were victims rather than victors. This adds to the long-contested narratives about the Channel Islander experiences during the war, including the extent to which various people collaborated with the occupiers, and the lack of resistance activity – both of which could also link more closely with, say, the French experience of occupation rather than the apparently unfragmented narratives relating to British victory.

There are studies relating to why people visit battlefields. Dunkley, Morgan & Westwood (2011) studied a group of people who were visiting the World War I battle sites of Ypres and the Somme. They studied the narratives of four from a group of 25 people to show how such tours provide opportunities for pilgrimage, collective and personal remembrance and the validation of events. All the participants already had an interest in the war, and they perceived the tour to provide the opportunity for complex, meaningful and sometimes life-changing experiences. Bull & Panton (2000) suggest that battlefields are poignant landscapes, where physical geography has been transformed into a symbolic space through tourism, memorialisation and pilgrimage.

Francois (2013) argued that the view that nineteenth century tourists visiting Waterloo were more authentic and later tourists were *mere* tourists is false. He suggests that British visitors in the nineteenth century were also searching for both authenticity and longing for the familiarity of the *beaten track*, the latter of which is the claim regarding modern tourists.

Willard, Frost & Lade (2011) explore the notion of battlefield tourism as simply sites for tourists. They suggest that there is an emphasis on (high) quality tourist experience which is essential for maximising customer satisfaction. They suggest that focusing on this niche market "creates opportunities for curators and marketers to competitively position battlefield sites in the marketplace, while promoting long term growth." (p. 1359) This takes battlefield tourism to a new level, one which I think is problematic, and is why I use the term theme park. Battlefields such as Waterloo, and to some extent some of the World War I and World War II battlefields, are very commercialised, and it is not clear that many visitors' understanding goes much beyond the tacky gifts in the inappropriately placed gift shop. Willard et al. also suggest that doing this will create an ideal experience, allowing for a "quality tourist experience." (p. 1359) Is this really why people should be visiting battlefields?

Atherton & Morgan (2011) argue that battlefield memorials are preserved in different ways, some of which may be contested. They are constructed by the victors to memorialise an act of conquest or victory, by the defeated as a memory of resistance, along with the more straightforward commemoration of the dead. They also argue that memorials must have a commitment to preservation and perhaps continuing ritual. This means they have an evolving life history. Memorials have an importance in national life. How we view particular battles and wars relates to the national psyche. We celebrate victories, even long ago victories, because these victories symbolise something we believe is important about our national character. While this is certainly contestable, these narratives are important for people to believe that their country is great, with the implicit suggestion that other countries are not so great. The classic example for the UK is a lot more explicit, regarding the Germans in relation to both World Wars – and usually the 1966 World Cup is thrown in as though it somehow has an equivalence to the two wars which killed more people than any other wars in history. This nationalism is still present whenever the English (in particular) have a football match against the Germans. While it is shameful behaviour to many, it 'shows what we are made of.'

There is no clear agreed definition of dark tourism, or even an agreed typology (Stone, 2012), though it is used as an academic lens to scrutinise broader socio-cultural considerations, politics and ethics. This brings us back to memorialisation at Waterloo. I focused on the general notions of memorialisation in Chapter 4. This chapter looks more closely at the purposes of battlefield memorials. As noted previously, there are a range of purposes relating to dark tourism, and this applies equally to monuments at battle sites. The Lion Mound was created in order to memorialise a particular person, the Prince of Orange. Memorials are usually put up to individuals either because they were killed in the battle or because they were the commander of one side or the other. The Lion Mound is different. The Prince of Orange was only wounded, and he was not one of the key commanders. He led the Netherlands contingent, but they were under the overall command of Wellington. The Lion Mound could only be put there because the battle took place in the Netherlands (this was before Belgium became a nation state), on Dutch soil. This is an important factor and one that has relevance to all battles. The form of memorialisation is significantly affected by the government of the country in which the battle took place. The Commonwealth war graves in France and Belgium, are on land that was given to Britain. This meant that they could decide on the form of the memorials. Now, when visiting First World War battlefields where the British and Commonwealth troops fought, there are many cemeteries dotted around. But in between these cemeteries there is relatively little left concerning the battle. There are exceptions such as Newfoundland Park or Vimy Ridge, but otherwise the land is now being farmed or it has been built on. Contrast this with the French battle at Verdun, where vast tracts of land have been left as they were as a memorial park. Even the villages have not been rebuilt but have been left as ruins. Visitors are not even allowed to picnic in this memorial park in order to show respect to the (French rather than German) dead.

With regard to Waterloo and its many memorials, the site has evolved over the last two centuries. I call it a battle theme park, Seaton (1999) called it a tourist "mega-attraction." Seaton proposes a model based on sacralisation, a quasi-religious mystique and a goal of ritual pilgrimage. Seaton suggests that tourists themselves can affect the stability and potency of this sacralisation process over time. It could be argued that Waterloo has entirely lost the sacred element of respecting those who died in the battle. Not that it is important, as the sacred is critical only to those who remember the men who fought. If we accept the 2 up 2 down approach of memory (discussed in Chapter 4) then it could be argued that Waterloo lost its sacred importance in the late nineteenth century and afterwards became a battlefield dark tourist attraction, or theme park.

Walking Waterloo

It is easy to walk the main parts of the battlefield of Waterloo. It is mainly rural, with roads, tracks and footpaths covering the key areas. This is a walking route that takes in the main sites. Start from the top of Mont St. Jean ridge. There is a car park on the right if you are heading towards Brussels. Cross the main road (carefully!) and head on the road along the top of the ridge towards the Lion Mound. There are plenty of opportunities for refreshment and for buying souvenirs. You are walking along the line of the British troops at the battle. After the mound there is a track which veers left, signposted Hougoumont. The track is wide and easy to follow. There are information signs at various stages. Stop at these and it is relatively easy to work out roughly where the troops were positioned and where they attacked through the day.

The track comes to a junction. Carry straight on past the wood to Hougoumont Farm. When I was last there it was being renovated. You could get inside most of it, but now it has been opened as a memorial to the British troops. If you have looked at pictures of the farm around the time of the battle and read about what happened it is easy to follow the details as the buildings are largely similar, though some features are missing.

Retrace your steps up past the wood and take the track on the right at the bottom of the ridge. This takes you to La Belle Alliance. You are walking across what was originally no man's land but was attacked across from right to left by the French cavalry and infantry. At La Belle Alliance you cross the busy Brussels road again. The buildings are largely the same, and there is a statue of Napoleon at the back.

Looking towards the ridge, turn right down a side road that heads to Plancenoit. A few metres down the road is a viewpoint, which is reputedly on the site from where Napoleon watched much of the battle. It provides a helpful French perspective on the battle. From here the difficulty of the French climbing the ridge can be seen, and why the British troops lying on the north face of the ridge were invisible to the French.

From here you can take the shorter route and head back to the main road, heading up the ridge. Again, this is the route of French attacks through the day. Just before the ridge on the left is La Haye Sainte farm. Again, this looks very similar to pictures contemporary to the battle. It is private, so please don't try and enter or look round. Return to the car park. From here look south to the French positions, and across to the south east, from where the Prussians arrived in the afternoon.

The longer walk entails going down into Plancenoit and exploring the churchyard. The churchyard walls were defended very effectively by the French troops, but when they lost the village the battle was effectively over. More Prussians were coming to the battleground from the east and Napoleon launched his Imperial Guard towards the ridge. They were his last gamble, and it failed.

Return back the same way and go up to La Haye Sainte.

There is no need of further detail as the number of information boards and memorials will provide sufficient information for the tourist to add further to knowledge of the battle. While in the area it is worth looking at the crossroads of Quatre Bras, with the farm buildings on the corner which were used as a hospital during the battle, and also to go to the village of Waterloo to see the museum of Wellington's headquarters.

Final points

One last significant point about the battlefield involves the battlefield conditions. The main monument on the battlefield is the Lion Mound. After it was built in the 1820s, Wellington visited the spot and said that his battlefield had been ruined. He had a point; battlefield archaeology has shown that the soil taken for the monument removed the top of the ridge, so it would have looked very different in 1815. The ridge, which Wellington chose carefully so that the French would struggle up the forward slope and his own troops could lie down on the rear slope, protected from French fire, was significantly higher, making attacking much more difficult for the French to advance up the ridge into the Allied fire.

The other factor to consider is the ground itself. It had rained very heavily the night before the battle and the soil was sticky and soggy – a little like the experiences of the troops at Ypres a century later – making it difficult for troops to advance, and also to control artillery. Every time a gun was fired it needed to be manoeuvred back into position, which would require maximum effort from 8 or 10 men on each occasion. This would have significantly affected their rates of fire, and the organisation of their gun line. Furthermore, once the artillery came into action, the balls were more likely to be buried in the muddy ground and have much less effect on the Allied troops.

Marshall Ney, Napoleon's key general at Waterloo was, it can be argued, traumatised by his experiences in around 70 previous battles. After the Russian disaster of 1812, Ney was the last man to leave Russia. He later led troops in Riga, where many died due to starvation. He had been wounded several times, and by the time Napoleon was being defeated in 1814, he was one who encouraged the Emperor to abdicate. He then declared loyalty to the King and was asked to capture Napoleon when he landed from Elba – but he joined him instead. At Waterloo, when Napoleon had to temporarily leave the battlefield presumably due to illness, Ney took over. His most important decision was to commit the Imperial Guard, Napoleon's best troops, and to order them to advance up the ridge. This failed and ended the battle and Napoleon's reign. Was it Ney's combat trauma that led him to make a wrong decision in committing these troops?

These are good examples of how we need to be careful, when visiting battlefields, to be aware of any significant changes to their appearance. The ridge that is now missing, and the guns that were difficult to control in the mud, may have had a significant effect on the outcome of the battle. Napoleon delayed his artillery bombardment because of the mud. This gave more time for the Prussians to arrive. If there had been no rain the night before, perhaps the French would have won the battle. It is down to such simple factors that history is made.

10

THE CRIMEAN WAR

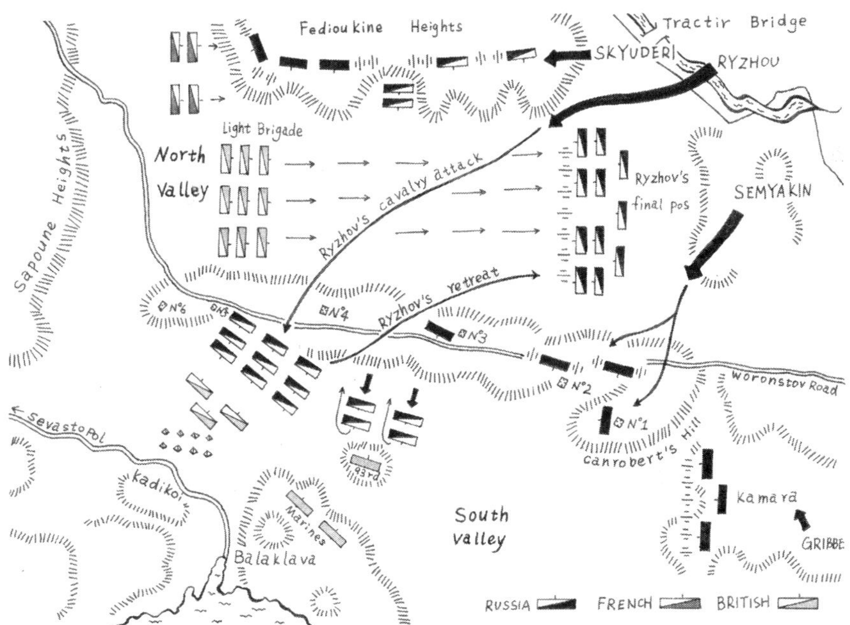

BATTLE OF BALAKLAVA. This is a battlefield fought over for longer and more intensely in the 1940s by the Germans and the Russians, and there is much evidence of this fighting. The best evidence for the Battle of Balaklava is the landscape itself. From the Sapoune Heights (from where Raglan tried to coordinate the battle), there is a good view of the Valley of Death, the key hills poorly defended by the Turks (including Canrobert's Hill), and down to Balaklava, in front of which the marines fought as the 'thin red line'. It is also the Sapoune Heights that contains much evidence from the 1940s' battles, from tanks and guns through to trenches and concrete emplacements. The Valley of Death is now a vineyard.

The Crimean War was a relatively small-scale war (though not for its participants) in the middle of a century that was, for the most part, relatively free of wars between the great European powers. After the defeat of Napoleon in 1815, the only significant direct conflict between these powers until World War I, apart from Crimea, was the Franco-Prussian War, dealt with in the next chapter. The Crimean War was fought over access through the Dardanelles for the Russian fleet. Turkey, Britain and France wanted to restrict Russian access. Russia needed access to the Mediterranean and beyond because it had few ice-free ports apart from Sevastopol on the Crimean Peninsula.

The Crimean War was not the finest of wars fought by the Allies. There were more casualties due to illness and disease than through fighting, and the strategy was less than ideal. This is not the book to deal with these things in detail. The focus here is on the impact on those who took part in the war, drawn largely from the personal recollections of the participants. It is worth noting that Tolstoy fought here at the siege of Sevastopol, with his experiences informing his later work, such as *War and Peace*. The position of his battery is still marked at the Malakov, with gun emplacements, concreted defence positions, and – if you climb over the top of the defences – some ditches with extant dugouts. It is difficult to know though whether these dugouts are from the Crimea or – perhaps more likely – the sieges of the city in World War II. There are naval guns positioned on the Malakov from that time.

Battlefield archaeology is often difficult. Accounts of battles in the distant past are sketchy, and lack accuracy. The problem in Crimea is that much of the ground fought over in the 1850s was fought over again – more ferociously with more soldiers for longer with more sophisticated armaments and a lot more explosives – in the 1940s, with Sevastopol besieged first by the Germans and then by the Russians. The remains of this war are scattered over the sites of the war of the 1850s; the two wars mingle in a way that is quite unusual, at least in most of the battles described in this book – though Northern France has seen warfare throughout history, with armies crossing the same land over and over again.

The war that was fought in the 1850s took place largely over a relatively small area of South West Crimea. Apart from Alma, fought while advancing down the coast from the landing point at Evpatoria, the key battles of Balaklava, Inkerman and the siege of Sevastopol all took place within a few miles and were inextricably linked in what could be argued was a single battle with multiple phases. The tour for this battle is by car. Some elements could be carried out on foot, but there are limited public rights of way across the ground apart from the roads, though I walked through fields and vineyards without being challenged.

Unless otherwise indicated the quotations are from Figes (2011), as are the page numbers. Figes selected a wide range of quotations from participants. The ones selected tell us something of the nature of war to the individual.

The first battle to be fought was the Alma. Around 35,000 Russian troops held the heights south of the River Alma (a very small river, not an obstacle in itself). These were attacked by 60,000 Western troops. The Russians had plenty of guns, but they failed to position them overlooking the cliffs on their left flank, and this is where the French climbed up to take that flank. The British launched an ultimately successful frontal attack to the left of the main road to Sevastopol. It was here that the incompetence of the generals on both sides were first shown. The British General Raglan was supposed to attack simultaneously with the French but – without informing the French – held back until they took the cliffs. The Russian General Kiriakov, who apparently was rarely sober, held a bottle of Champagne and ordered his men to fire on who he thought were French troops; but they were Russians who were forced to retreat under fire from their own men.

The Russians were surprised by the firmness of the British advancing in line. Chodasiewicz:

> This was the most extraordinary thing to us, we had never before seen men to be found with sufficient firmness of morale to be able to attack in this apparently weak formation our massive columns. (p. 211)

This demonstrated the power of discipline in an army. For troops to march in line, in good order, through severe enemy fire takes a lot of training. It is not something a civilian could do. Endless drill and training eventually leads to soldiers learning to respond automatically to orders, more or less without thinking (as thinking would surely undermine this firmness). It would have disastrous consequences half a century later on the battlefield of the Somme. Walking into machine gun fire was not an effective strategy. Unfortunately, the line broke when it reached the river, and chaos ensued among the British troops until General Codrington arrived on his white Arab charge and shouted at the men to fix bayonets and charge up the hill at the Russian Great Redoubt. All ideas of formation failed, but the troops managed to get to the Great Redoubt and take it. A Russian counterattack retook it and the British retreated. They failed because of leadership incompetence. There was no second wave to back up the troops. Raglan also made the foolish decision to ride ahead of the troops and watch from a position very near the Russian skirmishers. It is not clear how he survived that.

A second attack with bayonets followed. This also failed. Hugh Annesley:

> We had got within 30–40 yards of the intrenchment, when a musket ball hit me full in the mouth, and I thought it was all over with me; just then our Adjutant rode up with his revolver in his hand and gave us the order to retire; I turned round and ran as fast as I could down the hill to the river, the balls were coming through us now even hotter than ever, and I felt sure that I should never get away without being struck again; halfway down I stumbled and fell, then I was quite certain I was hit again, but I got up all right and went on. I lost my sword and bearskin here; at last I reached the riverbank and got under shelter, there were crowds of soldiers here. (p. 214)

Annesley lost 23 teeth and part of his tongue. The ball was lodged in his throat and he was unable to speak. The troops around him repeatedly failed to follow orders to attack up the hill again. Once morale is lost it is difficult to regain it.

The British succeeded when they disobeyed their officers by firing volleys at the Russians rather than charging up the hill with fixed bayonets. They were learning new tactics with a new weapon, the Minié rifle, which was more accurate to a greater range than any musket.

With the French advancing on the right flank and the British on the left, the battle was won, despite the incompetence of certain officers. The Russians were routed, without discipline. Figes (2011) argues that they were defeated not by the new rifle but by a loss of nerve among the men. According to Figes, Ardant du Piqu studied the French who had fought at the Alma and concluded that large bodies of troops tended not to engage with the enemy because at the last moment one side or the other would lose its nerve and run. This meant that military discipline was the most important thing in battle. The role of the officer was to maintain morale and stop the men from turning their backs and retreating. Comradeship also plays an important role, as men do not want to let each other down (Hunt & Robbins, 2001b).

The battle cost around 8000–9000 lives, British, French and Russian; but it meant that the Allies could advance to the outskirts of Sevastopol. Little remains of the Great Redoubt now. It is just a hill with vines growing on it. It has been reclaimed by agriculture. Near to the river there is a British cemetery which contains a grave noting the names of the first officers to die. There is also a mass grave which gives no indication of the number of troops buried, or their names. The distinction between officers and men was as strong as ever.

The Russian troops were in disarray, and if the Allies had pushed on straight after Alma, it is likely they would have taken Sevastopol and the war would have been over. Unfortunately, the generals again made a mistake, they delayed the advance long enough for the Russians to regroup (after looting the houses en route to the south), provide reinforcements, and set up the defences of Sevastopol, ensuring the war would drag on for a long time. This time it was the French; Raglan wanted to push on but the French had to go back and pick up their kitbags left on the other side of the Alma, and they were also worried they didn't have sufficient cavalry.

The Tatars in Crimea had for a long time been treated badly by the Russians. In the twentieth century they were expelled from the peninsula by Stalin, only starting to return after the fall of the Soviet Union. When I visited Crimea, they were generally very poor, living in hovels, with many of them spending their time ripping off the tourists. After the Allied invasion at Evpatoria in 1854, thousands of Tatars left their homes to join the allied armies, seeing them as liberators. The allies replaced the Russian governor of Evpatoria with a Tatar, Topal Umer Pasha. The Tatars supplied the allies with carts, mules and food supplies, in the hope of reward. Some worked as spies, others became marauding bands, attacking the houses of rich Russians and stealing what they had. They thought – wrongly – that the allies had invaded to get rid of the Russians and make the peninsular Moslem again.

The allies reached the outskirts of Sevastopol just as winter was setting in. While Crimea does not supply the same general winter that later supported the Russian armies of World War II, it does get very cold. The British set up their base around Balaklava Bay, the French to the west at Kamiesh Bay.

While British people are familiar with Balaklava, both the battle and the helmet, few people have visited in recent times. Balaklava is an interesting port, small, with a ruined Genoese tower overlooking the bay and the sea. During Soviet times it officially did not exist. It was not marked on maps because it was a restricted area along with the major port of Sevastopol. Only people who lived there and official visitors were allowed. Balaklava was part of the restricted area because of the top secret nuclear submarine base, which is now a fascinating museum. The submarines went through an underground canal from the open sea through to the bay itself, and inside there are bomb doors that weigh ten tons each, the remains of various weapons, and a museum to the Crimean War, right along the canal in a room to the side. It contains all sorts of remains from the war. The curator was very pleased to see us – I don't think he got many visitors, let alone English visitors – and insisted on showing us a film, in English, about the war. If you visit Balaklava, don't forget to visit this extraordinary place.

To get an impression of Sevastopol at the outset of the siege, it is helpful to read Tolstoy's *Sevastopol Sketches*. He was based there as an artillery officer during the siege, and the remains of his post at the Malakov is still there, preserved for visitors. Tolstoy provides a vivid description of the town just before the siege:

> As you approach the quay you are struck by the distinctive smells of coal, beef, manure and damp; thousands of oddly sorted articles - firewood, sides of meat, gabions, sacks of flour, iron bars and the like - lie piled up near the quayside; soldiers of various regiments, some with kitbags and muskets, others without, are milling around here, smoking, shouting abuse at one another or dragging heavy loads on to the ship that is lying at anchor, smoke coming from its funnel, by the landing stage; civilian skiffs, filled with amost varied assortment of people - soldiers. Sailors, merchants, women - are constantly mooring and casting off along the waterfront. (p. 230)

Sevastopol has always been a military naval town, the best ice free base in Russia. That is why it was fought over in the Crimean War, then the Second World War, and after being given to the SSR Ukraine in the 1950s by Kruschev, presumably assuming that the Soviet Union would always remain united, it was taken back by Russia in 2014, though Russia's naval fleet never left.

In the Autumn of 1854, Russia hurriedly built strong defences to withstand the siege the allies were preparing. Raglan wanted to attack immediately, before the Russian defences were complete, but the army's chief engineer disagreed, and the French agreed with him.

The bombardment finally began on 17 October. A civilian in the city wrote:

> I never saw or heard of anything like it before. For twelve hours the wild howling of the bombs was unbroken, it was impossible to distinguish between them, and the ground shook beneath our feet.... A thick smoke filled the sky and blotted out the sun; it became as dark as night; even the rooms were filled with smoke. (p. 238)

After a week, the Russians attempted to relieve the siege by attacking Balaklava. The British defended the port with six redoubts along the Vorontsov road (still the main way to Sevastopol from the east) on the causeway heights (from here you can see Balaklava off to the left and down to the Valley of Death on the right). They started by attacking the redoubts. Raglan had a grandstand view from the Sapaune hill, which is situated between Sevastopol and the battleground of Balaklava. The redoubts were defended by Turkish soldiers who defended for a time and then abandoned the posts. Figes (2011) provides an amusing example of how the retreating Turks were jeered at by the British wives, and one was given a good kicking for running over her washing. Like the mythological Italians retreating from Guadalajara in 1937, they kept running until they reached the sea. Figes does argue that they were ill-trained Tunisians who had only just arrived in Crimea. It would be unfair to castigate them as they would not have yet learned the discipline and obedience required in the army.

The Russian cavalry attacked down towards Balaklava. Instead of retreating or forming a square, the relatively few men of the 93rd infantry formed a line just two deep, relying on the Minié rifle and the discipline of the troops to hold off the Russian cavalry. William Russell, the *Times* correspondent, watched the fight from the hill above. He described:

> The ground flew beneath [the Russian] horses' feet; gathering speed at every stride, they dashed on to that thin red line tipped with steel. (Russell, 2014, p. 83)

Figes (2011) states that the original phrase was the *Thin Red Streak*, later changed to *Thin Red Line*. Whatever the case, the Russians had fled by the third volley. Again, the discipline of troops, who must have been terrified, with the horses rushing at them, suggests a great degree of trust in officers and in the men standing in the ranks. If one broke, all would break, and they would have been run down by the cavalry.

The Russian cavalry was going to attack again but were stopped by a charge of the Heavy Brigade, which never received the fame of the later attack by the Light Brigade, perhaps because of the lack of reporting and the fame of a certain poem. This charge almost certainly saved Balaklava for the British. There were relatively few casualties on either side. As was described at Waterloo, with large bodies of men victory concerns which side holds its nerve best. The other side breaks and runs. The Russians retreated. The battle seemed to be over, then Raglan saw that the Russians were removing the British guns from the captured redoubts, so he ordered Lord Lucan, the cavalry commander, to recover the heights and the guns. The orders were confusing, because they indicated infantry would be in support but there was none around. After 45 minutes of inaction Raglan again gave the order to attack and capture the guns. Unfortunately there were several sets of guns situated on various heights, and Lucan did not know which ones were meant. The Light Brigade was frustrated because it had not been involved in the fighting, and many were upset with them for not taking part. Captain Nolan, who had brought the order, when asked to indicate which guns were meant, pointed to the end of the valley – at least according to Lucan, as Nolan died in the subsequent charge, and so could be an easy scapegoat. We will never know the truth. The valley, the North Valley, had the causeways heights to the right and the Fediukhin Heights to the left, and guns on both. The situation, already looking like disaster, was to get worse when Lucan ordered Cardigan, the commander of the Light Brigade, to attack down the valley. Cardigan thought the order insane, but Lucan insisted. They were brothers-in-law who detested each other, so instead of trying to find a sensible solution, the Light Brigade, at 661 men, advanced down the valley, building up speed to a full charge.

> The smoke was almost blinding. Horses and men were falling in every direction, and the horses that were not hurt were so upset that we could not keep them in a straight line for a time. A man named Allread who was riding on my left fell from his horse like a stone. I looked back and saw the poor fellow lying on his back, his right temple being cut away and his brain partly on the ground. (p. 249, Sgt Bond)

It didn't last long. Figes notes that 113 were killed, 134 wounded and 45 taken prisoner. The notion that attack was a mistake was quickly turned into the master narrative of the battle by Tennyson that most people in Britain are still acquainted with:

> 'Forward the Light Brigade!'
> Was there a man dismayed?
> Not tho' the soldiers knew
> Someone had blundered:
> Their's not to make reply,
> Their's but to do and die
> Into the Valley of Death
> Rode the Six Hundred.

There are many valleys of death across the world. Yes, here there was a blunder; there usually is in battle, but it wasn't an unmitigated disaster. The purpose of a cavalry charge is to frighten the enemy off the battlefield, and many Russians did retreat in disorder from the valley. The failure may have been the failure to follow through on the Russian cavalry after the Heavy Brigade had routed them.

In October there was yet another example of the incompetence of leaders. The Battle of Inkerman took place to the north of Balaklava, on the same long hill as the heights of Sapoune, but at the northern end. Again the Russian plan was to relieve the siege of Sevastopol, but again it was not to succeed. The Russians were unable to effectively coordinate their troops, and also relied on a naval map of the area that had no markings on land. The initial commander, who had fought in the Napoleonic Wars, was very indecisive. The narrow ridge along which the Russians were to deploy was not wide enough for the 35,000 men, so at the last minute he changed the plans, requiring the Russians to climb the ridge at three points to attack the British from several sides. He then changed his orders again at the last minute, and one of his commanders decided it would not work so went back to his own preferred plan – so the commanders went into battle with different plans! They managed to take the British by surprise, but the latter held on, though outnumbered by the Russians and with weak defences. This is where deception came in. The British kept firing their guns to make the Russians think they had a larger force than they had. The Russians then lost three commanders in succession and so had no leadership. There was hand to hand fighting across the ridge, usually small pockets of men who found each other in the fog. Edward Hyde was in one battery, Sandbag Battery, that was attacked. The Russians poured over the parapet, shouting:

> We in the battery were not quit, you may be sure, and what with the cheering and shouting, the thud of blows, the clash of bayonets and swords, the ping of bullets, the whistling of shells, the foggy atmosphere, and the smell of powder and blood, the scene inside the battery where we were was beyond the power of man to imagine or describe. (p. 261)

The inability to describe a battle scene is common among those who experience it. Almost invariably the participant will claim that there is no way that a non-participant could understand what it is like to be in battle. This is what separates veterans from the rest of us. When I first started studying the psychology of war, interviewing veterans of World War II, it was very common for them to say that it was impossible to describe the experience, or that they could not make someone who had not been through it understand what it was like. The description, such as it is, often contains the phrase, 'there are no words to describe it.' Not, 'I cannot find the words to describe it,' but that the words do not exist that can put across the experience of intense battle. This applies not only to the physical description, but the emotions and feelings associated, such as stating that the word terror does not adequately describe being shelled. This is the point at which we experience a blockage in the narrative, an inability to communicate intense experience. This occurs in all traumatic experiences, though with more simple experiences such as a natural disaster, people can often describe the event in detail, but not the emotions. Perhaps this is because it is not possible to describe the impact of bullets and shells flying around and hitting people and objects.

This is a significant limitation of language and communication that we do not find in many situations. We usually rely on narrative to communicate, coherent narratives communicate a subject well, less coherent ones communicate it less well. The other factor here is that the battle itself is not coherent, so how can a person make coherent that which is intrinsically not coherent?

Sandbag Battery changed hands several times and became symbolic for both sides. The battle became increasingly chaotic and unstable, with both sides charging and countercharging along the ridge. There are reports that when the ammunition ran out it was hand to hand fighting, throwing stones, even biting and kicking one another (Figes, 2011). This brings us back to the need for leadership and cohesion among fighting soldiers. The Russians failed on both fronts; regiments became mixed up, instead of advancing they stopped to loot British belongings, and eventually they started shooting at each other.

The British meanwhile had called up French support. Bosquet commanded a mixed bag of French and African soldiers who were well disciplined. He advanced on the Russians at the front of his men and routed them. He then came to support the British at Sandbag Battery, where 100 British faced 2000 Russians (but bearing in mind the battery was at a height and the Russians lacked discipline). The combined force of British and French drove the Russians off the hill and the battle was over. Again, many fled in panic. Afterwards there were bodies piled one on top of the other, mostly killed by bayonets. It is relatively rare in battle that such a large proportion of the dead were killed in this way. Bayonet charges often end with either most of those charging being shot or the opposite side running away.

There were stories of Russian atrocities against the British, killing the wounded. The Russians responded that this was in response to religious outrage at the destruction of the Church of St. Vladimir at Khersonesos by French troops, and that the English troops had committed atrocities at Inkerman. Atrocity stories are common in battle, and care should be taken regarding both their veracity and their meaning. In terms of accuracy, both sides like to claim that the enemy has committed atrocities to encourage their own soldiers and civilians to support the fight against the enemy, to show that the enemy is in the wrong or evil; as Tajfel (1970) said, we need to strengthen the differences between ourselves (the in-group) and the others (the out-group) in order to show that we have the right cause, that we are good people, and so on. In a sense it doesn't matter whether the enemy have committed atrocities, it matters that they are the type of people who would commit atrocities.

In terms of the meaning of atrocity, there is a distinction between what is acceptable behaviour in civilian life and what is acceptable in military life. This is not always clear, though attempts have been made to draw up legal documents (Hague and Geneva conventions, for instance) to show what is acceptable in war. But it is more subtle than this. In war it is acceptable to do certain things that would lead to prosecution and outrage in civilian life. Killing people is the obvious example, but the actions are determined by the psychological state of the person in war. We have trained people from a very young age that hurting others is wrong, yet military training is all about it being acceptable in appropriate circumstances. During the terrifying experience of battle, soldiers will desperately attempt to kill the enemy before the enemy can kill them. If there is a danger they will be killed they are likely to fight more ferociously. Then, if enemy soldiers surrender, the soldier is expected to stop fighting, treat them with respect, and ensure that they are taken safely from the battlefield. This is not always physically or psychologically possible, so the only safe thing to do is kill the prisoners. While this is morally wrong, it is practically necessary. So, two thoughts are in the soldier's mind at the same time. It is both wrong and right to kill. We cannot put a civilian mind into a soldier in battle. We must accept that the soldier in battle is likely to behave in ways that are not acceptable to civilians – particularly civilians who have not experienced battle.

Many forms of atrocity are against civilians, and the laws of war indicate that civilians should be left alone. The difficulty with this is that fighters are often hidden among civilians, and how are soldiers supposed to know who is a fighter and who is a civilian? Many atrocity stories stem from this confusion. Of course, there are atrocities that cannot be described in any way other than that they are wrong, even for soldiers in battle.

The allied troops, though they had laid the siege of Sevastopol, and been successful at the battles of Alma, Balaklava, and Inkerman, were increasingly demoralised, wondering why an initial push for victory had not been made immediately after Alma. Lt Col Mundy:

> If the Russians are as strong as they say, we must quit the siege, for it is generally understood that even with our present strength we can do no good with Sevastopol. The fleet is useful and the work now so harrassing that when the cold weather comes on hundreds must fall to overexertion and sickness. Sometimes not one night rest do the men get in six and oftentimes are 24 hours on. It must be remembered that they have no clothing except a thin blanket, and the cold and damp are very severe at night, and the constant state of anxiety we are always in, for fear of an attack being made on our trenches, batteries or redoubts quite puts a stop to wholesome sleep. (p. 273–274)

With the winter and the general conditions, the rate of desertion increased, with hundreds of British and French soldiers surrendering to the Russians (Figes, 2011). This is a story little known among the British, that the conditions were so bad it was considered better to become a prisoner of the Russians. In all wars there are deserters from one side to the other, but there is something wrong when the numbers get into the hundreds. A few people will always consider surrendering to the enemy to get out of battle, or they might have sympathies with the opposite side; but with these larger numbers, something is seriously at error. In this case it was conditions overall. As we have seen, it was a lack of clothing, the cold itself, working long hours, and having limited food. The fear of the Russians was also important, as two large-scale attacks had been launched against the rear of the besieging forces. And this only got worse as the war and the siege dragged on. Even that first winter was made more difficult by the incompetence of those meant to provision the troops and organise their activities. The French also suggested that the English lacked resilience in coping with the conditions. The problem is probably that poor morale saps resilience, so the English troops were just unable to deal with even the ordinary stressors that life in camp brought. Again, the fault for that lies with the leaders and those who are meant to organise provisions and activities.

Another way disgruntled soldiers show their displeasure at the war they are being told to fight is through mutiny. For instance, large scale mutinies took place on all sides during World War I, with much of the French Army refusing to fight in 1917 after the slaughter at Verdun; and the British troops rebelling against the harsh training conditions at the Bull Ring near Etaples (the story of the Monocled Mutineer arises out of that example, again with a lot of fiction and twisted narratives). We hear little about desertion and mutiny on our own side, as we do not wish to think our army dissatisfied.

The Russians were also disillusioned in Crimea, thinking that the defeat at Inkerman would lead to the immediate fall of Sevastopol, and there were suggestions about surrender, but these were dismissed by the Tsar.

Treating the wounded

It is worth spending a little more time considering the wounded and the ill, as the Crimean War led to a fundamentally new way of considering their treatment. The numbers of ill were very high, mainly due to the men not having sufficient provisions, shelter and heating. This is why men were usually more likely to be ill than wounded, but they still needed hospital treatment. Up to the Crimean War, the care of the wounded was sporadic. Generally, army surgeons would be around to pull bits of shell and shot out of wounds and cut off any arms and legs that were mangled. Once a soldier was wounded, if he was not going to get fit enough to fight again, he was a burden, a useful mouth to feed and a man to transport. Relatively few commanders cared for their wounded and ill troops.

Florence Nightingale was born in Florence. Her family was from Derbyshire and she grew up wanting to find something to do to help people. After an experience among a Lutheran community in Germany she trained to be a nurse. When she heard about the conditions of the soldiers in Crimea she offered to take a team of nurses to care for the sick and wounded. She was ruthless in her selection. Younger women from the lower classes who would work harder than *sensitive* middle class women, and Catholic nuns with experience of nursing. They arrived in Scutari ready for the wounded from Balaklava. The conditions were terrible when she arrived, filthy, crowded and inefficient. She quickly turned things round, recognising that cleanliness and wholesome food are the key requirements to getting better. The medical care provided by the doctors was often (not always) crucial, but good nursing meant that medical attention could be put to good use. Although the death rate among the British troops increased in the first six months of Florence Nightingale being present, it quickly went down once it was realised the main hospital was built on a cess pit.

Florence Nightingale belongs to the mythology of the Crimean War. It made her famous, it enabled her to write numerous books about various aspects of nursing (and she was a good statistician), and she really did set the scene for modern nursing; but it should not be thought that she was fully responsible for making all these positive changes. The French, in that first winter of war, had a far lower death rate because they already knew about the role of both cleanliness and good food – they prided themselves on the soup they prepared for their sick and wounded.

Another factor in improving the health of the British troops was food. Alexis Soyer was a well-known chef who had written cookery books for the middle classes. He travelled to Crimea with Florence Nightingale (who became ill and had to return to Scutari) and took over the running of the kitchens. He also designed the Soyer stove, a mobile field canteen used by the British Army even after World War II. He trained a soldier in every regiment how to cook and taught them good recipes using standard rations.

Changing attitudes

The errors and mismanagement described previously ensured that the Crimean War would be a turning point in British military history. No longer would the aristocracy have it all their own way. They were demonstrably fallible. The old system of officers buying their rank was stopped, and promotion on merit was introduced.

The ordinary soldier gained a prominence never before known. He became important to the civilians at home. This was also partly due to the war correspondence bringing the war to people's homes on a daily basis. The improved conditions forced on the army after the first winter also reflected on the country's desire to look after the troops properly.

The Crimean War changed not only our attitudes to the ordinary soldier, but also our general attitudes about how society should be run. Soldiers often came from the lowest classes, and this was perhaps the first time they were being cared about by the ruling classes. This attitude also arose in the UK, with new laws coming in regarding giving some people the vote and also improving conditions of life. This changing attitude developed over the decades after the war and was fundamentally altered by the experiences of World War I, where all classes mixed in the trenches.

Topography

The topography around Sevastopol and Balaklava is quite complex. The bay of Sevastopol must be one of the most beautiful and practical in the world. Until the Russians regained Crimea in 2012, it was the base for both the Ukrainian and the Russian Black Sea Fleet. It is huge and well sheltered. To the east of the city there are hills which, if held by the defenders, form a useful protective barrier against the enemy, but if they are held by the enemy then Sevastopol is fully visible and virtually indefensible. This is the key geographical feature, and it is no wonder it was the scene of key fighting in the Crimean War (Inkerman, the siege itself) and in World War II, when it was fought over for long periods by the Russians and the Germans in their respective sieges. The hilltop itself is strewn with the debris of war. There is a museum and diorama of World War II, with plenty of equipment, guns, tanks, and also trenches. From the top of this hill Raglan observed the Battle of Balaklava, in particular the charge of the Light Brigade. The Valley of Death is straight in front of and below the hill. It is probably one of the better observation points of a battlefield anywhere.

In Sevastopol itself there is a painted panorama of the siege, showing the Allied assault on the Malakov Battery (where Tolstoy fought) in June 1855. It is worth a visit. It was painted between 1902 and 1904 and is housed in a building with a cupola in Sevastopol (The Defence of Sevastopol Museum). There is also a panorama of the World War II siege based in a building on the Sapoune Ridge, among a lot of weaponry and evidence from the war. This again is worth visiting. The painting contains images of key Soviet participants of the battle and at the bottom the painting blends into debris (e.g., rifles, barbed wire, bits of metal, broken trenches) from the battle.

In Balaklava there is a disused Soviet nuclear submarine base that looks like something out of James Bond, with an underground canal running from the bay to the Black Sea, doors weighing 10 tons each to absorb the blast of a nuclear weapon, along with dark corridors and rooms containing Soviet-era weaponry. Along the canal towards the Black Sea end, there is a museum within a museum, this time to the Crimean War. We were the only visitors and the curator put on a film in English for us. There are various uniforms, weapons, and other items from the war.

Outside, in Balaklava itself, I saw a fairground shooting gallery. It was not using air rifles, but Kalashnikovs.

Tour

This is a driving tour, with some walking. It covers the main battlefields of Alma, Balaklava, Inkerman, and the siege of Sevastopol. Balaklava and the Valley of Death are still recognisable, and a soldier who fought at Alma would see little change to the topography, apart from better roads. Sevastopol is fundamentally changed. The Sapoune Heights across to Inkerman are strewn with evidence of the sieges of the 1940s, from weapons and tanks through to concrete bunkers. The town of Sevastopol is greatly enlarged, and most of the fortifications have gone. The Malakov remains, complete with Tolstoy's battery and various guns – along with naval guns emplaced in the 1940s. It is now surrounded by the town.

We stayed on the south coast of Crimea, not far from Yalta, where there is the Lividia Palace, scene of a key Big Three meeting in World War II. The drive from the UK was a long one, and we did it just before Crimea was annexed by Russia. At the time of writing it is more difficult to drive across Ukraine and enter Crimea from the north.

It is helpful if you can read the Cyrillic alphabet, as otherwise it will be difficult to read road signs. It is not as difficult as it might appear. There are a few more letters than we have, but many of them are similar, so it is a matter of learning the sounds of perhaps 15 letters. That will also help with menus.

The tour starts at the site of the Battle of Alma. The road TD104 goes south from Viline towards Uhlove, crossing the River Alma in the middle of the assault positions, with the British to the left flank and the French to the right. The French climbed the cliffs near the sea to assault the Russians. The British crossed the river and attacked the heights – where a substantial defence position had been quickly built – eventually forcing the Russians to retreat. The River is very narrow where it is crossed by the road, but it widens to the east where the main British assault took place. The Russian defences on the heights have disappeared, though the position is clear. There is a car park from which you can walk to the top of the hill. Alma also has a British memorial garden (for want of a better word), where there is a grave containing the first five named officers to die. The rest of the men were buried in a mass grave with no indication of name – typical of the time.

Head south on the same road, then the T2707, T2701 and H06 to Inkerman. To get to the site of the Battle of Inkerman, cross the Chorna River, turn left and then right up Radyanska Balka St. The main battle took place on the ridge to the right, where the Russians were trying to dislodge the Allies, but also further up to the top of the road. The Russians were trying, without success, to remove the Allied forces from their positions dominating Sevastopol on what becomes the Sapoune Heights. At the top of the hill, and across the whole area there are remains of the sieges of the 1940s, including concrete bunkers. Little remains of the Crimean War battle. It is still worth a walk around here and along the ridge, where the most brutal part of the battle took place.

Continue south through Dergachi and turn left at a roundabout along the H19. Go straight over another roundabout and on the right there is the entrance to the war remains of the Sapoune Ridge. This is worth spending some time at. There is the diorama to the World War II siege, many remains from that war, and also the best view over the Balaklava battlefield, including Balaklava Bay, the site of the Thin Red Line, and the Valley of Death. This is the view Raglan had on the day of the battle. This is the kind of view every commander wants, but rarely gets. It also indicates how difficult it is to take Sevastopol, which lies behind the hill, as long as the defences here are strong.

Continue down the main road, and straight over a roundabout. Along here, on the right, in the middle of a field, is a memorial to the charge of the Heavy Brigade, largely forgotten, but critical during the battle at stopping the advance of the Russians along the crest to the right, which had been abandoned by the Turkish troops. Go down Yasna Street on the left, through the small town and you are in the centre of the Valley of Death. The Light Brigade charged down from the left, the Russian guns were on the hills in front, behind and to the right. Go down the valley to the right – there is a track – the Russian troops were positioned in and around the nearby village. The Light Brigade tore into them, disrupting their positions and forcing them to retreat. This was the successful part of the attack that is often not mentioned. It had a significant impact on the outcome of the battle.

From the village turn left up the TD105 back to the main H19 and turn right. To the left is Canrobert's Hill and the other redoubts attacked by the Russians and then abandoned by the Turks which had nearly led to the loss of Balaklava. Turn left down towards Balaklava. Just where the sign showing you are entering the town is situated, look right into the vineyards and this is where the Thin Red Line of British troops held off the advancing Russians. From the positions you have been in it is easy to see how vulnerable Balaklava was, and it was critical to the British as it housed their main fleet and supplies. The loss of Balaklava may have meant the end of the war, unless the British had joined with the French to the west.

Balaklava was a closed city during Soviet times, so it did not officially exist. Now it is much bigger than it was and is a holiday resort, popular with people with yachts. You can still climb up to the old watchtower for a view of the sea, or visit the nuclear submarine base. The bay itself is fairly well protected from the elements, though a great storm did cause significant damage during the war.

From here return back to Sevastopol via the H19 and H06. The city is much larger than it was, so most of the evidence relating to the Crimean War, and World War II, has disappeared. This too was a closed city during the Soviet era, as it contained – and contains – the main Mediterranean fleet. It is worth going to the centre and seeing the bay, which is magnificent. At the end of Lenina Street there is a memorial to Admiral Nakhimov, who was the commander of the Russian land and naval forces at the Siege of Sevastopol in the Crimean War. Nearby there is a huge memorial to World War II. It is also a good place to see the bay. Just south of here near Ushakova Square, is the park where the panorama of the siege is situated. Near here is the reconstruction of Bastion 4, where Tolstoy fought as an artillery man.

From here, go around the southern spur of the bay along Vokzalna Street. As the road turns north, stop near a bus station. On the left is a steam engine towing a large naval gun. On the side of the engine it says *Death to Fascists.* This was used during the first siege in 1942 to attack the German lines at night. Continue along this road, which changes names several times, until you reach a square, in front which rises the Malakhiv (the target for the Allies on the panorama). Climb up the steps and head through the park. There are various naval guns from World War II positioned here, as it was a critical defensive point in 1942 as it was in 1854. At the far end is the Malakhova Kurgana, a building which can be seen on photographs in 1855 and is still there. The views from the Malakov are very different to 1855, as most of the surrounding area is built up, but it still provides a useful impression.

While that is the end of the main tour regarding the Crimean War, there is a lot to see in the area. To the west, on the coast around the Leninsky District, are batteries from World War II. There are monasteries, the dachas and palaces on the south coast, the Swallow's Nest, the palaces of Bakhchysarai, the mountains, and the Livadia Palace, where the Yalta agreement was settled, which basically ensured that Europe was split in half after World War II – but these belong to other stories.

Conclusion

The critical change for the soldiers resulting from experiences in the Crimean War was in terms of basic conditions. The British soldiers who landed at Crimea and fought in the key battles were treated very badly. Their rations were poor (unlike the French, whose base was to the west of the British at Balaklava), their clothing inadequate for the winter, and conditions in hospital when wounded or ill were atrocious. Thanks to people like Florence Nightingale and Alexis Soyer, by the time the war was over conditions were much improved. In wars after this time the authorities at least tried to make the conditions for the ordinary troops better than it had been.

We do have a lot of accounts from the soldiers who took part in the war, and it was also the first war to be properly covered by the media, in the guise of William Russell of the *Times*, who sent back regular reports about the Crimea. He also was one of the people who influenced the Government to change the way the troops were treated. In no previous wars had newspaper reports been sent home while the fighting was on giving details of the atrocious conditions of the troops.

There is still no concern for the psychological welfare of the troops. This would not really start properly until World War I. Until then, soldiers would continue to write about their psychological state, but there were no medical or psychiatric facilities to deal with this.

11

THE FRANCO-PRUSSIAN WAR

The Battle of Sedan

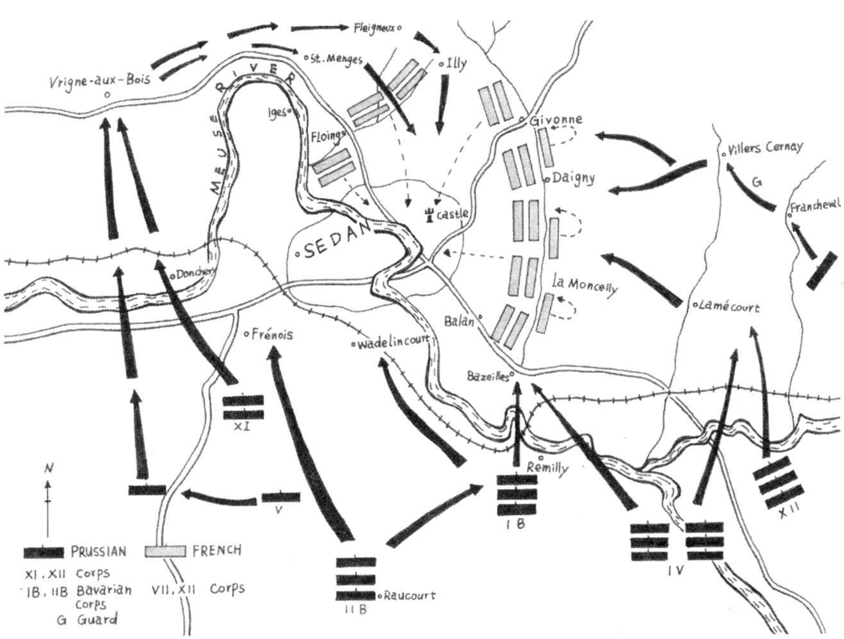

BATTLE OF SEDAN. Sedan is a somewhat scruffy town in northern France, but worth visiting for those with an interest in war. It was the scene of later battles, but the 1870 battle was a critical one in the Franco-Prussian War. The French retreated to the town, and then lost their chance for further retreat as the Prussians advanced to the west. To the north was Belgium. The French were caught in and around the town and the Prussians quickly surrounded them and bombarded them from the hills to the south (from where the Prussian commanders watched). There is quite a lot to see. The memorial at Bazeilles, where the battle started; the ossuary at Balan, on the road along which the Prussians advanced; the sites at Illy and Floing where the French cavalry attempted to stop the Prussians; and not least the fortress itself, thought to be the biggest in Europe. It was not defended during the battle, but has evidence of Vauban fortifications. The French Emperor, Napoleon III, was captured and met the Kaiser at Donchery.

This chapter focuses on the Franco-Prussian War of 1870–1871, specifically the Battle of Sedan. The town of Sedan, very close to the Belgian border in northern France, is unusual in that if someone was born in the 1860s and lived to be in their 80s they would have experienced three German attacks through the town, in 1870, 1914 and 1940. The French were defeated on all three occasions. Here the focus is on 1870, exploring our understanding of the individual in war using Émile Zola's novel, *La Débâcle*, a fictional account of French soldiers and civilians in the lead up to the battle, the battle itself, and afterwards in the siege of Paris and the Commune. The complexity of the impact of war is evident in this novel and can be seen because we have a complex understanding of the characters. Zola researched his subject well, exploring the area around Sedan and talking to people who had been involved in the battle, both civilians and soldiers. He also lived through the siege of Paris and the Commune (the basis for the final part of the novel). If you visit Sedan it is important to read *La Débâcle* to really get the flavour of the war as described by Zola. The quotations included in this chapter go some way towards an understanding, but are no substitute for the book itself, as it is important to get to know the characters that Zola creates, and see the events that unfold for each. The chapter has many more quotations than other chapters, and a large proportion require little further explanation. The art of the novelist is to concisely express events, people and feelings.

The town itself is dully attractive, a classic French town that looks like it had a heyday somewhere around a century or so ago. It has what is claimed to be Europe's largest fortress (it has a modern hotel inside; there are Nazi markings from the occupation on some walls; there is a museum). The town has a fascinating history. For centuries it was an independent state on the edge of France, and in more recent centuries it has been a frontier town for France, particularly in the years that Germany annexed Alsace and parts of Lorraine. There is evidence of all three battles to be found in the local area. The hill to the south of Sedan, the Marfee, was where the Prussian commanders, von Moltke and Kaiser Wilhelm, watched the unfolding battle in 1870. From here the whole area surrounding Sedan can be seen. In 1940, the French defences here were subjected to the largest German aerial attack on fixed defences of the war. Massed Stukas and other bombers relentlessly bombed the bunkers while the German tanks commanded by Guderian emerged from the Ardennes Forest and crossed the Meuse at three separate points around Sedan (the main one is marked by a plaque to the south of the river). The French panicked and fled, attempting but failing to launch a counterattack over the next few days. This rout is arguably responsible for the rapid defeat of the French in 1940, as Guderian's tanks sped towards the Channel, with no substantive armies to block their way, cutting off the British and French forces in the north, leading directly to the evacuation at Dunkirk. In 1870 Sedan was also the scene of the key battle of that war, with the French utterly defeated and their commander, Emperor Napoleon III (nephew of Bonaparte) captured by the Prussians just outside Sedan.

The 1870 battle was fought on all sides of the town and in its streets: From the southeast at the village of Bazeilles, up through la Moncelle, where both sides thought they could achieve a breakthrough, up to Donchery (the house where the Emperor and the Kaiser discussed terms is still there) and across the north of Sedan at Illy, where nearby the French cavalry charged the Prussians at Floing to the northwest of Sedan three times to try and break out. They were not successful, and these were the last cavalry charges of the French army. Nearby is the loop of Iges in the Meuse, where the captured French troops were kept in awful conditions until they were marched off to Germany, and just south of that the village of Donchery, where the Emperor discussed the terms of the surrender with the Kaiser. The house is still there, and looks much the same as it did in 1870. Throughout the battlefield there are memorials to events and people, many of them supported by helpful information boards. There are not only reminders of the battle of 1870, but also 1914, 1918 (the liberation) and 1940. There are military cemeteries for the Germans and the French, and a memorial near Wadlincourt commemorating the furthest advance of the U.S. troops at the Battle of Meuse-Argonne.

There is little left to see of the actual destruction caused by the battle. The armies swept through and left within a matter of days, so extensive fortifications were not built (though there are World War II era bunkers to the south of the Meuse). The French only intended to rest at Sedan and then continue their retreat, not realising that the Prussians were busily surrounding them and cutting off any intended retreat. It is possible to walk the main battle sites in a day though much of the walking is on main roads, and there is not much to see for some miles, so it may be better to tour at least part of the area in a car. You can also follow the route of the French army towards Sedan using Zola's book. There is also the battlefield at Beaumont-en-Argonne, where a preliminary battle was fought the day before Sedan.

La Débâcle is the penultimate book of the Rougon-Macquart series, where Zola explored human behaviour among people during the empire, the two decades ending with the Franco-Prussian War of 1870–1871, where the French were soundly defeated. The book has three parts: the march around France trying to find the enemy, the battle of Sedan, and the siege of Paris and the Commune. The novel follows several (mainly) fictional characters, both military and civilian, that the reader gets to know well before the battle itself. The characters are well-drawn and illustrate very well the boredom of marching leading up to battle, the battle itself, with the excitement and the terror, and the aftermath, particularly becoming prisoners of war, and the destruction of the town.

The tour incorporates the initial fighting at Bazeilles, which led to the destruction of the village, the attack via Daigny and Givonne from the east, the cavalry charges by the French towards Floing, events in the town itself, the building in Donchery where Napoleon III surrendered and the area where the prisoners of war were held after the battle, There is less focus on the fortress of Sedan because it played only a minor part in the fighting, but it is still worth a visit.

Zola

Zola's Rougon-Macquart series of twenty novels was an attempt to demonstrate the importance of genetic and environmental influences on people's thoughts, feelings and behaviour during the years of Napoleon III's rule, from 1848 to 1870. It was an early attempt at the scientific novel, attempting to show that literature can be used to illustrate and advance science; in this case the science of being human. This includes biology, sociology and psychology, along with anthropology and history. The books follow the fortunes of two interlinked families, the Rougons and the Macquarts. Zola began writing the books while he was still in his 20s and made little variation to the series as he originally planned it. The novels cover a whole range of human behaviour, exploring greed and gluttony, despair, murder, the conditions of industry, prostitution, the advent of the department store, and many other areas. The focus here is on *La Débâcle*, the story of the Franco-Prussian War, and the disaster it was for France as a whole, as well as for individual people. The Sheffield Weekly Telegraph described the novel as "probably the most realistic presentment of the horrors of war ever given to the world of readers. It exhibits in a panorama, vivid and most gruesome, the terrible drama of the last France-Germany war, from the tragic retreat on Sedan to the final collapse of Paris in a sea of fire and an ocean of blood.... [It] is also the most powerful argument against war ever presented in the guise of fiction."

The book is in three parts. The first part is with the French army, marching around eastern France trying to find the Prussians, hearing rumours of victory and defeat, only having maps of Prussia as they expected to be invaders rather than the invaded, and having difficulties with supplies and an inclination to mutiny. In this part Zola shows the grumblings of the ordinary soldier and the incompetence of the leaders, particularly Napoleon III himself.

The second part is about the Battle of Sedan, where the French army, hoping to retire from the town, is surrounded and annihilated; thousands are killed or captured, and Napoleon himself is captured. This is the key focus of this chapter.

The third part is the siege of Paris and the Commune. Zola himself experienced these events, which ended with the declaration of the new republic and the founding of modern Germany.

Zola conducted thorough research for his writings, particularly for *La Débâcle*, which was in many ways the final book of the series. The final book, Doctor Pascal, is really a roundup of all the key characters of the series. *La Débâcle* showed the end of Napoleon's time as Emperor. Zola read many books on the Franco-Prussian War, from strategy and tactics through to uniforms, weapons and equipment. He was very precise and wanted to get the detail right. He also interviewed many of the participants, obtaining detailed knowledge of various perspectives on the war. He visited Sedan and the surrounding areas – while also interviewing local participants – to get a feel for the battlefield (not dissimilar to the purpose of this book!). He marched the route of the army, asking local people for information. In Sedan he talked to anyone who would speak to him about the battle, including a doctor who had helped with the wounded (there is a detailed description of the removal of an arm in the book). He interviewed Charles Philippoteaux, who was the brother of the man who was mayor of Sedan in 1870 and himself the mayor of Givonne. Philippoteaux took Zola around the battle area and told him about seeing the Emperor at the farm at Baybel. According to Tancock (1972), he was the basis of Delaherche.

Zola took a scientific observational and empirical perspective on gaining, analysing and writing the book. It was fiction, but it was meant to be an accurate portrayal of the events of the time; and though the characters are largely fictional, they are based on real people's experiences; which makes the book an interesting data source to explore the psychology of war. According to Tancock (1972) locals believed that all the incidents in the book happened except the murder of Goliath. Zola gathered the facts and information and pieced them together using fictional characters.

The Pall Mall Gazette interviewed Zola in 1891, when he was preparing to write *La Débâcle*. They asked him about the length of time it took him to write a novel. His reply is interesting:

> About a year after I have got the whole thing definitely mapped out, I try to get the sources of accurate information about whatever subject on which I am engaged. If writing about the mining world, I go to both master and man; if about the stock exchange, I endeavour to see the successful millionaire and the ruined gambler – the line that separates all these good people is small.... Sometimes information is difficult to get, and even more difficult to use rightly. In writing one must try to give an impression of reality and truth. This is not always done by copying exactly what you see before you, exactly as you know it to be, in this the pen and the paint brush have a curious affinity.
>
> I prefer to do my serious writing at home, not in the milieu where my dramatic personae are to move and spend their lives. Everything is seen in better perspective at a distance, and a truer effect is gained of the whole.

This is a clear demonstration of the role of narrative construction in providing a coherent understanding of a given situation. Simply presenting the facts in no particular order does not help the reader understand a situation clearly. This applies as much to a doctoral thesis as it does to a novel and is a good example of the similarity of the two genres – particularly some types of thesis. It can be argued that *La Débâcle* is a truly scientific novel, in that Zola systematically observed and collected empirical information through the scientific means of the interview. His thesis, that war is unpleasant and to be avoided, and that soldiers merely represent the different types of people found in all society, can be seen as scientific. Zola's contribution to the science of the psychology of war is significant. His data collection is systematic; it is his analytic approach that is unusual. The way he structures and interprets the data, drawing on the device of the creation of fictional characters, is what makes this scientific thesis different from one constructed in a university. Any thesis on war involves interpretation and construction by the author. Zola's thesis is no different and would probably be deserving of a PhD if he had submitted it to a university.

La Débâcle not the first time that novels have been used to try and understand the experience of war, to create a narrative of war. Many novels are barely disguised works of biography, as many people want to tell their version of events, their experiences. I have tried to understand something of war trauma through an analysis of Remarque's *All Quiet on the Western Front* (1929), to try and demonstrate that PTSD is not a sufficient explanation of war trauma (Hunt, 2004). This attempted to build on the work of Shay (1994, 2003) who has carried out a detailed analysis of Homer's *Iliad* and *Odyssey* to understand the impact of war on individuals who go to fight. We can use *La Débâcle* in a similar manner, particularly because Zola took this scientific approach to understanding the war.

The use of data from novels is controversial in psychology, and most psychologists may reject such an approach, as the story is *made up* by the author. Hopefully I have demonstrated that this is not the case for *La Débâcle*, though in general the novelist has to describe human behaviour in the kind of detail not usually found in psychological texts. This may be the problem of psychological texts rather than novels. Humans are complex emotional and (sometimes) reasoning beings, and the fullness of behaviour is demonstrated through writing in a complex manner about them, rather than attempting to isolate variables and manipulate them. War is a good example, trying to understand the complexity of war trauma by examining the characteristics of PTSD is like trying to see what is in a room when it is dark. Some of the furniture may be visible, but the subtleties of colour and shape are missing. Shay (1991) argued that a book such as the *Iliad* provides us with a much more complex understanding of war and should be used by clinicians when treating traumatised people. According to Shay, the *Iliad* describes so much more than PTSD, namely Achilles' guilt about the death of his friend, his rage at his commander, and the ways he treats the enemy when he is traumatised.

La Débâcle

The first part of the book has the soldiers marching to and fro around eastern France, with the generals knowing the Prussians have invaded France but not knowing where they are. There are vague rumours of battles fought and won or lost, and the troops gradually get more disgruntled. Zola describes both the initial enthusiasm for war and the reality of marching with inadequate food in inclement weather (all weather is inclement for marching troops; too hot, too cold, too wet, too dry). Zola describes how the men were badly supplied with food and fuel and would end up washing down their dried hard-tack biscuits with brandy rather than having a proper meal.

The French were unable to keep the troops properly supplied and this was an important component of reduced morale. One of the biggest gripes of soldiers is that they are not being provided for adequately. A key element of enabling an army to move is logistics. Any army needs enough food and water for all its troops – bearing in mind that soldiers on active service generally require many more calories than the average civilian – and sufficient supplies of arms and ammunition to enable it to fight its battles. It also needs sufficient medical supplies. Usually, an army will also require lines of communication with its base, enabling many of these goods to travel safely along designated routes. In the late nineteenth century, the best way of supplying armies was via the railways, and the Prussian armies made good use of railways heading from Prussian territory into France. The French were not even capable of doing this within the boundaries of their own country. Add to this the almost random marching around the countryside and it was no wonder the army was insufficiently supplied. Much of the time they did not even know where they were as they had been supplied with maps of German territories, but not of France!

The key characters of the book are Jean and Maurice. Jean Macquart is a key character in another Rougon-Macquart book, *La Terre*, where he was an ex-soldier trying to be a peasant. His wife's family would not accept him, and eventually they murdered his wife and took his land away. The only option for him was to return to soldiering. He had fought at the Battle of Solferino, and so is one of the few in the book who has battle experience, though he could hardly read and write and had little ambition. He is a corporal, and so is responsible for a section of his platoon. The men initially have little respect for him because he is a peasant, but this does change to some extent through the book.

Maurice is a gentleman who joined up wanting to fight the Prussians. He has no experience of war, but critically for the structure of the book, has family and friends in Sedan. Initially Maurice and Jean do not get on, but their friendship develops quite quickly during the first section of the book, partly because Maurice begins to see the strength in Jean through the long fatiguing marches. The following quotations are taken from the 1972 translation by L.W. Tancock.

The book does not ignore the miseries of the civilians who are terrified of the coming fighting and only want to get way, becoming refugees in their own country.

> As soon as they saw the troops in retreat, this rabble of exhausted soldiers dragging their feet, the inhabitants got busy and hastened their own flight. (p. 52)

The civilians packed up their bags, loaded their carts, and fled, in scenes that would become common in 1914 and 1940, three times in a lifetime.

The soldiers became mutinous. Too much marching to no apparent end and a lack of supplies made life very difficult. Zola describes how units were disaffected and officers were insulted, with men refusing to salute.

This has shades of the mutinies of the French armies in 1917, armies who felt they had been through too much – particularly the Battle of Verdun – that their officers were making poor decisions, and that the war should come to an end. In 1917 forty-three mutineers were executed (around 3427 were court-martialled), and the whole thing was hushed up. In 1870, the soldiers were being mutinous before they had even experienced battle, demonstrating the problems faced by ill-trained, ill-fed, and ill-led soldiers.

Jean's responsibility as corporal was to look after his men, whether that was to ensure they had adequate food and ammunition or whether there was an injury. He notices Maurice has problems with his feet because his shoes were worn out. Jean inspects the foot carefully and tenderly, noting that the feet and legs are the most important parts of the body for an army. Jean notices the problem recurs as they are marching and advises Maurice to walk barefoot. Later, in the evening:

> [Jean] knelt down, washed the place himself and dressed it with some clean material from his knapsack. And his movements were like a mother's, He had the gentleness of a man of long experience whose big hands can be delicate when need arises.
>
> Maurice could not help being overcome by a great tenderness, his eyes went misty, and the language of friendship rose from his heart to his lips in an immense longing for affection, as though in this clodhopper he had loathed some time ago and despised only yesterday he had found a long lost brother. (p. 99)

This is a crucial part of the book, where the middle class Maurice recognises the value of the poor peasant Jean, where their relationship, their comradeship, is established. This was often talked about in the World Wars; how soldiers of different classes learned to respect and like one another.

Towards the end of the march, after Zola has been describing the route they are taking, and the constant changes, the soldiers realise they are repeating their steps, going over the same ground, and they have had enough. He describes the march through the hills and woods of the Ardennes, the difficulties, the changes in course, the grumblings of the men, the lack of knowledge of the officers regarding local territory, ignoring advice from local fighters, and finally making contact with the Prussians as they are trying to reach Mouzon to cross the Meuse. As they near Beaumont they hear firing, and Maurice

> … had never felt so worked up. Each round made his heart leap, lifted his spirit and gave him a desparate urge to be there, to be in it, to get it over. (p. 133)

This is a common feeling of young men who wish to be involved in battle – but usually only before they have been in battle. The experience of war generally changes this view.

They soon come across fleeing troops:

> Wounded officers, soldiers out of control and without weapons, supply wagons galloping, men and animals all in flight, panic-stricken before the wind of disaster. (p. 134)

This caused some alarm among the troops, not knowing exactly where the Prussians were, whether they were going to attack or be attacked, whether they would get across the Meuse before nightfall. They had been marching for 12 hours. During the night they were shelled as they passed the villages of Raucourt and Haraucourt on the way to Sedan.

Zola provides, through the civilian character Weiss, the positions of the various army corps, and the suggestion that they should immediately retreat through Sedan to Mezieres – which was what Napoleon III was criticised for not doing after the battle. Instead they allowed the Prussians to surround them instead of retreating to Meziers. The only alternative was to cross into neutral Belgium and be interned. Through Maurice, Zola demonstrates the despair of the ordinary soldier after marching for so long around the countryside, suggesting they were cowards and should give in. Weiss argues that the battle must be fought, though French soldiers will die, and that they should ensure they kill as many Prussians as possible – an easy comment for a civilian to make. To get the alternative view Zola relies on a woman's character, Henriette, Maurice's sister, who argues that nations should sort out their arguments without fighting.

Through these discussions Zola provides a detailed account of the worries of the night and the movements of the troops and cavalry into positions along the road between Bazeilles and Givonne, and beyond that to Illy and round to Floing. In the morning the attack starts from the direction of Bazeilles, beyond which the French had failed to blow the railway bridge, though it was mined and ready. The battle is lost from the beginning. At the same time as the Prussians (actually Bavarians) advance across the Meuse to Bazeilles, other troops are cutting off the potential French retreat to Charleville-Mezieres. The Germans attack Bazeilles from several directions, the meadows towards the river, and the road from Douzy, and after a severe fight which destroys much of the village, they take it. They then advance up the road towards Balan. Held up at various points by the French, such as in the house (inn) now known as *La Dernier Cartouche* (the last cartridge), defended as suggested and now a museum with one room kept as it was after the battle, with severe damage to plaster and furnishings due to rifle fire. The Battle of Bazeilles is told partially through the eyes of Weiss, a civilian, who fights with the army and is captured. As he is a civilian, he is shot. His wife is Maurice's sister Henriette, who observes it all.

Zola uses the viewpoint of the Kaiser and his generals, situated on the hills south of the Meuse, to provide an overview of the battle. He then returns to Jean and Maurice, who are on the plain of Algerie with VII Corps, near Floing.

They experience artillery and musket fire, and their behaviour and things change.

> Eyelids fluttered over worried eyes, and voices went thin as though they could not get out properly. (p. 209)

Even though there are shells and bullets flying everywhere, Maurice wonders whether it is a battle. He does not know what a battle is. He couldn't see the enemy, and a peasant was calmly tilling his field.

Once the battle starts Zola describes, through Maurice, the response of the novice soldier, and the response of the veteran, Jean. As the firing continued:

> Maurice was seized by fear, insane fear. At first he had not this cold sweat and painful sensation of collapse in the pit of the stomach, the irresistible urge to get up and run, screaming. Perhaps even now it was only due to thinking too much, as happens in sensitive and nervous natures. But Jean, who was keeping an eye on him, gripped him with his strong hand and made him stay near him, reading this fit of cowardice in the worried darting of his eyes. He swore at him softly and paternally, trying to shame him out of it with harsh words because he knew that you put courage back into men by giving them a kick up the backside. (p. 215)

The battle of Bazeilles took longer and was more difficult than the Germans expected, and they did not look kindly on civilians fighting. When a civilian was caught with weapons they were shot without trial, as they violated international law. Weiss was one of these. Due to the resistance put up by the French at the village, the Germans were provoked to reprisal. Zola described how there was blood everywhere, with the dead piled in the streets and houses, and how if the Germans had to take a house by assault they would burn it down afterwards.

To the north of Sedan, Jean and Maurice remained lying on the ground, frustrated by the lack of action, though the shelling had killed several of their comrades. Eventually though, they did advance under heavy fire. Maurice's reaction changed:

> [Maurice] no longer knew whether he was afraid or not, carried along at a run by all the others, with no will-power of his own except to get it over with at once.... Instinct took over, his muscles ran amok, obeying every wind that blew. (p. 256)

There is a lot in this single quotation about the experiences of men who fight; the inability to think, the fear, the desire for panic but not panicking, the sense of being out of control but his body behaves automatically. This was discussed in detail by van der Kolk (2015) in *The Body Keeps the Score*, how memories are held by the body even if there is no connection to the conscious mind. Zola had researched his topic well – as he had not been in battle himself.

Zola also describes in vivid detail the brave and pointless cavalry charges, introducing the character Prosper as a cavalryman, who is one of the soldiers who charge the Germans on several occasions across the plain to the north of Sedan, all to no avail, as there was no way to break through the German lines. Prosper also experiences the dissociation felt by the foot soldiers, the separation of mind and behaviour, the automatic response to orders.

> He was riding in a dream, feeling as light and disembodied as a man in his sleep, with an extraordinary vacuum in his brain which left him without a single idea - in fact a machine functioning with irresistible impetus. (p. 269)

Armies often pride themselves on not leaving a man behind, whether wounded or dead. This was, according to Zola, not the case in 1870. Jean is wounded in the head, not badly but he is unconscious. Lieutenant Rochas had no interest in taking him along as they retreated because a wounded man is worth nothing. Fortunately, Maurice helps him. Those wounded who made it to the makeshift hospital in Sedan at least had a chance of survival, though not very high. The hospital was overwhelmed with wounded, many of whom required amputation. Zola describes these operations, and the piles of arms and legs, the blood everywhere, and how many soldiers died before even receiving treatment. Again, Zola's detailed description demonstrates how well he did his research. For instance, in describing an arm being removed, he provides the detail of how, once chloroform was applied, the surgeon cut through the flesh of the arm, then disarticulated the joint at the shoulder with a single stroke. The arm came off, the assistant grasped the brachial artery which the surgeon sealed, a flap of skin was brought down and stitched to cover the wound and they moved on to the next patient. The survival rate isn't given.

In the meantime, Jean and Maurice return to battle and narrowly escape death before the battle ends. The bombardment of Sedan, and the advance of the German troops on all sides, led to the capitulation in the afternoon of 2 September, and the surrender of Emperor Napoleon to the Kaiser, effectively ending the war, though it would go on for some more months, including the siege of Paris described later in *La Débâcle*.

What is missing?

It is not possible in this short chapter to do justice to the detail that Zola presented in sections of the book. The first section contains a lot more of the philosophy of the soldiers; the intrinsic belief in the superiority of the French soldier over the German, yet also the utter ignorance of Germany. It has many details of the difficulties people had exerting their authority over such a disparate group that had not had time to form into cohesive units. There are many characters described by Zola who present important psychological information but who have not been mentioned. There is discussion of other battles fought, of the characteristics of the Emperor and his unsuitability to lead an army, and the social differences between the characters.

The second part of the book, the Battle of Sedan, is very detailed, particularly about certain aspects of the battle, Bazeilles, the Plateau, and the cavalry charges near Illy, but largely and understandably ignores other elements, as it focuses on the key characters in the book. It is written from the French perspective, so we see little of the Germans, apart from portraying them as monstrous attackers. (When Zola was writing the book, Alsace and parts of Lorraine had been taken from France, and there was still a great deal of animosity between the nations.) The surrender is provided in some detail, apparently resulting from the continual bombardment of the town and the high casualties, including civilians, that this caused. There are also, as shown previously, vivid descriptions of medical and surgical procedures. Towards the end of the second part of the book, both before and after the surrender, Zola describes the chaos as units retreat, fall apart, men disappear and get drunk, some are looking to escape to Belgium which is only a few miles to the north.

The third part of the book, begins with descriptions of the Frenchmen, particularly Jean and Maurice, captured by the Prussians and held prisoner on the peninsula of Iges, a loop of the Meuse to the west of Sedan. As the men are marched away to captivity in Germany, Jean and Maurice escape, and make their various ways to Paris, where the remainder of the book is set, focusing on the siege of Paris and the Commune, a very different set of circumstances to the Battle of Sedan. Jean and Maurice are still present, though usually not together. The focus of this last part of the book is on the problems faced by besieged Paris, the confusion, and the politics of the Commune. It provides a grand ending to the series of novels with the fall of the empire and the establishment of the republic.

La Débâcle is the longest book in the series and could easily be split into two books, with the Battle of Sedan and the capture of the emperor as one book, and the events in Paris the second. The latter may even have benefited from bringing in some of the characters from the earlier books, and perhaps this should have been the final book in the Rougon-Macquart series.

The tour

As mentioned earlier, much of the tour should be done by car. It can all be walked, but a lot of the walk would be relatively uninteresting, much of it taking place along main roads without pavements. Start at Bazeilles, where the fighting began. Explore the area around the church and observe the monument to the battle in the main square. Much of the village was destroyed in the fighting. The German soldiers then pushed up the main road towards Sedan, with fighting taking place all the way.

On the right there is a good museum to the fighting, the *Dernier Cartouche*, where French soldiers – as it says –fought to the last cartridge. One room still looks as it did after the battle, with bullet holes and marks on the plaster, and damaged furniture. There is useful information about the battle here. Nearby, down a side road on the opposite side of the road there is an ossuary containing bones from both the French and German troops. The French bones are still visible. The German bones were encased in concrete when the Germans occupied Sedan in the 1940s.

Drive back down to the La Moncelle road on the left and on to La Moncelle. The house on the right at the crossroads is present on a contemporary photograph, where the Prussians are advancing behind the house (coming from Bazeilles and northwards through Rubecourt and Villers-Cernay), and the French are to the left of the road – which were daybreak positions on 1 September. The French believed they could break out of Sedan here. Unfortunately for them the Prussians saw this as the ideal position to attack the French and split their army. The Prussians succeeded.

Continue north to Daigny and to Givonne. The French positions were to the left of the road. Note the heights behind – the French should have been in a position to defend these effectively but were not because they did not expect to remain in Sedan for long, just to rest. They were planning to retreat. Add to this the incompetent leadership and we can see why the Prussians defeated them so readily.

After Givonne head to Illy via Olly. In Illy take a left turn at the centre and then another left turn towards Sedan. At the top of the hill there is a Calvary. It is from here that the French cavalry charges described so vividly in *La Débâcle* began. There is a memorial and an information board. You can turn around here and head back to Illy and on to Floing or continue along the road to the edge of the wood and turn onto a track (4 × 4 or walking recommended). At a crossroads turn right. This is the Plain d'Algerie. It was at the Floing end where Jean and Maurice's unit was situated when they had to lie down in the field for hours. This area would have been full of troops, particularly when they were squeezed from all sides by the Germans into an ever-smaller space. To the right is the area of the cavalry charges towards Floing.

Continue to the tarmacked road. Take the left fork. Just along here is a memorial to General Margueritte, who also has a statue in Floing, and who was commander of the Reserve Division of Cavalry, wounded during the cavalry charges above Floing, which managed to reach this point and no further. (If driving on the main road via Illy then you need to take a left turn to this point as you reach Illy.) A little further along this road is a series of memorials to the African regiments that fought alongside the French. Go down the hill to the left. Along here on the right there is a World War II French cemetery. The graves are mainly those of the men killed defending Sedan and the Ardennes against the Germans in 1940. A little further along on the left a cemetery dating from 1870, again with an information board. During World War II a tank came through this cemetery.

Go to the bottom of the village and find the statue to General Margueritte. You can take a detour here to the village of St. Menges to the north, through which the Prussians came to surround the French and prevent them from retreating to Meziers. From St Menges there is a good view of the area within the bend of the river where the French prisoners were held, often without food, after the battle. This is described in *La Débâcle.* From Floing you can drive into Sedan and explore the town, particularly the fortress.

There are other things to see in the surrounding area. There are French and German war cemeteries (not 1870) at Noyers, and by the French cemetery there is a path to the Marfee, the site where Kaiser Wilhelm and Bismarck observed the battle. It provides a view of virtually the whole battlefield. This is also the hill the Luftwaffe attacked as Guderian's tanks appeared from the north. The French panicked, abandoned their posts, thus contributing to the ease by which the Germans conquered Sedan and crossed the Meuse. This was also the point the U.S. Army reached in November 1918 when the armistice was signed, ending the battle of Meuse-Argonne. Their objective was Sedan, but the French got there first. There is a memorial commemorating this on the main road at the bottom, just south of Wadlincourt.

To the west of Sedan, the village of Glaire provides a route into the bend in the Meuse where the prisoners were held. The road goes to Iges. It is also at Glaire that a side road takes you to the Meuse, only a few hundred metres from the canal junction, where there is an information board indicating where the German tanks first crossed the river in 1940. Take the road to Donchery. Here there is the house where the surrender negotiations took place between Napoleon III and Kaiser Wilhelm. It looks much as it did at the time.

Another route worth exploring is that taken by the Army of Chalon in the days before it entered Sedan. Zola describes this in detail, and it is still easy to follow. It is best to follow it by car rather than attempt to march it as the soldiers did, though the choice is yours. Zola spends the first part of the book on the descriptions of the march, but the final march went from Vouziers (itself worth exploring. It was almost totally rebuilt after World War I), through tiny villages such as Authe, St-Pierremont, Oches, La Berliere, La Besace, Raucourt and Remilly (you do need to read the book for the detailed descriptions of the surroundings and the experience of marching). There are diversions to Le Chesne, where Maurice saw the emperor and his baggage. There is a building on the site of where the emperor stayed. I have no idea whether it is the same building. It is now a hotel restaurant. It is also worth diverting to Beaumont-en-Argonne, where a significant battle took place before the Battle of Sedan. The French were routed, and the retreat is described by Zola. The church has significant war damage, but whether that is 1870 or 1914 is not clear.

The central part of this tour can be walked in a day, or the main sites can be visited by car, taking walks at appropriate points. The focus is around the town of Sedan itself, though there are interesting sites a little further away that are best visited by car. The latter part of the route taken by the French Army of Chalon went through the Pass of Stonne to the south of Sedan, heading for Beaumont-en-Argonne, where a significant battle took place two days before the Battle of Sedan, which led to the French armies heading across the Meuse at Mouzon and Remilly and retreating to Sedan. There are contemporary photographs showing how the road into Mouzon in 1870 looked very similar to how it looks today.

Around Noyers, just to the south of Sedan, there are German and French cemeteries containing the dead of both World Wars. This is the point reached by the U.S. troops in the Meuse-Argonne battle of September–November 1918 at the Armistice. It is also from these heights that Wilhelm II and Bismarck watched the unfolding of the battle in 1870.

Conclusion

La Débâcle provides some very good descriptions of the life of soldiers during the Franco-Prussian War. Much of this applies to other wars of the time, and to all wars at any time. While many psychologists may reject the use of a novel as data to try and explain something of human experience, in this case war, the counter-argument is that Zola conducted a research programme to ensure that his account was as accurate as possible, but allowing for interpretation – no different to how psychologists interpret their data apart from constructing a narrative flow. As noted, Zola interviewed participants, he walked the battlefield and surrounding areas, and he lived through the siege of Paris and the Commune, so he had direct experience of the events in the last third of the book. While his research took place 20 years later, the memories of those who were involved would inevitably be very strong, as memories of war tend to be some of the strongest retained, though perhaps with some confabulation.

Nevertheless, Zola's account is rich in the description of the participants, their behaviour, thoughts and feelings. This was one of the most important books of the Rougon-Macquart series, as it brought it largely to a close with the end of Napoleon III's empire. There is a case for a closer psychological examination of the whole series and its depth of understanding of the human psyche.

12

WORLD WAR I AND THE WESTERN FRONT

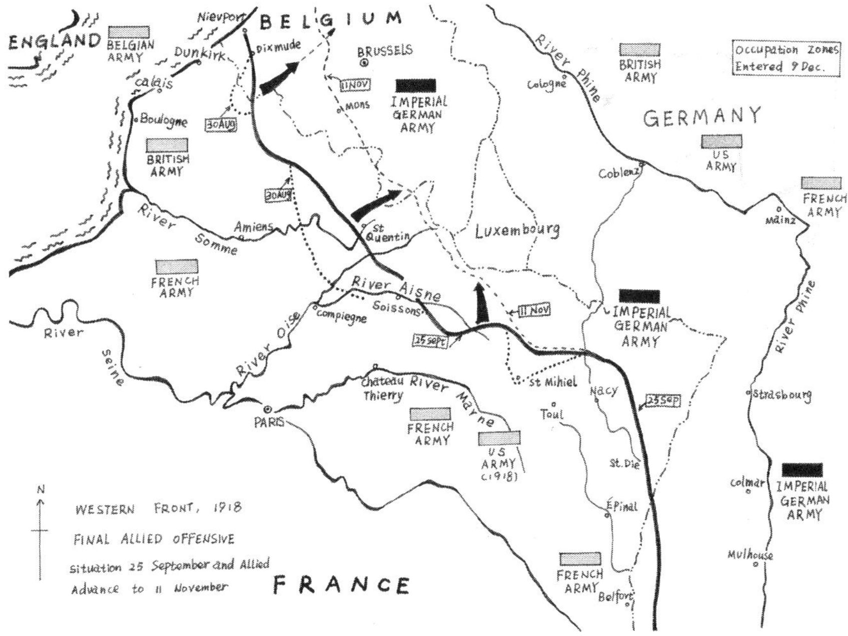

THE WESTERN FRONT. This is a rough indication of the length of the Western Front in the First World War, stretching from the English Channel to Switzerland. In the UK, we largely focus on the part down to the River Somme, a relatively short section of the whole line. The rest was held by French (and French colonial) troops for most of the war, with the United States joining in for the last few months (basically from September 1918). There are many sites beyond Ieper and the Somme that are worth visiting along the line.

My father was born during World War I, and he was in the RAF from 1939 to 1945. I got to know him in the late 1960s, and from then until he died in 2012 his obsession was World War I. Even though he had fought throughout World War II, it was World War I that mattered to him. Like perhaps most people in the UK, his interest was centred around the Western Front. Furthermore, it was not the whole of the 440 miles of the Western Front from Nieuwpoort to the east of Dunkirk through to the Swiss border southeast of Belfort, but that relatively small section in Belgium and Northern France from the North Sea to the Somme, focusing in particular on those seminal battles of Ypres and the Somme, along with Loos, Lens, Arras, and so forth.

A brief note on spelling. The place names in Flanders were commonly spelled in the French way (Ypres) and that is the way we usually know them when discussing World War I. In the modern world, the Flemish spelling is used more often (Ieper), so I have used the Flemish form when referring to the town, and the French form when referring to the battle.

Ignoring the Eastern Front, the Italian Front, the Far East, Africa, and the sea war, World War I is, through British eyes, largely focused on this short stretch of the Western Front. I am also going to be guilty of ignoring the war in the rest of the world, but I will attempt a brief look at some other areas of the Western Front, largely fought over by the French and Germans, but also including the British (including the Empire troops) and the USA, for those who are interested in touring the length of the Western Front.

This short stretch of the Western Front is the only area most British people are interested in that was fought over by the French and the Germans is Verdun, though relatively few British people visit the area. It is the largest preserved battle site in France, perhaps the world, with museums, cemeteries, an ossuary, and several ruined villages that were left undisturbed after the war. It is a huge memorial park with strict rules of behaviour (no picnics, etc.). But there are other interesting places to visit all along the route. We will start at the beginning, with a visit to Nieuwpoort, followed by the area of the Ypres battles, Arras, the Somme, and then on to the French areas, Chemin des Dames (where the British also fought), the Butte de Vauquois, Verdun itself, Meuse-Argonne (where the United States fought at the end of the war) and Le Linge in the Vosges mountains near the German border.

The tour is necessarily by car, with routes on foot in the particular areas. After examining some of these sites, we will examine the notion of memorialisation and World War I, along with a consideration of why we bother to continue with remembrance after 100 years.

The tour

The tour provides general directions and routes, stopping off at various points. Throughout the length of the front there are memorials, museums, and the remains of the battle. To stop at everything would take a very long time. The front also moved significantly at various stages, particularly at the start of the war: when the Germans attacked along the Marne, getting close to Paris before being beaten back; when the Germans retreated to the Hindenburg line in 1917; when the Germans attacked in the 1918 Spring Offensive; and when the Allies counterattacked in the last 100 days of the war. This route follows the line roughly. Detours will be necessary to see alternative sites.

The tour starts in Nieuwpoort, which was near where the trenches met the North Sea. This is where the Yser meets the sea. While the town was largely destroyed, there are few remains of the trenches, but there is a memorial to King Albert I, which was built with the support of the Belgian veterans' associations. There is a modern visitor centre here that explains the role of Nieuwpoort in the war, including the importance of flooding the area. Nearby, there is a memorial to the British soldiers who died in the defence of Antwerp and in the defence of the Belgian coast who have no known grave. There are also Commonwealth cemeteries such as Ramscappelle Road to the east of Nieuwpoort. This contains 841 casualties of World War I and was designed by Sir Edwin Lutyens.

Ieper

Head south through Diksmuide to Ieper. You will pass much evidence of the war, including Essex Farm Cemetery, and the nearby dressing station where John McCrae served and wrote the poem "In Flanders Fields."

The area around Ieper was fought over from virtually the beginning of the war during the rush to the sea in late 1914 to the end of the war in November 1918. There are many reminders of the war in this area, from sites that were left as they were after the war to the numerous memorials and cemeteries; and the tourist attractions such as museums and cafes.

Passchendaele is a small town on top of a ridge to the east of Ieper, and it was the target for the offensive launched on 31 July 1917. Though the distance from Ieper is only a few miles, it was not captured until November. This battle became known as the Third Battle of Ypres, after the first in 1914 and the second in 1915. All the ground gained in 1917 and more was lost to the Germans in their Spring Offensive of 1918.

Ieper is worth a visit even if you are not interested in the war. Its fortifications were modernised by Vauban's workers in the late seventeenth century and were used during World War I for shelter and storage. The town was destroyed by 1918 and rebuilt as an exact replica over the next few decades using whatever plans were available, along with photographs and people's recollections.

A tour of the battlefield can be undertaken by foot, bicycle or car, and there are organised tours. The battle cannot be fully comprehended in a single short tour. To get an impression of the battle, there are certain places that should be a priority. It is worth visiting some of the many museums in the area, from the main city memorial in the Cloth Hall in Ieper to the one in Zonnebeke with a reconstructed dugout or the museum at Sanctuary Wood, with numerous stereoscopic pictures of the battle, and some genuine (though reconstructed) trenches. In terms of a driving tour, the places to include, running roughly from south to north around the Salient, include the Messines Ridge, site of the attack in June 1917, where 19 mines were set off under the German positions and the Allies managed to capture the ridge on the first day. The northernmost mine was at Hill 60, where a portion of the battlefield was left as it was and has grassed over. There is a museum here. Then there is Sanctuary Wood, so-called because at the beginning of the war it was a sanctuary for the troops – but not for long. There is a good museum here with stretches of trench. At Hooge there is Crater Cemetery and another museum. This is where Hitler fought in World War I. For a time, he was opposite Anthony Eden.

After Hooge, move on to Polygon Wood and Zonnebeke, followed by Passchendaele and Tyne Cot cemetery. Then Langemarck, with the German cemetery, and finally back to Essex Farm.

Drive south along the Messines Ridge, where the 19 mines were set off (one exploded in the 1950s and another is still buried) to Mesen, Armentieres, south through Lens to Vimy.

Vimy Ridge

This is an enormous site, carefully tended by the Canadians, to whom it was entrusted after the war due to their part in taking the ridge. At first sight, it appears that the Canadians were solely responsible for this important action, which drove the Germans from the ridge which meant the Germans lost their oversight of the Arras battlefield, and gave the Allies oversight of the northern trenches around Lens, but the reality was that the Canadians were one part of the (largely British) army that took the ridge. After the war, trees were planted, one for each Allied soldier who died here. There are a lot of trees; but add the German casualties and the forest would be twice the size. One hundred years after the war there is no recognition of the thousands of Germans who died here. This is true for many battlefields on the Western Front.

I have a problem with Vimy Ridge, and some of the other sites, in that they are kept in pristine condition. Visitors are told to behave *appropriately*; the trenches have been shored up with concrete. There is a permanence about the site. I would prefer to see the site gradually decaying, the trenches falling in, the undergrowth allowed to flourish, perhaps much of the site being returned to the farmers. Vimy is somehow less real than some sites along the Western Front (though others are also preserved similarly). There has been a debate about the camp at Auschwitz-Birkenau, which is gradually deteriorating, particularly with so many visitors, with many thinking that it should be allowed to slowly return to nature. As those who recall these terrible events die off, perhaps so should many of the sites of mourning. We cannot preserve every site that has been the scene of massive human destruction, nor should we want to. There is good in the world too.

Just to the north-east of Vimy is the French military cemetery of Notre Dame de Lorette, built on top of a hill the French fought over early in the war, from the first Battle of Arras in October 1914 to the 3rd Battle of Artois in September to October 1915. This is the biggest national war cemetery for French troops in the world, containing the remains of more than 40,000 soldiers, some with graves, some within an ossuary. It is possible to get inside the Necropole and see coffins that used to be guarded by members of the French Resistance. There is also a vast round memorial containing – unusually – all the names of the soldiers (French, German, British, Empire) who died in the Nord Pas de Calais area during the war. It is called the Ring of Memory and contains 576,606 names of soldiers from 40 different nationalities. It is made of 500 steel panels arranged in an ellipse. Each panel is nearly three metres high. The names are listed alphabetically, with no consideration of rank or nationality. It was opened in 2014.

Arras

Just to the south is Arras, a town fought over several times during the war. The front line tended to be just to the east of the town. The Grand Place, which now has restaurants and hotels, is seen in wartime photographs as little more than rubble. Underneath Arras and the surrounding area are many underground caves. These were quarries from before the war which were extended by the Allied troops to provide protection, particularly before the Battle of Arras (1917), where the tunnels were extended so that the troops could enter from the town and emerge in the front lines to attack the Germans. They were called the Wellington tunnels by the New Zealand troops who were stationed there. The entrance to the new museum is near the centre of Arras. Outside is a memorial wall to those who fought in the battle.

Most of the area of the Battle of Arras is to the east of the town. Some areas have been built over, most of the rest is farmland, with cemeteries dotted around. Arras also has an intact Vauban fortress. Sadly, the main citadel is not normally accessible to the public.

The Somme

Head south on the D917 and you arrive at Bapaume, which was the initial objective for the British Army on 1 July 1916 but was never attained during the five months of the Battle of the Somme. Turn right down the D929 towards the British lines. Shortly after the Warlencourt British cemetery on the left is the Butte de Warlencourt, which is the furthest point reached by the British during the battle. From the top there is a good view (from the German viewpoint) of most of the battlefield. After a Canadian memorial on the right there is the site of the windmill of Pozieres, which was heavily fought over during the battle. The rubble of the windmill is still all that remains. There is a tank memorial on the opposite side of the road commemorating the first tanks used in battle at nearby Flers-Courcelette. The familiar names of the Somme villages are on both sides of the road here. The next village on this route is La Boisselle, which was heavily fortified by the Germans. The aim on 1 July was to bypass it on either side. There are deep tunnels dug by the Germans to the south of the village, and to the south-east is the Lochnagar Crater, privately owned but accessible. This is the remainder of one of the British mines blown under the Germans on 1 July. When I first visited this site, there was very little there; now there are many memorials to the dead.

At La Boiselle head on the Authuille road to the north-west. At the point where you turn right on the D151 there is a place to park. The woods here contain the remains of dugouts built by the British troops for protection from the German guns. It is mostly covered over, and people use the area for motorbikes, but it is worth exploring.

Continue to the Thiepval Memorial, which was designed by Lutyens and contains the names of 72,337 Allied soldiers with no known grave. Nearby is a museum. Little remains of the old village of Thiepval. From here head west on the D73, stopping at Mill Road and Connaught cemeteries, where noticeboards indicate some of the action in the area. Near the former is the Schwaben redoubt, which the Germans used to hold off the attacking forces. Nearby is the Ulster Tower, commemorating the 36th Ulster Division which took part at the start of the battle. The woods on the other side of the road are private, but contain the remains of trenches and dugouts, little touched since the war.

It is worth walking this whole area, including the parts below, to give a better impression of the battlefield.

It is worth crossing the river to visit Beaumont-Hamel, specifically Newfoundland Park, another Canadian memorial with a large field containing the remains of trenches. In recent years these have been fenced off. Within the park is Hawthorn Ridge Cemetery Number 2, with Hawthorne Ridge Cemetery in a field behind. There is a track to the cemetery from the D73. Just beyond this cemetery is a copse, which is actually the site of several mines, set off under the German front lines on 1 July 1916. It is sort of fenced off but accessible. There is talk of making this another World War I theme park (I mean memorial site) so it is worth visiting before that happens. Walk through the craters to the other side. There is a path down to the road. Turn left and then right on a track leading to Beaumont-Hamel British Cemetery. Just after the first turn onto the track, the embankment to the left is part of *White City* an area forward of the British lines, where tunnels were dug through so the troops could get closer to the German lines in safety. It is from here that a cameraman shot the famous exploding mine – the first Beaumont-Hamel mine. If you have seen the footage you can tell where it was taken from. Imagine the British troops crossing the ridge from right to left to attack the crater, facing the German machine guns. The village in the dip, Beaumont itself, wasn't captured until much later in the battle, indicating there were no real advances.

Walk down the road into Beaumont and there is a track leading back to Newfoundland Park. There is so much still buried from World War I in these parts that it is difficult to get away without finding something, whether that is a piece of barbed wire, a bullet, or sometimes a human bone. It is now illegal to remove anything from the battlefield.

It is worth visiting Albert and then the villages on the other side of the battlefield. The Somme itself is a disappointing river, being little more than a canal and some marshy areas. The Somme marked the boundary between the British (and Empire) forces and the French for much of the war. In the 1916 battle the French advanced next to the British. It is worth visiting Peronne, another town with a good museum on the banks of the Somme and north to Cambrai, the site of the first massed tank battle (to the south and west of the town).

To the French sector

From the Somme, head south-east, perhaps on the A26 for speed, past Laon, to the Chemin des Dames, a ridge (or rather a plateau) which runs west from Corbeny to the N2 at Vauxrains, fought over several times. The Aisne River flows to the south of the ridge. The First Battle of the Aisne in 1914 was an Anglo-French counteroffensive following the First Battle of the Marne. The Second Battle of the Aisne took place in 1917, and the Third Battle of the Aisne took place during the German Spring Offensive in 1918. The Germans stopped the Allied offensive on the ridge in 1914, taking the whole of the plateau by early 1915. It is worth travelling along the ridge to visit some of the sights, such as the Caverne du Dragon, which was the list sight held by the French in 1915. There is a good viewpoint on the Plateau de California which offers a good viewpoint of the battlefields. The village of Craonne was destroyed in the fighting and was left as rubble, which is now grown over. There are signs indicating the various buildings of the village. Nearby, the Battle of Craonne took place in March 1814. This was a victory for the French over the Prussians and the Russians – perhaps more of a pyrrhic victory because while Napoleon and his men retained the field, at the end of the day they failed to stop Blucher taking Laon. There is a statue of Napoleon along the main road near Craonne. There are walks available all around the area.

From the Chemin des Dames head east past Reims (which was behind the French lines) along the D931 past Sainte-Menehould to the heart of the Argonne, which saw severe fighting throughout the war. There are the two forests of Lachalade and Haute Chevauchee. In these forests there are many remnants of the war. To the north there is l'Abri du Kronprinz, where the German headquarters were situated. There are concrete bunkers and trenches, some intact, some damaged by shellfire. There is the Kaisertunnel, built in 1915/16, which was used by the Germans for two years to send up men and supplies to the front. It was 350 metres long plus extensions. It still contains the remains of a first aid station and a telephone exchange, among other things. There is a walking trail nearby, enabling an exploration of the trenches and the mine craters of the area, including an ossuary built by the track, with the remains of mine craters behind.

Touring the Argonne and Verdun regions

As already mentioned, it is difficult to suggest a single tour that takes in all the sites that are worth visiting across these two battlefields. This is an area you can spend a week exploring, without seeing all the main sites. It is a matter of picking and choosing. There are ample guides available in English and/or French for both areas. In the following sections, I provide a brief outline of a few of the more interesting sites.

The Argonne forest

The Argonne forest had been the scene of war since 1914, when the lines settled down at the southern end of the forest. The Germans had built substantial fortifications, training grounds, dugouts, trenches, and rest areas within the forest and nearby. While they were used throughout the war, as the lines did not move from the end of 1914 to September 1918, many were used for the soldiers fighting at Verdun during 1916 to rest and recuperate.

Start at Varennes-en-Argonne (where there is a monument to the Pennsylvanians who fought in the area – it was rather unkempt when we saw it), and head west on the D38 towards Vienne-le-Chateau. A little way along the road there is a sign indicating the shelter for the Crown Prince 700 km along a track to the right. The track is in good condition to the shelters. They are easy to miss if you don't spot another sign on a tree to the right. Explore. There are numerous bunkers and trenches, with some original barbed wire fencing, and evidence of shell damage, presumably from when the Allies advanced in September 1918. These shelters were used for Wilhelm, Crown Prince of Germany when he was here in command of the Crown Prince Corps during the Battle of Verdun. His accommodation is obvious. It is more luxurious than the rest, with the concrete shaped a little more decoratively than usual. The site is not well-maintained and has no information signs, perhaps because it is German.

Head back to the road, turn right, and a few kilometres later turn left where there is a sign indicating the Kaiser Tunnels and the Haute-Chevauchee. There are various signs and monuments as you go down, so be observant. Eventually there are the German trenches, quickly followed by the French trenches. The lines ran east-west at this point, a little south of Varennes. The lines barely moved between the end of 1914 and September 1918.

There is a car park enabling further exploration by foot. There is a large monument which is also an ossuary, and behind that a large mine crater – actually, there are several craters mostly joined together as you move away from the road behind the ossuary. The entrance to the ossuary is at the back of the monument, and a light illuminates the stacked bones on either side. On the other side of the road there are the remains of trenches and also the Kaiser Tunnels. These are underground bunkers that have been rebuilt and are the only part of the site that has opening times and an entrance fee.

Further south on the road there is the Ravin du Genie, which was a supply depot situated on an old Roman road in the rear of the French lines. There are various bits of evidence around this area. Further down the road is a French war cemetery, opposite an old forester's cottage. The track to the right here goes to Lachalade. Turn left and there is a monument to the Italian troops who fought alongside the French here in the early part of the war. Nearby, there is the site of an Italian cemetery. Presumably the bodies were either shipped back to Italy or taken to another, larger, cemetery.

Head to Vienne-le Chateau and then take the road to Binarville. Just outside Vienne is a French military cemetery containing more than 8000 graves and two ossuaries with more than 3200 remains between them. Further along is the monument to the Lost Battalion. It is a rather unusual monument, but there is a helpful information board which explains how the battalion broke through enemy lines and took up positions in the Charlevaux gorge. Unfortunately for them, the Germans repaired their lines, cutting the battalion off. They remained isolated for five days, undergoing several heavy German attacks, before being relieved.

Drive to Apremont and then on to Chatel Chenery. Head on the road towards Cornay but while still in the village note a sign to the left. This is a display indicating the actions of Corporal (promoted to Sergeant for his actions) York, who received the Medal of Honor for an attack to the west of the village. There is a route laid out, along which information boards provide further information. The U.S. troops headed west out of the village, attacking the German lines. They were stopped by German machine gun fire. Seventeen men, including York, attacked and silenced the machine gun, breaking through the line and taking 70 prisoners. A machine gun then opened fire on them from the hillside, after shouting at the German prisoners to lie down. Several men were shot, including the commander of the unit. York was then in charge. He attacked the machine gun post up the steep hill, himself coming under a bayonet charge. He defended himself with his Colt 45, took out the machine gun, and captured another 62 prisoners. The U.S. troops returned to the village with their 132 prisoners. York was promoted and awarded the medal.

It is fascinating how men can bring themselves to charge a machine gun post. This is something few normal civilians would ever do (I assume that is the case; I do not have the evidence). Such an act depends on a number of factors: very good training so that one acts automatically in a dangerous situation, caring for one's comrades, bravery, foolhardiness, fitness, agility, and a lot of luck. We hear about those who successfully take out machine gun posts. We do not hear about the (probably vast) majority who get killed while trying unsuccessfully to do so.

Nevertheless, York was rightly recognised for his actions in taking the machine gun next and coping with the bayonet charge. Regarding the capture of the Germans, it is likely that they lost the will to fight when they lost their machine gun. They would probably have surrendered to anyone.

The problem with the previous story is that it is highly contested. One version, which has York take out 35 machine guns, is perhaps taking it too far. Other soldiers who fought with York on that day claim that they too took prisoners, and that his role was not as important as portrayed both in his diary – which was serialised in the 1920s – and in a film starring Gary Cooper which was released in the Second World War, when positive propaganda was essential for the war effort. We will probably never know the truth of the story, but it shows we should be wary of accepting the truth of any individual. They may have deliberately changed the facts to suit their own purposes, or the facts may have been changed for other reasons, whether forgetfulness, propaganda, or any other reason.

Take the road through Exermont up to Romagne-sous-Montfaucon, where there is a World War I museum and the largest U.S. cemetery in Europe (52 hectares, 14,246 graves, including 486 unidentified soldiers and the names of 954 soldiers whose remains were never recovered or identified).

During both World Wars, the United States had a policy of allowing next of kin to repatriate their dead husbands and children, though the majority let them be buried in the region they died. The Montfaucon cemetery, in the classic way of U.S. memorial sites, is not exactly understated. On entering between two huge gateposts, the road splits and there are avenues of trees. The graves are on the right hand side, spread wide in the classic U.S. manner, taking up a lot of unnecessary ground (the French, British and Germans have their graves much more closely together). In the centre there is a pool. And up on the left there is a visitors' centre. Inside the visitors' centre there are two rooms of information, one about the war (or at least the part the U.S. army was involved in) and one about the cemetery, its construction and the families who visited after the war.

Head south on the D998, turning left on the D104 for another very large U.S. monument at Montfaucon d'Argonne. This mainly consists of a high tower with steps up the inside. From the top there is a spectacular view of much of the battlefields both of Verdun and the Argonne Forest. The tower is on top of a hill that was captured by the Germans in 1914 and subsequently well-fortified. There are bunkers all over the site. The village was situated on top of the hill but was destroyed in the war. Now there are the remains of walls, largely covered in ivy, and the ruins of the church behind the U.S. monument. Within the ruins of the church there is a German observation post, built atop a part of the wall and strengthened with stones from the church and iron girders and rails. From inside the post (it is a scramble to get inside) the Germans would be able to observe much of the Verdun battlefield and presumably would have had some weapon control from here. Several of the other bunkers at this site also have observation ports.

The U.S. troops attacked this fortress on the first day of the advance in September 1918, but – understandably, given its position on a high hill with good visibility all around – they failed to take it immediately. After a few days it was taken and the advance continued.

These sites are all important either for the duration of the war, as in the French/German trenches around the Haute-Chevauchee, or for the first phase of the battle of Meuse-Argonne (the U.S. sector). The battle continued, with the Allies advancing northwards, until Armistice Day, when the French had taken Sedan and the United States were on the heights to the south of that town. Interestingly, a tour of the more northern battle sites of World War I covers similar ground to much of the first part of Zola's *La Débâcle*, in which the Army of Chalon is marching backwards and forwards towards Sedan.

Butte de Vauquois

Just to the east is the Butte de Vauquois. This was a hill which overlooked the front lines and so was heavily fought over by the French and Germans. The village of Vauquois was on the top of the hill. It was completely destroyed. The hill was split in two by deep mine craters, which run the whole length of the hill. The trenches still remain on either side of the craters, particularly on the German side, where there are virtually intact fire steps with steel armour and bunkers that are still accessible. Within the hill itself there are many tunnels that are accessible for guided tours. This is one of the most impressive sights on the Western Front.

The Germans took the village early in the war. The French fought back. Both sides needed the top of the hill: the Germans so they could observe the main railway line from St. Menehould to Verdun, and destroy any traffic attempting to supply Verdun; the French so they could observe German troop movements to the north. In the end neither side dominated and both remained entrenched on the top of the hill until the final Argonnes offensive.

The site is worth visiting for the extent of the remains. It is not only the tunnels and dugouts, but it has the largest set of mine craters I have seen on the Western Front. There are good examples of trenches, complete with fire steps, smaller dugouts that are sometimes accessible (take a torch and tread carefully), a trench mortar, rusty remains of barbed wire entanglements, and a whole series of concrete bricks used by both sides in different theatres of the Western Front.

Verdun

The battlefield of Verdun is a sacred site for the French, not surprisingly, given the extent of the destruction and death. There are signs saying no camping, no picnicking, and no music on many of the roads, though I am not sure how picnicking is somehow disrespectful to the dead. If people come to pay their respects to the site and to the dead, then presumably they are still going to need to eat.

Wherever you go, there is evidence of the battle. Much of the site is covered by forests, but beneath the trees there are still miles of trenches, shell holes, and general damage due to the war. Much of the area is out of bounds and has been since World War I. It is known as the Zone Rouge (there are areas along other parts of the Western Front, but it is mostly around her, to the north of Verdun), and is still littered with unexploded ordnance and toxic to most plants due to the poison gases used. Housing, farming and forestry were forbidden. The area is much reduced, but still extensive.

There were several villages here, but all were destroyed and abandoned. Now they are heaps of stones covered in soil, with trees growing around and among them. At Douaumont there are signs outside where each house stood, showing who lived there. The people never came back. Presumably they made their homes where they were evacuated to, or perhaps came back as far as Verdun. It is not clear what happened to those who wanted to rebuild their homes because they didn't get the opportunity to do so. There are several such villages, dotted around the heights to the north of Verdun.

These *villages that died for France* have an official population of 0. The area around was made uninhabitable during the war and some has remained so. The French decided to leave several villages permanently ruined. To the east there is Fort Vaux. Driving there you will pass several marked sites of other forts and positions. This is open to the public. To the west is the ossuary, the main site on the battlefield. This enormous Art Deco building, in front of which is a French cemetery containing more than 16,000 dead, contains the bones of thousands of French and German soldiers, mixed together. They are visible through the windows. The tower can be climbed, and there is a shop and a museum. Nearby is the ruined village of Douaumont, and Fort Douaumont, which was captured within three days of the start of the battle by the Germans and was regularly fought over. It bears the marks. Douaumont had been built in the 1880s and just before the war had been rearmed and provided with an extra cladding of reinforced concrete. It was one of around 70 forts constructed in the region as a response to the French defeat in the Franco-Prussian War. While Verdun is well inside the borders of France, it was still considered a border town. The Vauban citadel inside Verdun is further evidence of that.

From Verdun to the Vosges

The route continues to head east from Verdun, then just west of the then German town of Metz (near the battlefield of 1870 at Mars-la-Tour) it cuts south, leaving Metz in German hands, then cutting east leaving Pont-a-Mousson in French hands, then south-east roughly along the 1914 border into the Vosges mountains, the tops of which comprised the border. In the southern half of the Vosges, the French had pushed forward off the mountains, with the line heading south from Colmar to the west of Mulhouse.

In the Vosges, in January 1915, the French pushed forwards to take the mountains. They attacked along the length of the Vosges. One of the key points was Le Linge, which remains as a museum and a series of trenches at the top of a mountain. Between July and October 1915, the French and Germans fought for this small piece of ground. More than 17,000 men were killed. The lines then stayed much as they were for the rest of the war. The museum has a range of personal items, weapons, models and maps of the battlefield on display.

The trenches themselves are well-preserved and contain many of the accoutrements missing from most of the preserved trenches. A lot of the trench armour remains, along with the concrete emplacements and bunkers that were built up over the years of the war. What is quite shocking is how close the French and German trenches were. The Germans held the top of the mountain, and the French attacked up the western slopes, gradually getting closer until at times the trenches were within 10 metres or so. Exploring the trenches provides an indication of the difficulties faced by the troops.

To the Swiss border

The line of the Vosges provides the line of the trenches through the war. Colmar remained in German hands, and the line went to the Swiss border just east of Pfetterhouse in the foothills of the Jura mountains by a river called Le Largue. Pfetterhouse is where, before the war, the three countries of France, Germany and Switzerland met. During the war, the Swiss built a series of bunkers within their boundary to keep watch on the opposing forces. The bunkers, which contained trenches to protect the Swiss troops from stray bullets, flew Swiss flags so the French and Germans knew where the border was. The area is called Kilometre Zero. A series of bunkers and observation posts have been rebuilt in the area.

Memorials on the Western Front

Memorials are examined in Chapter 4. This further discussion concerns how memorialisation takes place on the Western Front. If you visit any area of the front you will find memorials. Some of them are huge, such as the Canadian memorial at Vimy Ridge, the Thiepval monument to the missing on the Somme or the ossuary at Verdun. There are many cemeteries to the soldiers of all sides – though the German cemeteries are far fewer with on average many more graves. The French and Belgians did not want to hand over too much of their land for the bodies of their enemies. Then there are the more personal memorials, which might be to a particular regiment, a small action, or to a group of individuals or an individual. It might be thought that most memorials were constructed in the years immediately after the war, when the memories of the dead were raw, but this is not the case. A large proportion of the memorials present on the Western Front are relatively new, in many cases very new, commemorating the 100th anniversary of the war. There is a difference, however, between the British and the French (the Germans are less likely to be allowed to monumentalise the war). There are far more newer memorials in the British sector than in the French sector. Does this tell us something about the differences between the French and the British or perhaps about the different ways in which they wish to remember the war (see the following discussion)?

Throughout the British sector of the Western Front memorials continue to be constructed. At one level, it is understandable that people create memorials on the anniversaries of key events, but there are an increasing number of memorials relating to particular individuals, often family members, who fought in the war. This is claimed to be a form of remembrance. How can someone be remembering a person who died long before they were born? Why do they want to *remember* them in any public sense? There is an interesting narrative going on around the notion of memorialisation, commemoration and remembrance in the UK. The notion of remembrance seems fixed and unalterable. To suggest that we remove the cemeteries on the Western Front or change the remembrance service on 11 November is seen as utterly unacceptable. Anybody who does suggest it may be ostracised, given that the feeling about remembrance is so strong.

Memorialisation, commemoration and remembrance of World War I in the UK

There is currently an obsession with World War I remembrance in the UK. While this is in some ways understandable, given that we have recently seen the 100th anniversary of the war, there is something more subtle, more difficult to understand. Why are people constructing new memorials to the war? There are even new memorials in towns and villages commemorating the deaths of people who died 100 years ago. Why would anyone want to do this? We never did it for wars prior to World War I. There are memorials to Waterloo or to Crimea, but they are relatively rare and are largely forgotten. People do not usually put wreaths or poppies on a Waterloo memorial; so why do they continue to do so with World War I memorials, from the Cenotaph in London to towns and villages all around the country? It is understandable that after a war the people who are grieving their loss wish to have a service of commemoration, but it is not readily understandable why people do it for those who they cannot remember.

After World War I, the country had experienced so many deaths that there was a narrative involving a huge outpouring of grief for the dead and relief that the war was over. There was a sense of needing to create a national memorial, which became the Cenotaph; but that was not accessible to most people, so the wave of memorialisation swept across the country and people built war memorials in virtually every city, town and village, inscribed with the names of those who had died and sometimes with a roll of honour of all those who had fought. The religious ceremony that started at the Cenotaph was copied around the country and most memorials held the ceremony on Remembrance Day, initially 11 November, later the closest Sunday to 11 November. Two decades later, when the country's master narrative was still about the enormous losses incurred during

World War I, there was World War II, a longer conflict with fewer casualties, though there were still deaths from most communities. These names were added to the memorials, and the services continued as before, except now people were grieving for a new generation of dead.

World War II had the effect of removing World War I from the master narrative, which now focused on World War II and the losses associated with it; not only people, but the massive destruction of cities and towns, and the enormous economic cost, which the country would be literally paying the USA for until the twenty-first century. The veterans and those who remembered World War I started to die out in the next few decades, and they were the ones who ensured the services were well attended. The World War II generation attended, though a little less enthusiastically, because they understood that the ceremony was about World War I. After this the services became less and less well attended, until by the 1990s relatively few people attended.

It was only in the twenty-first century, when the UK went to war in Iraq and Afghanistan, that the Government recognised that the central narrative of the population was not only against these wars but against the armed forces, in a way they had never been before. There was an active drive to resuscitate these services (along with other means of getting people to like the armed forces again), which were naturally dying out with those who remembered the world wars.

It was by this means that we now have a revived Remembrance Day service, but one which is virtually unchanged from the one for World War I and is not fit for purpose in the twenty-first century. The service focuses on a Christian god, on British military power, and on monarchy; all topics that are contested in a world where the British Empire is heavily criticised, British military power is virtually meaningless alone, and the monarchy is – or should be – on its last legs as an inappropriate means of governance (even if that governance is largely symbolic). After all, royalty does in reality symbolise a family who got into the position they are for having ancestors who were better thieves, rapists and murderers than the ancestors of the rest of the people.

Longer-term psychological consequences of war

World War I was the first time we recognised not only the mass psychiatric casualties of war, but its longer-term impact. The psychological impact of war does not end with the ending of the war. After World War I, there were so many millions of men (and women) fighting that there were many who suffered the psychological effects long after the ending of the war. Psychologists and psychiatrists wrote a lot about shell shock and related disorders during and in the immediate aftermath of the war, but within a few years these disorders had been forgotten. Many men returned from the war and lived apparently normal lives. They do not show up in the medical or legal records, but it is unknown how many of them continued to suffer for years. Novels were published that indicated continued suffering, but these were relatively few, though sometimes provided a sophisticated account of how war-related problems could continue into civilian life. Unfortunately, most of these accounts are about the middle and upper classes, rarely about the ordinary soldier, who continues to have little voice in society. There are accounts in newspapers throughout the 1920s regarding soldiers who get into legal trouble and blame their shell shock for their actions. Unfortunately, there is rarely any further information about the evidence for this. Most people just lived with it and made their families live with it.

The evidence for continued problems is strongest in the United Kingdom and in France. The Germans and the Russians were busy trying to build new societies, so there was limited space for the consequences of the war. The best evidence we have relates to those soldiers who received treatment after the war, and the relatively large numbers who were committed to asylums, sometimes for long periods. There is evidence that there were still World War I veterans in asylums up to the end of their lives in the 1960s and possibly beyond. The added dimension for the French is that their performance in 1940 may have been affected by the master narrative relating to the destruction of Northern France in World War I and the desire for that to not happen again, which may in part explain their quick surrender.

The psychological impact of the war in the United Kingdom

After the war, it was recognised that many thousands of soldiers had experienced problems, usually labelled as shell shock, though that is a simplistic label. This is not the place to provide a detailed account of the psychological impact of fighting in the trenches, instead I am going to briefly examine the post-war impact. The horrors of war did not disappear when the war ended. The nightmares, the memories, the behaviour continued well into the post-war period.

The most significant document to arise out of the post-war interest in the problems faced by those affected by war psychologically was the report of the War Office Committee on Shell Shock. In 1920, Lord Southborough called for an investigation into the causes and treatment of shell shock. In his speech, he recognised that many people were still suffering from the effects. The findings of the Committee were reported in 1922 (HMSO, 1922). The report, while important, was heavily biased towards the upper and middle classes, with most of the committee and most of those who gave evidence representing the officer classes. Out of the 60,000 men receiving mental-health related disability pensions, only six (four officers, two OR) were called on to give evidence. The findings were ambiguous. There were no clear recommendations regarding the causes of shell shock or the treatment, let alone the longer-term consequences, which were largely ignored. The advice that was given largely related to the experience of soldiers in wartime, such as the importance of unit cohesiveness, officer awareness of psychological problems, ensuring military medics had some training in the treatment of the disorder and, perhaps most importantly, the abolition of the term *shell shock*, which clearly did not represent a single disorder, and its descriptive wording was just wrong.

These findings were not particularly new, as various psychiatrists had described several disorders and several treatments (though the evidence for effectiveness was not very good). The controversies emerging from the report were not new. The notion of cowardice remained, along with the idea that people of a neurotic disposition were often not willing to become good soldiers – leaving the fault for the traumatic response in the hands of the soldier rather than the experience – so someone accused of cowardice should still expect the full force of the law rather than a recognition of psychological difficulty. According to Barham (2004), the military establishment wanted to wash its hands of the problem of shell shock, basically "putting Tommy Atkins in his place." (p. 233)

There are two main groups to consider when looking at the longer-term psychological impact of the war. The first group we know very little about. They are the ones who went home and somehow got on with their lives, managing their problems themselves, with their families and friends. The second group we know more about, because they had regular contact with the medical services, particularly the asylum services. This second group were treated in several ways, from very positive to very negative. Knowles Stanfield, a medical superintendent speaking in 1919, made his views clear when he said that soldiers suffering from mental disorders after the war were disturbed before the war. This represents another example of leaving the responsibility in the hands of the soldiers themselves, failing to recognise the war as an essential and important cause. His view was that the problem was allowing these disturbed people into the forces in the first place, with the consequence that the medical board was now responsible for many thousands of mental health pensions.

Government policy was that servicemen would not be sent to asylums, and this was reiterated in the Shell Shock report of 1922. Asylums were supposed to be for the hopeless and incurable mental cases. The reality was, according to Barham (2004), that many were already entering the asylum system, often from workhouse infirmaries or other Poor Law institutions.

The government in the 1920s was in a difficult position regarding veterans with mental health problems. On the one hand they were trying to claim that the service personnel themselves were to blame for their problems, but at the same time they recognised their responsibilities by awarding many thousands of mental health pensions. The other difficulty was that officers were still being given labels of shell shock or neurasthenia and being treated with psychotherapy, while ORs were considered to be insane and locked up in asylums where they would receive very little treatment. The so-called bringing together of the classes in the trenches was again shown to be a lie. The rich look after themselves, even in the area of psychiatry.

Barham (2004) makes a good argument for the failure of the authorities to acknowledge the *normality* of many of the ex-servicemen who were committed to asylums. Taking the Wandsworth infirmary as an example, he identified a group of 120 ex-servicemen who were admitted between 1918 and 1925. While the authorities' argument was often that these were men who already had problems before enlisting, Barham shows clearly that in most cases there was no evidence of mental health problems before their service. Most had served abroad for at least three years. A large proportion were married, often with children, and so the trauma of war was shared with a family. Barham provides individual details of many of these people, demonstrating how ordinary people became ill due to their war experiences. The difference in language between then and now is well illustrated by a case presented by Barham (pp. 247–248). Frederick Hill, 38, had served in the Machine Gun Corps, was twice wounded and promoted to staff sergeant instructor. In 1923 he told his wife that he felt queer and was losing the use of his legs. He later came home from business one evening and said his mind had gone. A doctor saw him that evening and said, "he is acutely depressed, can give no reply to questions, makes no effort to think, says despairingly that he cannot, buries his face in his hands and sobs convulsively. No attempts to comfort him are of avail." (Barham, pp. 247–248) He was sent to Long Grove Asylum a few days later. His story is typical of men of the period. There is no medical diagnosis that makes sense and not much effort to try and make sense of the problem – another example of the lack of care about the ordinary soldier.

While there is evidence of thousands of ordinary soldiers who were sent to asylums for varying periods, there were relatively few officers sent, around 300, though that may be because the evidence swings towards officers whose families were not financially able to support them (Barham, 2004), in other words, officers whose background was probably that they had joined up from the working classes as privates and been promoted through the ranks.

The problem of failing to recognise the difficulties faced by ex-servicemen lasted a long time. In the 1930s there were still many thousands of veterans locked up in asylums

We all lived with the psychological consequences of the war. I remember growing up in my village, there was a man we called George who spent his time pushing a pram around the roads of the village. The pram had wing mirrors and might have contained a dog, some food, or nothing at all, but George would push his pram all day, abused by ignorant children, and taking little notice of what went on around him. He was a World War I veteran who had never recovered. This was the 1960s. My Dad said that when he was growing up in the 1920s and 1930s there was a man who stood in an alley who would accost all the boys and show them his arm. He would roll up his sleeve and stick his finger through a hole left by a wound. This was deliberately done to frighten people. These are normal stories. After World War II they were obviously blended with stories of World War II veterans who had problems but who, like the World War I veterans, received little care. Every one of my age and older probably grew up knowing a few traumatised World War I and World War II veterans in their community.

The psychological impact of war for the French

The French suffered terribly in World War I. Most of the Western Front was on French territory. There were many French civilians caught behind enemy lines, who somehow had to live through four years of occupation. Thousands of square miles of land were devastated. Towns and villages were erased or so badly damaged they needed to be totally rebuilt. The economy of the North, based on coal and iron, was badly damaged, and millions of men were killed, maimed and wounded. Many of the psychological casualties would never be fit for work or family life again. Many were destined to spend the rest of their lives in asylums or shunned by their families. Many maimed men would never get married and have children because they were crippled, whether this directly affected their ability to have sex, or whether because of facial or other injuries they were unable to find – or want to find – wives. This is arguably why the French collapsed in May 1940. The children of the World War I generation could not face what their fathers had faced. They had seen the consequences.

While we will never really know why the French collapsed so readily in 1940, when they had superior weaponry, tanks, transport and men compared to the German Army, at least part of the explanation must be what happened in World War I. Alongside the German boldness in the *Blitzkrieg*, with generals such as Guderian ignoring the dangers of leaving flanks exposed and running ahead of supplies (to get over the latter, tank crews fastened ammunition and fuel to their tanks as they advanced – seems rather dangerous to me), it was at least in part the French fear of repeating World War I. As already noted in Chapter 11, the French were well dug in on the heights to the south of Sedan, but when attacked from the air they basically ran away, even though they were well-protected in their bunkers, and experienced few casualties. This itself may be the reason for the quick defeat. Once the Germans had crossed the Meuse, there were no armies in their way before they reached the Channel at Abbeville. But I believe it is more than just this single failure.

France was almost destroyed by World War I. They had about 1.4 million military deaths, lost 27 villages and towns, with many more very badly damaged; a large part of their population was subjugated by occupation; many key industries were in German hands. After the war they were angry with the Germans and wanted to make them pay for every bit of damage they had caused (or the French perceived them to have caused – there are two sides to every war), whether that was damage to the roof of a house, the destruction of a town, or the financial costs of looking after a crippled veteran or the loss of earnings relating to a man who had died at the age of 20. On top of the anger was the fear that it might happen again. The French wanted to ensure that Germany would never again be able to threaten them. They wanted them disarmed, they wanted to remove their factories, and to turn them into simple peasants. They did not succeed in doing this, and as a consequence they remained frightened about the potential for a repeat; and when that repeat finally did come, the German army, with fewer and poorer quality tanks than the French, fewer men, and limited vehicles available to transport men and supplies, overran France in about six weeks. The extent to which this was caused by a general fear of a repeat of 1914–1918 cannot be known, but it is certainly part of the story.

Conclusion

The aftermath of World War I is all about narratives. There were the millions of individual narratives of war, which were taken home and lived with either more or less successfully, narratives of courage and heroism, confidence and cowardice, comradeship and fear. These narratives on occasion led to significant psychological consequences and on occasion they did not. The master narrative of remembrance, particularly in the UK but also in other parts of the world (particularly among the victors), became an important part of the nation's story, and even though it is, in the UK, riven with god, monarch and militarism, it remains as powerful now as it was in the years following the war. World War II gave it prominence given the vast numbers of casualties, but for some reason we have been unable to move on from this fixed narrative of remembrance. It is important we start to think about this, start to think about changing the remembrance service to reflect modern times, and perhaps to think about removing the military cemeteries of World War I and returning the land to the farmers from whom it was taken in the first place.

13

THE SPANISH CIVIL WAR AND THE BATTLE OF THE EBRO

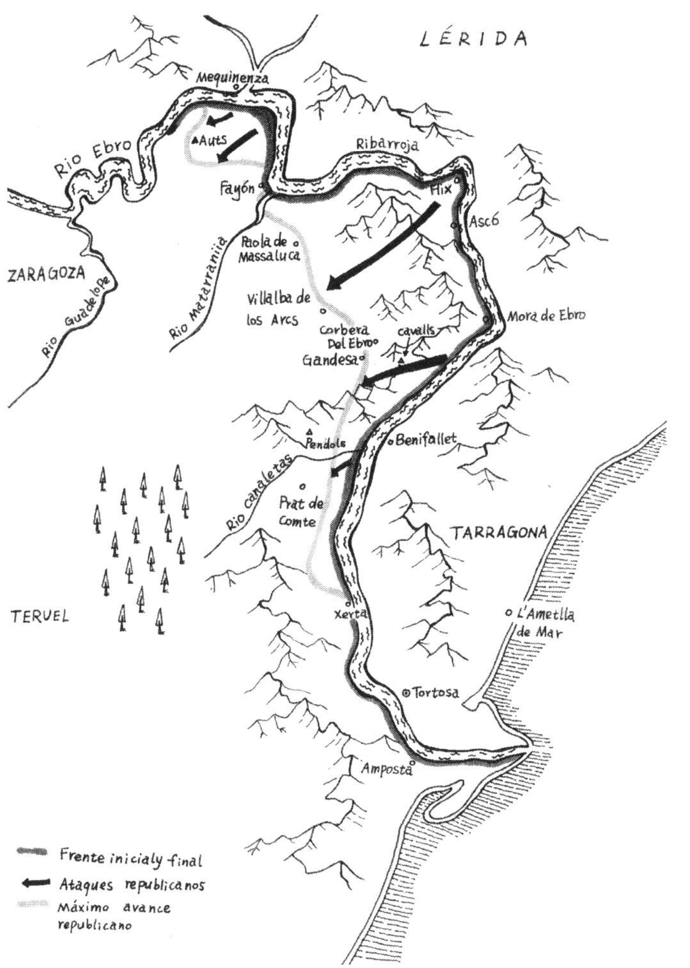

BATTLE OF THE EBRO. The Ebro was a critical battle for the Republicans. It was not an attempt at defeating Franco, but an attempt to draw others into the war by showing the Republicans were still strong. Until relatively recently there were only Francoist monuments in the area. Now there are more monuments to the battle. The town of Corbera del Ebro is worth visiting as it was destroyed by the Francoist forces towards the end of the battle and later rebuilt in the valley. There are stories in the local museum from people who lived among the ruins after the war. The mountains to the east and south of Gandesa were heavily fought over, often involving the International Brigades. While local walks are useful, the whole area is best explored by car.

The Spanish Civil War of 1936–1939 was particularly brutal, as many civil wars are (see Chapter 7 for the British Civil Wars). Hundreds of thousands of people died, many thousands died in battle, civilians starved to death or were caught up in the fighting, both sides executed the enemy and Republicans continued to be killed in large numbers even after the fighting was over. There are many good general accounts of the war such as Preston (1984) or Beevor (2012); books such as Orwell's *Homage to Catalonia* (Orwell, 1938) and hundreds of personal accounts written by participants and others. It remains popular in the arts and humanities, generating a great deal of interest despite it taking place before World War II. This is perhaps due to the political nature of the war, and that many British and other international people volunteered to take part, mostly on the Republican side.

This chapter focuses on the Battle of the Ebro, which was the last great attempt by the Republicans to defeat the Fascists and the decisive battle of the war. The key aims were to show the Western powers that the Republic was worth fighting for, to keep the war going until the general war between Germany and France and the United Kingdom started and to relieve the pressure on the Valencian front. They failed. The Republican Army was beaten in 115 days. By the end of the battle there was no real Republican Army left. The International Brigades had been disbanded on the orders of the powers that constructed the Munich Agreement, which meant many of the more experienced soldiers returned home. The fighting was over before Germany went to war with Britain and France.

This chapter also considers social memory, how the memory of the war was suppressed under Franco, and how, through the Law of Historical Memory, it is only in recent years that Spaniards have started discussing the war and memorialising it in a modern way. I have explored some of this elsewhere (Hunt, 2011).

The Battle of the Ebro was a critical battle in the European 30 Years Civil War. It was here that democratic values, fought for across Europe for centuries with generally increasing success, were defeated by the totalitarian regimes of the right. First, they were defeated by Franco's Fascists, who held firm after the first attack and then successfully pushed the Republicans back to their start line. Second, they were defeated by the German and Italian regimes, who had lent substantial practical military support to Franco. But they were also defeated by the democracies of the West, particularly by France and Britain, who refused to help the Republican cause. Then, in the midst of the Battle of the Ebro, they met the German and Italian leaders in Munich where they not only betrayed Czechoslovakia by handing the Sudetenland to the Germans, but also agreed that Franco's forces had effectively won the Spanish Civil War and that they should work towards a peace in that country through recognising Franco's government. This led directly to the Republican government withdrawing the International Brigades from the fight at the Ebro and, after a parade in Barcelona, sending them home. This weakened the Republican forces and effectively led to the final defeat at the Ebro and shortly afterwards to the end of the war. It also gave the German and Italian governments greater confidence regarding the push towards what became the Second World War. Their equipment and men had been tested on the battlefields of Spain and shown to be effective. After Munich, Hitler had claimed that he was seeking no further territory – he had already occupied the Rhineland against the terms of the Treaty of Versailles, he had taken Austria in the Anschluss, and now he had the Sudetenland. Munich showed that the British and French would not intercede against the Germans – they had not helped the Spanish government, and they allowed the transfer of the Sudetenland – so they were unlikely to bother too much if Germany invaded Poland. Thus, it can be argued that the failure of the British and France with regard to Spain – and particularly the Ebro – led indirectly to World War II.

The battle, the biggest in the Civil War, was fought in north-east Spain at a bend in the Ebro river between July and November 1938. Tens of thousands died – we do not know how many – and many more were wounded or captured. There were possibly 40,000 casualties on each side. This was a large-scale battle. The key target for the Republicans after crossing the Ebro was the town of Gandesa, an important road crossing point. The Republicans got to the outskirts but had to retreat to the mountains of Pandols and Cavalls. There followed a war of attrition, often fought in trenches reminiscent of World War I. The town of Corbera del Ebro, between the river and Gandesa, was utterly destroyed by the Fascists as they advanced to regain territory lost at the outset of the battle. The ruined town still remains as a memorial, as the new town was built down the hill.

Around the battlefield there are numerous monuments commemorating some aspect of the battle. Many of these are newly erected.

Why was it that people were not allowed to remember the battle? Citizens of Franco's Spain were clear, until he died in 1975, that the surviving Republicans should not be allowed their interpretation of what happened in the Civil War. It was really only in the 1990s that Spain started to think about the atrocities and to dig up some of the mass graves of people shot by the Fascists. This section will focus on the so-called *pact of forgetting* in Spain, which came after the death of Franco in 1975 as a means of not going over old mental wounds. This chapter again illustrates the importance of the long-term effects of war, some of which do not go away until all the participants are dead.

The Spanish Civil War did not officially end until 1948, nearly a decade after the end of the formal fighting – though there were still guerrillas fighting in the mountain ranges until the 1950s. Between 1939 and 1948, perhaps 150,000 people had been killed by the Franco regime for being on the wrong side. Many were summarily executed and buried in mass graves on the outskirts of towns; many others were worked to death in slave labour camps. When Franco died in 1975, there was a long transition to democracy, during which time people found it difficult to *remember* the civil war. Younger generations were looking forward rather than backwards, and many of the participants on both sides were still alive. As noted in the chapter on landscapes, the battlefields were largely ignored, the trenches and military architecture left to rot away. It wasn't until the 1990s that people started to think more seriously about the war and its consequences. As the generation that fought in it died, this perhaps became easier. It has been argued that being able to study war-related objects can lead to closure (Gonzalez-Ruibal, 2007), and perhaps it is time that the Spanish were able to look back at the war with a critical eye.

While Franco was alive, he had no interest in healing war wounds He focused on punishing the losers and on the construction of monuments to his own dead comrades. Where the Republicans had committed atrocities there were also memorials and ceremonies commemorating these events. Nothing was done for the losers. After the death of Franco, the transition to democracy meant amnesty for the perpetrators and amnesia for everyone (Reig Tapia, 1999). While this meant the transition was relatively smooth, it was perhaps a mistake. Most people would probably agree that the best way to build a democracy is to revisit and debate the past and attempt to resolve the collective trauma by constructing collective shared narratives about the traumatic past (Alexander et al., 2004).

The Ebro

The Law of Historical Memory has made a difference to Spain, and academics and others throughout the country are starting to explore their Civil War past. There are now monuments being erected, sites of historical interest being recognised, and museums of the war being opened. A good example of this is the Battle of the Ebro. This site is unusual because it has always had a site of historical interest protected from development. The town of Corbera del Ebro was destroyed in the battle when Franco's troops advanced against the Republicans. After the war the town was rebuilt at the bottom of the hill, leaving the ruins untouched. This area is also unusual because not only are there Franco-era monuments to the war, there was also a monument to the International Brigadiers who fought in the battle erected shortly after the battle in the mountains of the area. Perhaps it was in such an obscure place that it never came to the attention of the Francoist authorities, so it was never destroyed. In recent years it has been restored.

The Battle of the Ebro has received recent attention, with the development of a number of battlefield sites and a museum at Corbera under the auspices of COMEBE (Consorcio para la Musealizacion de Espacios de la Battle del Ebro), which was founded in 2001 to recover the historical memory of the areas in which the Battle of the Ebro took place and to promote awareness of the battle and its sites. There are several sites that have been excavated and renovated, and COMEBE provides walking trails and explanations, along with a museum in Corbera del Ebro.

The Battle of the Ebro was the largest battle of the Spanish Civil War. It was also the last gasp for the Republicans. Defeat here meant defeat in the war. The Republican forces crossed the river Ebro in the middle of the night on 25 July 1938, starting the longest battle of the war. The Republicans had three objectives. They wanted to stop Franco's advance to Valencia, which would cut the

Republican area of Spain in two. Attacking on the Ebro was designed to divert Franco's forces. The second objective was to revive morale, to make dissenting voices who were calling for peace realise that the Republicans could still win the war. The final objective was to show the world, which was worried about Hitler, that the Republicans were useful allies, and that might encourage Britain and France to send arms to help the cause.

To begin with, the attack was a success. A large area of land was occupied on the right bank of the Ebro and Franco suffered heavy casualties. But it did not last long. The Fascists stabilised the lines around Gandesa, and the Republicans had to give up the offensive. The battle became one of attrition, with Franco's forces gradually wearing away at the Republicans, though it took them more than 100 days to recover the ground they lost on those first days. On 16 November, 115 days after the offensive, the Republicans retreated back over the Ebro. There were around 120,000 casualties on both sides, including around 30,000 dead.

The International Brigades

The International Brigades had formed soon after the start of the Civil War and consisted of people from many nations who came to Spain to fight for the Republican cause. It was initially a spontaneous rising of people, generally of the left, who realised the need to fight against the Fascist cause that was rising across Europe, particularly when their own governments refused to help.

The Battle of the Ebro was to be their last major battle. The British battalion was told they would be involved in the battle in July, just before the offensive. They made rapid progress, capturing Corbero late in the evening of the first day. They planned to move forward to Gandesa the following day, but they faced intense opposition from the Fascists, particularly when trying to take Hill 481, overlooking Gandesa, that was heavily fortified. By 3 August they gave up the attempt and were removed to the reserve. On 24 August they returned to the line, taking over from the American battalion on Hill 666, the key height of Sierra Pandols near Gandesa. They survived heavy bombardment and two Fascist attacks before themselves attacking Hill 356 in Sierra Caballs, which they successfully captured against heavy opposition. The battalion had one last duty. They took over from the 13 (Dombrowski) Brigade which had suffered heavy losses at Sierra de Lavelle de la Torre. Again, they suffered a heavy bombardment and Fascist crossfire. They were eventually overrun, but they maintained their positions until the end. After withdrawal and assessment of losses, they found that in three days they had suffered more than 200 men killed, wounded or missing. After this action the International Brigades were disbanded and repatriated by Juan Negrin, the Prime Minister, who realised they would suffer dearly if the Republic was defeated, which looked increasingly likely.

In recent years academics have begun to explore the battle in detail, and in different ways. Castell & Falco (2002) discuss how the Battle of the Ebro is not only a complex battle, but that it transcends its time and place to become a cultural reference, a symbol both of Franco's success and of the anti-Fascist resistance. They argue, and visiting the battlefield today their argument makes sense, that the Ebro remains "incomprehensible, strange and invisible." (p. 257) This is partly because of the long years of silence about the battle. Even now, as I write 15 years after their article, understanding of the battle is elusive. Perhaps it will always remain so as those who experienced it could not talk about it during their lifetimes except in terms dictated by Franco. In a sense, though the Battle of the Ebro is in many ways as important as the Somme or Normandy, it is invisible.

Nevertheless, the fairly recent memorialisation of the space by COMEBE and others has made it possible to explore the physical reality of the battlefield. This continues through battlefield archaeology – a subject ignored through the Franco years and afterwards and only recently becoming important (e.g., González-Ruibal et al., 2015, with archaeological work taking place throughout Spain at the key battle sites.

The International Brigadiers (IBs) left a detailed legacy of their experiences in Spain. There are numerous books, journals and other accounts, many published, some not, some probably awaiting discovery in an attic. The Brigades contained a large number of writers, perhaps because they drew on many from the intellectual left. Baxell (2012) has brought together a lot of this material in an extremely readable book. The quotations in the following section, unless otherwise indicated, along with page numbers, refer to his book.

There was optimism among the IBs at the start of the battle, because it was initially so successful. George Wheeler noted:

> Our army advanced on a one hundred and fifty kilometre from to a depth of thirty kilometres. Over five thousand prisoners were taken together with large quantities of military equipment. The fascists were well and truly on the run. (p. 324)

This was – at that point – a major turn-around, and Wheeler, while somewhat exaggerating the success, hoped the world had taken notice. Unfortunately, the world had already seen the Republican cause as a lost cause. No temporary military success would change that. The Ebro was somewhat like the Battle of the Bulge a few years later, a last chance.

The initial crossing of the river took place on precarious temporary bridges or boats, and the Nationalist air force was a constant threat. Bob Clark:

> The sky was overcast by scores of black enemy bombers all heading for the river. A deadly sickly feeling was in the pit of my stomach as I watched those black hordes with hardly any opposition, except for a dozen or so AA guns on the opposite side of the river, droning their way towards that fateful stream. The low, dull rumbling of many bombs hitting the ground

> made even the hill on which we sat tremble with the concussion. Over four hundred tons of bombs were dropped in one afternoon. (p. 326)

Like the bombing of Guernica in the previous year, bombers and fighters that strafed the ground were changing the face of battle. They comprised a dreadful new weapon against which people had little effective defence, leaving them powerless, which created a greater degree of fear.

Percy Ludwick, in typical British fashion, worried more about the mules trying to cross the Ebro than the men:

> They panicked, reared, brayed pitiously and many were slaughtered, if not by the bombs, then by merciless strafing. (p. 327)

Baxell (2012) reports one particular mule was called Chamberlain because he kept wandering off towards the Fascists.

The Republic still had civilian support, even at this late stage in the war. As the troops marched towards Corbera, on the way to their target of Gandesa, Bob Clark:

> We were surprised to find quite a large number of peasants, men and women, lining by the side who loudly cheered us on. (p. 327)

The British IBs attacked Hill 481, known as the Pimple, which overlooked Gandesa. It was well-fortified. Billy Griffiths described the task:

> It was a small hill, hardly enough room for a dozen or so men on the top. Yet the flanks were protected by covering fire from Gandesa. A frontal attack left little room for the deployment of many men and was well protected by 4 ft barbed wire fence and booby traps. When this position was reached one was met with showers of hand grenades. With artillery, or a supply of mortars, or concentrated attack from low flying aircraft, they could have been blown out. These we did not have. We had to depend on small arms. (p. 330)

Bob Clark watched what was happening:

> Suddenly the cry 'Adelante' was given and Britishers and Spaniards, among whom were youths of seventeen years, with loud yells clambered over rocks past trees from which the leaves were dropping like a day in a park in autumn cut by thousands of bullets. The whole crest of the hill was a death trap. The whining of bullets was amazingly consistent. A number of heavy mortar bombs sent up cascades of earth and stones. There was the cry of wounded and the plaintive cry of a Spanish youth who kept calling for 'Sanidad'... the fire was overwhelming. (p. 330)

It is these aspects of battle that we who have not experienced war cannot comprehend, such as the descriptions of facing continual fire, wondering how anyone could survive. Jack Jones:

> The bullets of the snipers whizzed over, grenades and shells were striking the ground, throwing up earth and dust and showering us with shrapnel. Suddenly my shoulder and right arm went numb. Blood gushed from my shoulder and I couldn't lift my rifle. I could do nothing but lie where I was.... U was taken with other wounded men down the line to an emergency hospital at Mora del Ebro where I was given an anti-tetanus injection. The place was like an abbatoir; there was bloode and the smell of blood everywhere. (pp. 330–331)

The descriptions of where the wounded are treated seems to vary little over the centuries. The wounded always talk of blood and damaged bodies, perhaps limbs lying around. The developments of medicine over the centuries may have little impact on when one initially sees the inside of an emergency hospital at times of battle when medical staff are often overwhelmed. One interesting phenomenon is that, over time, surgical procedures get more sophisticated, requiring more personnel, more equipment, more time and more space. To go from simply hacking off a limb and tying a tourniquet through to the sophisticated cuts of later years (see the Waterloo chapter), followed by the tying up of arteries and stitching a flap of skin and muscle across the wound requires not only increased expertise but all these other factors. Triage has always been important – differentiating between those who will die, those who can wait for treatment and those who need immediate treatment – and has gained in sophistication over the years as medical practitioners have developed techniques and medicines that enable a greater proportion of the wounded to survive. In the modern world, nearly all wounded soldiers are expected to survive if they are quickly moved to hospital facilities – the initial hour is critical.

It is also worth noting that war is a good means of finding ways to improve the treatment of the wounded. Just like technology in other areas, developments in surgical practice move much more quickly when there are a lot of damaged bodies to practice on. This applied to the Spanish Civil War as much as any other.

The soldiers fighting in Spain did not only have to face the bullets and shells of the enemy, they had nature to contend with. Walter Gregory:

> Twelve hours of lying on rocky soil, every fragment of which seemed intent on burying itself in our bodies, of being continually shot at, of having nothing to eat or drink, of being driven half-mad by the ceaseless attraction of the most malevolent flies in the whole of Spain, and of hoping that by staying still the attention of a Fascist marksman would be distracted by movement elsewhere. (p. 331)

Soldiers often talk of the physical conditions making a bad situation much worse. It doesn't matter where the battle took place. The ground itself, insects and rats create conditions that would, under normal circumstances, be very difficult to bear. Equipment can also be a problem. Fred Thomas:

> My boots, issued to me in Murcia, somewhat tight from the beginning and only worn rarely since, soon began to hurt, a nail in one foot, a blister on the other. Second-hand (or more) when I got them, this was hardly surprising. My blanket choked me, my packstrap cut into my shoulder, the night was stifling hot – in short, I never felt less like a revolutionary in my life. (pp. 324–325)

The conditions at the Ebro were particularly bad. Peter Kerrigan:

> From the 25th to the morning of the 30th they had nothing to drink but a little water, sometimes going for a day without this.... They are fighting and marching over mountains, the rocks of which have cut their Spanish shoes to pieces. Many are literally barefoot as well as being in rags because of wear of clothes. Nobody has had a wash since the start of the offensive. (p. 334)

Or John Peet:

> The state of our uniforms at this time was medium to catastrophic. We were all that time haunted by lice We had in most cases no change of clothing which meant that you were sleeping in your clothes and encouraging the lice. Shoes were an extreme problem. The alpargatos were war economy alpargatos... [which had] a very poor composition rubber sole which inevitably split after a few days' use. (p. 334)

The battle did not go well. The British battalion was moved back into reserve on 6 August. The killed and wounded amounted to 408 out of the original 558. It was at this point it was recognised that the war was probably lost and that it was time to think about shipping the International Brigadiers back home. But they still had to continue to fight at the Ebro, taking over from the Abraham Lincoln Brigade in the Sierra Pandols at Hill 666. The awful situation here was described by John Longstaff:

> The higher I walked the more I could smell the dead. It was getting darker and only a few Republican soldiers could be seen. The entire position was bad. The few bits of brushwood showed signs of have been burnt. I then realised when the smell was; burnt bodies, for the dead could not be buried in the rock.... It was evident that both the Republican Army and Franco's

> forces had suffered heavy casualties for, despite the height and strong winds blowing, everywhere was the stench of those burnt bodies. (pp. 335–336)

After a vicious fight, they were relieved by Spanish troops; some were sent home, but the battalion had one more battle to fight while the Republicans retreated to the Ebro. This was another difficult fight where a number of men were killed, men who were to have been sent home shortly afterwards.

The experience of the International Brigadiers in Spain was unlike any other war. While many wars have mercenaries, these men were fighting for an ideal of democracy or Communism. They came from around the world to fight. Most of them were not trained soldiers, but they had to learn quickly. Many of those who survived would go on to fight in World War II.

The Spanish Republicans were not so lucky. Many thousands were captured by Franco's troops and for years afterwards carried out hard labour. Those who escaped to France were mostly put into concentration camps by the French, and many were then captured by the Germans after June 1940. Others worked in the French resistance.

The tour

This is a driving and walking tour. The area of the Battle of the Ebro is so vast it is not feasible to explore the whole area in a single day. Driving around provides some understanding of the scale of the battle and walking in the mountains provides evidence of the difficulties the troops had in those areas, with steep hills, cliffs, few paths, and a ground so hard it was often impossible to dig trenches and foxholes. There is no attempt to explore the whole of the battlefield. If you have time, there is plenty of information available about further sites and activities. I would recommend a 4 × 4 that you can use up the mountains and elsewhere if you are going to explore some of the tracks. While a normal car can get to many of the places, there are some areas only suitable for a four-wheel drive.

The tour begins at Mora del Ebro, which lies on the west bank of the Ebro and is a good base for exploring the area. The Republican troops did not cross the river here. They crossed further south, and then approached the town from inland, forcing the Fascists to surrender. Go south on the T-324 to Benissanet. The relatively flat landscape shows why it was easier for the Republicans to cross the river around here rather than where the riverbanks are steep. Carry on to Miravet, where there is a spectacular castle, which looks very defensible, but the Fascists surrendered here immediately. These easy surrenders in July are partly because the area was defended by relatively few Fascist troops, and the Republicans had successfully infiltrated the area in relative secrecy and so appeared suddenly, surprising the defenders.

From Miravet continue on the same road to El Pinell de Brai. Throughout the battle this was an important staging area for the Republicans, bringing in reinforcements and supplies, and it was also one of the key medical centres. There is a museum to the medical services in the town.

Head towards Gandesa on the C-43. Gandesa was the key objective on the first day of the battle, but it was never attained. We are following the route of the Republicans as they tried to cross the mountains. It is obvious how difficult it must have been for the soldiers as they fought in these mountains. The terrain is steep, rocky, and has relatively few paths. Initially the Republicans took most of these mountains, the Sierra de Pandol, on the left of the road, and the Sierra Cavalls, on the right of the road.

During the battle, while the Republicans held the key heights, one of their objectives was to protect the road. One day, a car was seen driving at speed, pursued by Fascist bullets. The car stopped, two men got out and ran up the mountain to the Republican base, still being shot at. One of them was Ernest Hemingway.

Look carefully and you'll see a sign on the left indicating the Pandols in the Civil War. Take this road, which leads past a picnic area, and follow it until there is a junction. The tarmacked road goes to the right, an unsurfaced track to the left. This leads up the mountain to the monuments at Hill 705 and to the Ermita Santa Magdalena. These two places were fought over during the period 9–15 August. The Fascists attacked the Republican positions on these hills, eventually taking Hill 705 on 14 August. The Ermita was an important position because it was the only source of water on the mountain. It changed hands several times during the battle. It has been completely rebuilt. The Republicans finally stabilised the position, retaining Hill 666, which can be reached by going back down the mountain for a few hundred metres to where the road turns sharply left. There is a track to the right which leads to an aerial on the next hill – Hill 666.

Throughout this area there are many signs of the battle. There are the remains of the foxholes that were scratched out of the ground. There are also shell holes, left there as the Fascists relentlessly bombarded the Republican positions before attacking them. The main monuments are on Hill 705, but it is difficult to find the monument to the International Brigades on Hill 666. It is not at the top, but in such a position that under Franco's regime it was never found by the Fascists. Presumably if they had found it, they would have destroyed it. It lies next to the grave of a Captain of the International Brigades.

Returning to the main road, an optional drive for those with a four-wheel drive vehicle is to tour around Hill 481, the key point above Gandesa for the Republicans. From where the track joins the main road, turn right, and a few hundred metres further on turn left (second left, the first leads into what appears to be chicken sheds). Follow this track for some time, with Hill 481 to the left and the main mountains of the Cavells to the right, until a junction is reached with a signpost that indicates Corbera and Gandesa to the left. Take this route. The track is less well made than the previous one, but it is perfectly passable with a four-wheel drive vehicle. As you go along the track note the face of Hill 481 to your left and Gandesa and Corbera to your right. The Republicans initially took Corbera and got to the suburbs of Gandesa before being driven back to Hill 481. Just before you drop down into the town of Gandesa there is a track sharp left, just before a barn. Follow this. A few hundred metres on there is a fork, take the right fork for another few hundred metres. Where there is a sharp right stop and park at the beginning of the track to the left. Walk along this track. It takes you part way up Hill 481. There is a sense of destruction here, showing the effects of the Fascist bombardment, with fragments of stone everywhere and ruined terraces. Don't read too much into this though. Much of Spain has fragments of stone and ruined terraces without experiencing war! This is one of the difficulties of reading a battlefield: it is all too easy to interpret something as the effect of war – when it is simply decay or neglect.

The track comes to an end at a pylon. From here, to reach the top of Hill 481, it is a matter of struggling through the brush. It is better to have long trousers and boots as it gets very prickly. Again, imagine the experience of the Fascists fighting their way up this hill with very little cover and being fired down on by the Republicans at the top.

There are easier ways up to Hill 481 – paths go from either end of the mountain.

Return to the car and drive to Gandesa. Take the N-420 towards Alcaniz. Only a few kilometres away there is a turning for Poblat Iberic. Take this turning, go under the road and turn right onto the old road. A few hundred metres on the right there is a stone obelisk with a Fascist symbol at the end of a small road to the right. Take this road to the top. This is Col de Moro, where Franco and his generals would watch the course of the battle, as much of the battlefield can be seen from here. In the latter half of the battle Franco would come every day to observe. He was billeted 50 km away near Alcaniz. The monument is defaced, and there are some old trenches in front of the memorial.

Return to Gandesa and take the TV-7231 towards Villalba del Arcs. The road roughly follows the front line, with the Fascists to the left and the Republicans to the right. Villalba was heavily fought over, and the front line for most of the battle was to the east of the town. The Fascists held the town and the Republicans held the hills to the east. Just before the village, you have to turn left. Stop here. This is Cuatro Caminos, a critical point of the battlefield. At this point there are two small hills. The one nearest the village was held by the Fascists, the one further away by the Republicans. The Republican hill had four machine gun posts, trenches for snipers, and several rows of barbed wire. The first attempt by the Fascists to take it failed, and many were killed. There are Fascist memorials at each site, both of which have been defaced by people of the left. When I last visited, the Fascists had placed a concrete tablet commemorating the 75th anniversary of the battle. This had been smashed and covered with graffiti, such as the anarchist sign and *no pasaran* (meaning, they shall not pass).

Drive to the village. Take the TV-7231 towards La Pobla de Massaluca. Just over 2 km from Villalba there is a turning to the right, marked trincheras . Take this track and follow it for 2 km. On the left there is a small car park and some reconstructed trenches. These are interesting as most of the trenches we see have been left to nature. They show how they might have looked in 1938. Only a small section has been reconstructed; the trench system itself stretches for some 700–800 metres either side (they are worth visiting). This area did not experience severe fighting. The Fascists did not try to retake it until towards the end of the battle when the Republicans retreated.

Return to Villalba dels Arcs. Take the last turn into the town, Carrer Roquetes, and go down the road to the bottom, following it to the left at the base of the village. From here there is a good view of the cemetery, which was heavily fought over. The Fascists had mortars by the church. At the end, turn right on a track which goes to the cemetery. Park near the building and go into the cemetery. From here the hills to the east are Republican territory. Near the start of the battle this cemetery played an important role. It was fought over and changed hands several times. The Republicans never made it to Villalba, and for most of the battle the front was stable. Note the battle damage to the side of the chapel.

Continue along the track, with the cemetery to your left. Go to the end. Turn left onto TV-7333. At the next junction, turn right towards Mora del Ebre on the TV-7331. Note the Fascist memorial at the junction, usually defaced. A few hundred metres after the junction on the left there is a short track with dugouts clearly visible. Stop here and explore. These are part of the defences of La Fatarella. There are reconstructed bunkers and trenches and various shell holes. To find the more interesting parts that have not been reconstructed, walk up the hill.

Follow the TV-7331 to the junction with the C-12B. Turn right. A few hundred metres on there is a monument on the right. This is the key memorial to the battle and is called Los Camposines. It contains an ossuary where the remains of those still occasionally found on the battlefield are placed. This is a general memorial to those who fought and died and tries not to support one side or the other, though this is difficult in Spain. This is a monstrous creation in concrete – very effective for a memorial to a vicious Civil War. At the top there is a viewpoint, and it can be seen how the old trenches are becoming part of the concrete memorial.

From here turn left to the junction with the N-420 and then turn right, to Corbera del Ebro. This town was utterly destroyed in the Fascist counterattack in September. After the war it was rebuilt lower down, so the ruins have remained virtually untouched. It is now an official memorial site and is worth exploring. Most of the houses have been flattened or at least have lost their roofs and much of their walls. There is artwork dotted around, and poems in Spanish and Catalan. The church contains photographs of the inhabitants after the war when they were rebuilding the village.

In lower Corbera there is also a good museum about the battle, where you can get leaflets about many of the places you have visited today.

That is the end of the tour, which is around 90 km. To do it thoroughly will take at least two days, longer if you are spending time walking the battlefield. If you are in the area for longer, there are other sites to see. The tour has not explored the battlefield to the north, focused around Asco and Flix. There are interesting sites in those areas. The intention of this tour is to focus on the key objective of the battle from the Republican side, taking Gandesa and cutting the key roads that pass through the town – the objective that was never attained.

Conclusion

The Battle of the Ebro was a disaster for the Republicans. It marked the beginning of the end of the war. The last main Republican Army was destroyed in the vain attempt to join up with the Republican forces in the south. The International Brigades were disbanded, and the volunteers went home. Finally, it would only be a matter of months before the rebels pushed through Catalonia and took Barcelona, finally defeating the republicans. Once the war ended, Franco's forces locked up many thousands of those who had fought on the Republican side. Many people disappeared – their bodies to be found many decades later in mass graves around the country – and the Francoist era began. It did not end until 1975, when Franco was almost the last European dictator to go.

In terms of understanding the war, the many accounts written by international people who took part are significant in terms of studying the war because most Spanish people were unable to write about their experiences, particularly if they were on the losing side, though Franco pushed the narrative that it had been a good war and it had reunited the nation. This was definitely not the case. In some ways the Spanish nation is still divided. There are still people who are on one side or the other. The 1978 constitution was a compromise to try and keep all sides happy after Franco's death, but it is at least in part responsible for the divisions between parts of Spain, for instance Basque or Catalonian separatists. As with the British Civil Wars, it is taking generations to heal the psychological wounds, the contested master narratives, of the Spanish Civil War.

14

THE BATTLE OF NORMANDY

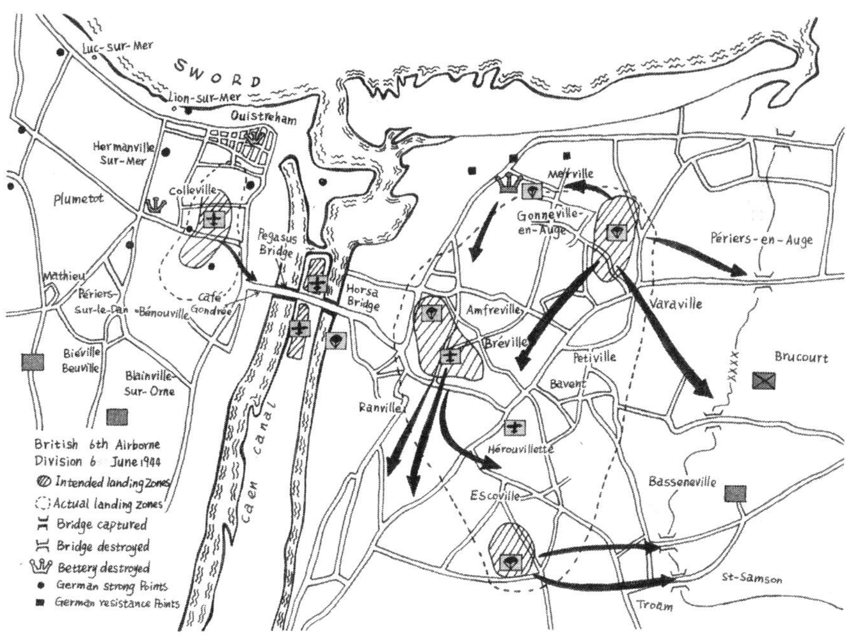

NORMANDY. This is only a small part, the eastern part, of the site of the Battle of Normandy. It is the area taken by the 6th Airborne Division, landing mainly to the east of the Orne, and the 3rd British Division, landing on Sword Beach around Ouistreham. The walk, starting from Pegasus Bridge, can be done in a day, or a car can be used between the main sites. Ranville has the largest British cemetery in the area, and to the north is the flat land used by many of the gliders. The Merville Battery is largely intact and a good museum. The area from the south of Escoville, up through Bavent and northwards, formed the front line of the paratroopers from June to August 1944. This was trench warfare similar to the Western Front in the First World War.

This chapter focuses on the Battle of Normandy, fought between the Western Allies and Germany from June to August 1944, starting with the air and sea invasion of Normandy, and ending with the breakthrough leading to the liberation of most of France. Participants accounts were derived from interviews with mainly British participants that I carried out in the 1980s and 1990s, and from letters, journals, published and unpublished accounts. Most of the material is unpublished, and it provides an interesting insight into the experience of battle, including the psychological elements – the excitement of battle, the boredom, comradeship, on so on, along with experiences of trauma. This chapter also touches on the very long-term effects of war trauma and how a person is often traumatised for life, as it builds on interviews conducted with older survivors of the war. Some of the material has been previously published (Hunt & Robbins, 1998, 2001a,b; Hunt, 2010).

The scale of the battle is such that it is not possible to describe it in any detail – there are many books which do this, such as Belfield & Essame (1967), Hastings (1984) or Keegan (1982). If you want to explore the whole battlefield, it is possible to drive the 80 km length of the landing beaches in a day if you do not stop too long at any particular site. It is probably better to either stay for a few days or to focus on particular areas of the battlefield. While the areas to explore will depend on interests, the focus here will mainly be on the area taken by the 6th Airborne Division in the east (the left flank of the Allied forces). They landed before the main seaborne forces in the middle of the night of 5–6 June 1944 to take strategic points such as the bridges over the Canal de Caen and the River Orne, the area between the Orne and the River Dives to protect the flank against German counterattacks, and to knock out the battery at Merville on the coast to ensure it could not jeopardise the landings in the morning. These sites were crucial to the success of the battle; defending the key left flank was critical as this was the direction most German reinforcements would come from, though the Airborne troops were lucky that they did not face a major counterattack during the two and a half months they held their positions. For much of the time the 6th Airborne were engaged in trench warfare not unlike that on the Western Front in World War I, though they had limited time out of the trenches, at least in the early stages (The U.S. Airborne Divisions, 82nd and 101st, whose objectives related to the right flank were removed from their positions almost immediately after the invasion and sent back to the UK).

While most people know about D-Day – the seaborne invasion – many do not realise that the fight for Normandy lasted so long, over such a large area. It was first of all a battle to ensure the troops could land and hold their ground, rather than be pushed back into the sea as was the aim of Rommel. Second, it was a race to reinforce and supply the various armies, with the need for the Allies to reinforce and supply across beaches with no ports, and the need for the Germans to reinforce and supply using the roads and railways of France. The critical need here was for the Allies to disrupt the German transport – which they did very effectively – and for the Germans to sink as much shipping as they could in the English Channel – which they failed to do because of Allied air and sea superiority.

Many of the Allied soldiers who landed at Normandy had not been involved in fighting before. They often had spent years training in the UK. However, there were exceptions. Montgomery, as Commander of the Land Forces, wanted men of his 8th Army, who had fought across North Africa, Sicily and Italy, to take part in the landings, as he thought them excellent experienced soldiers. This was not what many of the soldiers themselves thought. Many thought they had done their duty and it should be the turn of others, those who had spent years training in the UK without fighting. This illustrates a point made by Xue et al. (2015) with respect to the length of time soldiers can effectively fight. Using a meta-analytic approach, they showed that war-related PTSD is linked, among other factors, to the number and length of tours a soldier has undertaken. In World War II there were no tours, and soldiers were expected to be able to continue to fight indefinitely. As one of my interviewees noted, the only ways out of the fighting were to be killed, wounded or captured – not a particularly pleasant set of options.

Many of the men who fought in Normandy described the sheer size of the fleet that crossed the Channel on D-Day. There were around 7000 ships and thousands of planes. Many troops had spent several days in their landing craft, with the invasion held up by bad weather. Many were seasick and actually described preferring to face the German machine guns on the beach than spend more time on the rough seas. When they actually landed, they often faced extreme danger:

> Columns of water were now shooting up between our landing craft and the sound of battle grew louder. Can't be long now. I can hear the small arms fire; then suddenly, the beach appeared before us, tanks and landing craft on fire, men moving up the beach as quickly as possible, no doubt remembering Lord Lovat's words, 'If you wish to live to a ripe old age, keep moving.' There were those lying there that just didn't make it. Only seconds to go now before we hit the beach; the noise and smell of gunpowder, flashing of guns. The naval ratings both port and starboard were firing at the enemy targets oblivious of the enemy fire which was now raining down on us. Landing craft to the left and right had been hit and were now on fire. This is it - ramp down, let's move, we're a sitting target. Naval personnel scamper back to the rear of the bridge for safety. What's the hold up? Let's move. Bren gunner has frozen at the top of the ramp. Won't move. Hit him out of the way. (Pte Jones, Sword Beach)

The Airborne landings were also the largest airborne invasion up to that point in the war. The airborne forces were to protect the left (British) and right (United States) flanks of the invasion beaches. The 6th Airborne Division landed by glider and parachute during the night of 5–6 June, with a general success in achieving their objectives. The first to land were the Ox & Bucks Light Infantry under Major John Howard. They successfully took the bridges over the Orne river and the Caen canal, the latter being renamed Pegasus Bridge in honour of the airborne troops. Howard, up to the end of his life, would regularly visit Pegasus Bridge, where he landed, and describe the experience to the increasing numbers of tourists who visited the beaches. I met him in 1994, on the 50th anniversary of the invasion, and he was as enthusiastic as ever. Howard and his men were relieved by 4 Commando under Lord Lovat. They, including Pte Jones quoted previously, had landed at Sword Beach. Bill Millin, the piper who accompanied Lord Lovat to relieve the bridges, played his pipes to encourage the troops. In 1994 he was doing the same again, though this time it was rather more peaceful, if no less busy.

It was an interesting time, being in Normandy for the 50th anniversary; so many veterans were there, and the Parachute Brigade did a display landing at Ranville where the main body of Airborne troops had landed 50 years before. On the way over to Normandy, I travelled with large numbers of paratroopers who, demonstrating they still had a zest for life, first of all drank the ship dry, then they – men in their 70s – climbed on the tables and jumped off to demonstrate how to do a parachute roll. They were tough. I'm glad I wasn't a German in Normandy in 1944. To finish it off, the wives were not to be outdone so they climbed on the tables and started dancing. British riotous drunken behaviour is not a modern phenomenon.

Having said that, there were psychiatric casualties. Major Howard noted the problem:

> Chaps began to go bomb happy. At first many of us tended to regard it as a form of cowardice and we were highly critical. I remember that I tended to take a very tough and almost unfeeling line about it. But after time, when we began to see some of our most courageous comrades go under, we soon changed our minds. We could see that it was a real sickness. Men would hide away and go berserk during bombardments, and they became petrified during attacks. They could not be used for patrols, or even sentry duty, and the only answer was to hand them over to the medical officer, who, once he was satisfied it was a genuine case, had the man evacuated as a casualty. It was pathetic to see good men go down.

Howard was a commander of one of the toughest and best trained units in the British Army, and this did not stop men from becoming psychiatric casualties. As he noted, it was often after some time that men started to become ill; they could take the fighting for a certain period but would start to have problems if they were fighting too long. This is similar to what Montgomery found when he insisted on using his 8th Army – that had been fighting since early on in the war – in the invasion. He believed they were the best troops, they had fought well but fought too long, and many experienced forms of battle shock. It was the less experienced troops who, in the end, proved the more effective soldiers.

It was difficult to deal with men who might break down in battle. While Howard suggests one approach, Lt Beckman reported:

> There were very few cowards... peer pressure was enough to eliminate any show of cowardice.... On a very few instances a man would say, 'I'm just not going to the front line and get shot. You can arrest me, shoot me, or anything, but I am not going.' On these rare occasions I had a letter I told him I would send to his home town paper, his parents or girlfriend. The letter, composed by an army psychologist stated (if memory serves) basically that this man refuses to fight for his country, is a coward, etc. This type of letter would never have been sent but it worked with one exception. This man was so frightened that he could not stand he was shaking so badly that I really believed it would be possible to die of fright. I sent him back on the same truck that brought the replacements.

The comradeship and the threats of consequences could keep soldiers going for as long as possible, but there was a general acceptance in the Allied forces that there were limits to endurance. In the UK we did not shoot anyone who broke down in or before battle. Men coped the best they could. John Allison notes:

> The most remarkable thing is the adaptability of the human spirit to circumstances. One lived day to day, and tried not to look ahead to what might happen. If our friends were killed, we were sad but we accepted it. On the surface at any rate we felt that it would not happen to us.

Bearing in mind that the men I interviewed were all older people who had lived decades after the war, there are aspects to recall that means we must question their veracity. While most probably told the truth as they see it, many must inevitably have had their memories affected by what happened in the intervening years. Perhaps my favourite example is a parachutist, Sgt Jackson, who I interviewed in the 1980s, then interviewed again in the 1990s, perhaps 10 years later. In his first interview, he described many events in detail, enthusiastically recounting what happened, both to himself and to others. It was only when he started talking about events that took place some miles away that I began to doubt him. Then I saw all the books and videos around his living room and realised that his narrative of war was not just constructed of what he remembered happened to him, but also elements that had been incorporated from his reading and watching. He was not lying, but his narrative was somewhat confabulated. On the second occasion I interviewed him, the house was very different. His wife had recently died and everything – including himself – had deteriorated. The house could have been cleaner, Sgt Jackson himself had lost his vitality. This man, who previously told me about his 42 parachute jumps and his battle experience, had lost most of his interest in the world and seemed ready to give up and die. It was a shame, but it perhaps shows the difference between young old age and older old age – or the difference between a man with his wife looking after him and a widower.

The tour

As already noted, there is no attempt to cover the full battlefield. What follows is an area that can be walked or can be visited using both driving and walking. If you were to spend a few days in Normandy then your tour can be more extensive, though do not think that you can cover the battlefield in a week or two. It is a very large area, from the beaches to the heart of Normandy, and the evidence of the battle varies from fairly extensive at the beaches to little or nothing in many inland areas.

The focus here is on the 6th Airborne sector.

The walk

As even this area is such a large battlefield, I have split the walk into four components, Ouistreham and the landings, Bénouville and Pegasus Bridge, Ranville, and the ridge. You can walk the whole route. It is about 20 miles and could be done in a day, but that would not allow time to stop and explore the key areas and visit the museums. I recommend driving between the components and probably taking two days to complete the tour.

Ouistreham and the landings

This walk is mainly along the coast of Riva Bella – part of the landing beaches for the British 3rd Division on D-Day. It includes the main bunker complex, the commando memorial, and two museums – the Commando Museum and the Bunker Museum. The commando memorial is positioned roughly where Lord Lovat and his troops landed early on D-Day. Their task was to break through the enemy lines and move up to support the troops who had taken the bridges over the Orne and the Canal de Caen, leaving the infantry to secure the town and advance forward. They succeeded. Lovat was accompanied by his piper Bill Millin. When Millin got off the landing craft into waist high water (dressed in a kilt), he followed Lovat to the beach and took cover from the bullets and shells which were flying everywhere. Lovat told him to stand up and play his pipes while marching up and down the beach. Millin wasn't too impressed but obeyed, fully expecting to be hit. Fortunately, he wasn't, and later, when some captured Germans were questioned, they were asked why they had not shot Millin. "Because we thought he was mad," was the reply. They quickly got off the beach and headed inland, reaching Pegasus Bridge at the appropriate time. The bridge was still under fire from the Germans, so they had to run across it. Later, Millin stated that the bridge was the longest one he had ever crossed.

Walk from the memorial and see the remains of a large battery. This was a typical coastal battery. From here head east along the beach, remembering that men ran up this beach under fire on D-Day, with many of them reporting that they preferred running up the beach under fire than the previous three days on a boat in rough seas.

There are various museums, including the Commando Museum and the Bunker Museum.

Bénouville and Pegasus Bridge

Pegasus Bridge, the bridge over the Canal de Caen, is one of the most famous sites of the Battle of Normandy. It was the first place taken during the night of 5–6 June, along with the Cafe Gondree beside the bridge (Arlette Gondree, a little girl during the battle, still owns the cafe, and has served me coffee and food several times during my visits).

The walk starts at the Pegasus Museum car park. You will probably have already driven over the bridge, so walk back towards it. To the left (south) of the bridge there are the markers where the gliders of Major Howard's Ox & Bucks Light Infantry landed. The gliders needed to be landed as close to the bridge as possible in order to retain the element of surprise for the attacking troops. The first glider, containing Major Howard, landed around 50 metres from the bridge, the two other gliders landing in line behind it. This was one of the best acts of flying in the Second World War, especially given that so many other landings went wrong that night due to the weather.

The troops from the gliders quickly overran the defenders at the bridge, taking both sides with few casualties – though the first death of D-Day was Lt Brotheridge, now buried in Ranville church cemetery (discussed later in this chapter).

There are various other memorials and sights to see, including a 50 mm German gun.

The bridge is not the same as the one on D-Day; that is now in the museum where you are parked. The original was moved in 1994, the 50th anniversary, and many people, particularly veterans, were upset that it had gone. For several years it rested in a field, roughly where it is now, until the Pegasus Museum opened in 2000.

You can have a drink and snack at the Gondree Cafe, buy souvenirs, and see that apart from the souvenirs it is still the same as it was in 1944. As the first house liberated on D-Day, it achieved a rapid fame, which it has retained until the present day. While some may see a tacky gift shop, this is actually a very important *lieux de memoire* for a generation of men who fought in the battle and for those of us who still go there. It is a good example of how memory is transmitted across generations before an event is consigned to history. I was born 19 years after D-Day, but I have spent many a happy – and unhappy – hour here with veterans of the battle. It was here I met Major Howard (who visited most years until his death in 1999) and many other veterans. It was here in 1994, the 50th anniversary, that I saw the present day paratroopers land across at Ranville, and then come over to Cafe Gondree to join with the veterans, talk, drink and eat, while I was with my 11-year-old wide-eyed nephew and my 3-year-old son. It was at the side of the cafe on the same day that I interviewed a veteran who could not stop crying because he was thinking of his dead friends.

The main part of the walk is around the perimeter of the 7th Battalion, who parachuted in the early hours of D-Day and whose task it was to protect the Western approaches to the bridges. The 7th Battalion was commanded by Lt Col Pine-Coffin, a tall man with a strong presence among the troops, who had the ability to cohere the men into a single fighting unit because they respected him. Airborne commanders cannot fight from the rear, they are in the front line with their troops. I have his unpublished diary.

This rectangular walk is only around one mile, but it represents the area that a single airborne battalion had to defend until relieved by the troops landing on Sword beach, around four miles away. This was an active defence, with the Germans regularly attacking the position until relief arrived.

Opposite the Cafe Gondree, take the canal towpath. Walk along this for a few hundred metres, then cross a small footbridge to your left. On the bridge, look to the left where there is a strange arrangement of bricks and a pool. It is an old washing place, where women would bring their clothes to wash. There is a reconstructed one further along the walk. Walk up the path to the church. Before you get to the church there are older houses on the left and new houses on the right. The troops took positions in the houses to defend against the Germans. Go into the churchyard. Just inside are a number of British war graves. Go further into the cemetery and you will find a row of British graves. These are all unusual because they were left where they were originally buried – most were reburied at Ranville cemetery. The graves include that of a padre who was killed defending the wounded when they were being overrun by a German attack on D-Day.

The churchyard was a key defensive position. The walls were used as protection. This was the corner of the defence line. Go left along the road to the centre of Bénouville. This is roughly the line held by the 7th Battalion. At the centre there is a memorial to the Battalion, and it was around here that Lt Col Pine-Coffin had his headquarters. The French memorial to the First World War victims was badly damaged during the battle. As my wife said when we were there, it looks like some of these men died twice, once in each World War.

The town hall was the first to be liberated on D-Day. It says it was liberated at 23:45 on 5 June, but this may be a little optimistic, as the bridges were taken around 00:15 on 6 June. Go along the street to the left of the town hall. Half-way along there is a small sign on the right to the Highlanders, artillerymen who were situated in the garden of a lively house. While we were reading the sign a girl of around 20 asked what we were doing. It transpired that she lived in the house, and her family were there during the war. She showed us into the garden, where a sign said that a Scotsman died of his wounds.

At the bottom of the hill, turn right and then left on Rue 5th Juin – again this is the line held by the 7th Battalion. It was along this road, which comes from

Caen, that a German attack with three tanks was made. A Bren gunner, the man whose grave is in Bénouville Cemetery, stood in front of the tanks, firing at them. While this did no damage, it distracted them sufficiently for others to destroy the first tank. This action was described to me by Sergeant Jackson, mentioned previously.

At the end of the road, at a cross roads, turn left next to the chateau, with its high walls, still the front line. This was a maternity hospital in the war and the scene of counterattacks by the Germans. The big wall surrounding the chateau is damaged in some places and has been repaired with concrete slabs. I do not know whether this is a result of war damage, but my own narrative of the battle would like to believe so!

Turn right past the reconstructed lavage to the canal. On the right there is a good view of the chateau. It was around here that one of the key Bailey bridges was constructed to help tanks and other vehicles to cross the Orne to prepare for Operation Goodwood, the big tank battle of July. Walk left and return to the bridge.

This is probably a good point to mention the film *The Longest Day*. It was filmed about 15 years after the war and has strong links with the people who took part in the battle. The parts about the 6th Airborne, about Pegasus Bridge, were filmed at Pegasus Bridge – it is unlikely that could happen again, as it is now a memorial garden! The fight scene at the bridge was filmed there, and the German gun that is still at the site was used in the film. Major Howard was played by Richard Todd, who was with Howard during the battle. At one point in the film, the actor Howard talks to the person he was. Major Howard was an advisor on the film, and Lord Lovat went one step further and played himself!

Ranville

Ranville was at the heart of the airborne operation. It was in the fields to the north of the village that many of the men landed. It was here that General Gale established his headquarters; and it is here where most of the airborne troops who died are buried. The Commonwealth War Graves Commission (CWGC) cemetery at Ranville contains around 2500 men, including more than 200 Germans. The civil cemetery of the church contains a number of war graves, including Lt Brotheridge, mentioned previously, the first British soldier to die during the battle.

The ridge

The ridge was the main objective of the airborne troops and the commandos. While there were other objectives, such as the Merville Battery and the bridges over the Dives, in the end the troops were to hold the ridge. When you visit the ridge, you see why. If the Germans held the ridge, they would be able to see not only down to Ranville and the landing grounds, but beyond to the crossings over the Orne river and canal, to the sea beyond the estuary and much of Sword Beach and the inland areas towards Caen and Carpiquet airfield. There is a view across the airborne area to Colombelles, the industrial area to the east of Caen that the Germans used to great effect for observation of the British lines.

The walk starts from Amfreville. Park in the car park by the side of the Marie, near the church. This is Le Plein, an area used for assembling the troops. The walk is linear, along the top of the ridge. Go behind the Marie, taking a left dog leg out of the car park and towards the north, with a school and library on your right. The path is easy to follow and flat. You go through what were once gates to the Amfreville chateau, of which nothing remains. The path then takes you to the right of a large wall belonging to the chateau, and you pass uneven ground on the right. This is the area held by the commandos and the airborne troops from D-Day through to the breakout in August. At the end of the path there is a chateau, which was for a time the headquarters of the troops here, but it became difficult to hold. Take the road to your left for 100 metres or so. After the trees there is a viewpoint. To your left there are the chimneys of Colombelles, which were held by the Germans for much of the Normandy campaign. As you are at the opposite end of the lines it is easy to see what a small area these troops were holding. To the right of Colombelles is Caen, again held by the Germans until after the middle of July. To the right of that is the area towards Carpiquet airfield, taken by the Canadians after intensive fighting. In the valley below is the Orne and the bridges. To the right is Ouistreham. On this side of the river is an area where there are several bunkers, in varying states of damage and decay.

You have a choice here. You can return the same way to Amfreville, or you can extend the walk by going back to the chateau and taking the road to the left and then the main road down the hill to Salanelles. You have walked through the British front line. Salanelles was occupied by the airborne troops on D-Day but was abandoned shortly afterwards and was in no man's land for the rest of the campaign. It was eventually taken by Belgian troops in August during the breakout.

Returning to Amfreville, the square has several monuments. To the right (west) of the church there is a monument to the commandos. The church itself was used by the troops to rest before attacking in the direction we are walking, towards Breville–St. Mont. Face away from the church door and head forwards to the left. There is another commando monument near to a farm. The farm itself was used by the British during the fighting. Lord Lovat and several other officers watched the attack on Breville from near the farm. A shell, probably a British shell, landed among them, killing several people and severely wounding Lovat. The farmer helped carry Lovat to the farmhouse so he could be cared for. More than 40 years later, I visited the farmhouse and met that same farmer and his wife and shared a drink and a chat in their kitchen. Lord Lovat survived.

Facing away from the farm, turn left, and perhaps 30 metres away there is an alley on the right. It doesn't go anywhere but go down anyway to the end. From here you can look across the battlefield of 12 June, when the British attacked

Breville, supported by the artillery that fired some shots short, severely wounding Lovat, and by several tanks. The tanks moved from your right to left, towards Breville, stopping in the middle of the fields and firing at the village. The troops ran up behind the tanks, waiting until they finished firing before attacking the village.

Go back up the alley. Turn left, pass the farm and go along the narrow road. At the end turn left. The British attacked in this same direction. Breville is now a bigger village, and what would have been fields at the time are covered with houses. Walk along the road to the village. Go into the churchyard. Here we find two CWGC graves and a ruined church. The graves were not moved to Ranville cemetery at the request of the Breville people. One grave was dug by a man who returned 40 years later and was surprised to find the grave had not been relocated. The ruined church was the only one not rebuilt in the area. This was because it had been too severely damaged, being at the heart of the fighting for a long time. This area was the front for more than two months. Leave the churchyard and carry on in the same direction beyond the crossroads (where there is another memorial). A few hundred metres on, you will see a chateau to the left across a field. Keep going. Look to the right. You are looking down on the landing grounds, on Ranville, and over the Orne. This was critical territory. It could not be lost to the Germans, otherwise the battle of Normandy itself might have been lost. The soldiers understood this, which is why they fought with tenacity throughout the battle to keep this ridge – fortunately they succeeded, but it did mean trench warfare for more than two months.

A little further on there is the driveway to the chateau, unfortunately now private. It was here that some airborne troops, supported by elements of the Black Watch, fought a difficult battle with the Germans around 12 June. The Germans continually attacked the position. The British troops lost more than 100 men in two days; the Germans considerably more. At the driveway entrance there are a number of memorials, including a statue of a piper of the Black Watch. Across from the drive there is a sunken lane. It was here that Lt Col Otway, who had commanded the raid on the Merville Battery six days previously, was seriously wounded by a shell. Note the water tower here. This can be seen for miles around, and if you are touring the area it is worth noting its position.

Complete the walk by retracing your steps to Amfreville.

Before visiting these sites, it is important to read a detailed account of the 6th Airborne Division at Normandy to get a fuller appreciation of the sites.

Further visits

While the previously described tour provides a good day of exploration of the area in which the 6th Airborne fought, it is a very small part of the battlefield. Head south beyond Caen to the plains towards Falaise where the tank battles Epsom and Goodwood were fought, or west to the main battlefield, the beaches, towns and fields that were fought over for so long. That is beyond the scope of this book, but some of the remains such as Pointe du Hoc or the various gun emplacements are worth visiting, as are the museums. The cemeteries contain the remains of troops of all sides who fought in the battle. Perhaps the most poignant cemetery is the British cemetery at Bayeux, opposite the Normandy museum. This is the largest of the British cemeteries.

Conclusions

The battlefield of Normandy is significant for a number of reasons. The battle was fought relatively recently so we have a lot of information about it. It took place in a distinctive region, and though there are relatively limited remains, it is possible to read about the battle and explore the landscape to understand the battle better. The flatlands to the south of Caen were ideal tank country. Much of the western end is very good for defensive purposes because of all the hedgerows and embankments. A map indicating the positions of troops and tanks while walking around the battlefield can be illuminating.

There are many stories of the men who fought in Normandy. I was lucky to collect a number of these and to know the men who were involved. When I met them, they were mostly ordinary men – the citizens' army of the United Kingdom. It was difficult to think that many had once been involved in such fighting; but this is the nature of war. Most people are not warriors. They go to war because – for whatever reason – they have to. Most will eventually go home, but some will be maimed and scarred going forward, whether physically or psychologically.

15

REFLECTIONS

Most research on the psychological impact of war has focused on war trauma, on the negative impact of war on individuals who are involved in war and has approached the subject from the perspective of psychological or psychiatric analysis. This is a good approach to the subject, but there are several problems. First, this approach focuses on psychological theory regarding the impact of war, and second, it has a narrowness of understanding of what constitutes psychological data. There have been previous attempts to broaden the approach. Jonathan Shay (1991, 1994) did precisely this when he suggested that PTSD does not adequately cover the range of symptoms and problems faced by people in war – and it does not necessarily consider the range of responses the soldier has. In order to broaden the approach to understanding the human consequences of war we need to focus on what we mean by data and the question of whether psychologists should use what is traditionally considered as not data – journals, novels, biographies and so forth. Hopefully this book has broadened that perspective. Yes, it has examined the traumatic aspect of war – that is unavoidable, as war is by its nature traumatic – but that is not the only consequence of war. War is also exciting, adventurous, interesting, dirty, boring, drawn out, fast and furious, tedious, and most other descriptive or emotive words that one can think of. People gain friends, comrades, enemies, love, hate, indifference. It provides an opportunity to travel, to see new places, and have new experiences. In many ways it encapsulates the breadth of human experience, particularly the intensity of human experience (and I include the intensity of boredom here). I hope that at least some of this is portrayed in the battle chapters.

This is still not enough. The landscape itself is important. If we want to understand the experience of battle, the site of the battle is important, as it shows something of what soldiers experienced. It is difficult to put across how much visiting battlefields can help in understanding at least something of the experiences of the people who took part in the battles. Seeing a deep World War I dugout gives at least an impression of the experience of being stuck in one day after day, sometimes under bombardment, where the terrors are difficult to control, sometimes doing nothing, reading, killing rats, eating. The privacy of defecation is lost in the trenches; privacy of any kind is lost. What effect does that have on a person, both in the short term and in the longer term? How does it change them when they go home after the war?

The complex effects of war need to be recognised. It is not just war trauma. People are affected in many ways, as we have seen. Most people are not traumatised, but they are affected; their lives may fundamentally change. This might be an inability to adapt to civilian life after a war. It might be changes in the ways they relate to people, and so on. While war trauma may affect a minority of participants, these other, more subtle and less obvious effects may affect most if not all participants. This means that instead of just looking at the impact of war on individuals we need to think about the impact of war on societies as a whole, and how it changes them. The narratives that have been discussed throughout are not only personal narratives, they are societal and cultural (or master) narratives. A cultural narrative at least partly experienced due to war may have a major impact not only on the participants in that war, but the rest of the population, and may also affect later generations.

World War I did not end on 11 November 1918. Apart from continuing wars in Eastern Europe and elsewhere, the soldiers who went home did so changed. They had experienced war and would not forget it. While most psychologists and psychiatrists wrote about the war in its immediate aftermath, few considered its longer term effects. If we examine records from the 1920s and 1930s we find strong evidence of the continuing impact of war. There were many veterans who remained locked up in asylums because societies did not know what to do with them (e.g., Barham, 2004). These were just the worst cases. Others had problems adapting to life at home or to civilian work. If we examine the newspapers of the time, there are many judicial cases where the defendant claims shell shock as a defence. Whether they were shell shocked or not is usually difficult to say after this lapse of time, but some undoubtedly were and some may have committed a crime because of this.

World War II had a fundamental effect on perhaps most of the population of the world because it affected so many regions. With so many nations taking part, so many areas being severely damaged or destroyed by the war, and so many people killed or wounded, there were few totally unaffected. Apart from the impact on individuals as for World War I, what was the impact on nations and cultures? How are our countries different now to how they might have been had World War II not taken place? These are questions that need to be addressed by sociologists, anthropologists, historians, psychologists and others. There is a body of work examining the first years after the war from different perspectives or focusing on particular groups (e.g., Goodrich, 2014; McCawley, 2015), rather than thoroughly exploring the changes. We know the Cold War took place and the impact the end of the war and the Cold War had on country boundaries, and we know something of the impact of the war on individuals, but we know little about the longer-term societal or master narrative effects.

Another key question that arises from exploring the impact of war across many centuries is the extent to which the psychological effects of war are universal and the extent to which they are cultural. The difficulty of ascertaining this is illustrated by the changing language we use. As we have seen, the terms we use to describe the impact of war (PTSD, anxiety, depression, coping, stiff upper lip, misery, suffering, etc.) are not the same terms that were available to someone describing the Hundred Years War, or even someone describing the impact of the Peninsular War 200 years ago. Some of the words are the same. Some of them even mean the same thing; but others are new. They are the terms invented or adapted by psychologists to described precise psychological states.

We infer from what someone described hundreds of years ago that they were having problems relating to war experience. Sometimes this is very clear, particularly when a Civil War officer or Shakespeare describe war-related nightmares. These are the same, or at least similar, symptoms. The difficulty is inferring that the full range of symptoms are the same. Only 100 years ago, in the First World War, symptoms were very different to what we see now. Some of the hysterical paralysis (e.g., the *funny walks*) observed in the old films of World War I veterans is highly unusual by modern terms. We might suggest that it is culture that suggested to these people that the only way to respond to the fear of the trenches was to have a physical reaction, as physical disability or illness is the only recognisable form. Psychological illness is unacceptable. That is to some extent certainly the case given that we used to shoot people as cowards. If there is such a difference over a period of only 100 years, when there was a fairly mature psychological science, then what are the differences likely to be many hundreds of years ago?

To some extent we can only speculate about the impact of war many hundreds of years ago. We can read the documents written by participants and others, looking for statements that relate to human behaviour, thought and emotion, and we can sometimes deduce symptoms. Perhaps this is easier when it is fictional, as in Shakespeare. The difficulty, and perhaps this is an area where some historians have fallen into the trap, is inferring that people are traumatised because of the difficult experiences they went through. There are descriptions of the horrors of war from hundreds of years ago, but these are descriptions of events, awful events, but they remain descriptions. They are not telling us anything about the human reactions to these events. We should not infer that participants will be traumatised just because they have been through a serious battle. In many cases we will never know about the psychological impact of a war because nobody has written about it.

In these cases, perhaps the thing we might infer is that participants in battle were not considered important as individuals, and so any notion of psychological impact is nonsense, because no one matters. There is of course a distinction between officers and men that was still prevalent in the way people were treated in World War I (officers were more likely to have talking treatment, men were more likely to have physical treatments such as electric shock or be prosecuted for cowardice or desertion). In the English Civil War, Major Withers described his nightmares. We do not hear about the ordinary men having nightmares. They were usually peasants who couldn't write so why would anyone care? This is more than just a throwaway remark. If the narrative of a society is such that the ordinary person, the soldier or peasant, does not matter as an individual, then to what extent does that individual see themselves as an individual with all the psychological responses we now take for granted?

Ethics of war

There are temporal differences relating to the ethics of war, which have developed over many centuries. Up until the nineteenth century, siege warfare was governed by a fundamental rule. If the besieged gave up without resistance, no one would be hurt. The soldiers would most likely be allowed to return home, and the civilians in the town would be untouched. If the besieged resisted then if the resulting siege was successful, once the town was taken, the troops would be given a free run to drink, steal, rape and murder for a period of time, often a few days. There was nothing special about this. Everyone knew the rules. The besieged might take a risk and hope they would be relieved; the besiegers had to get on with the job before the town received such support. This is what happened in the Peninsular War on more than one occasion; though perhaps the most famous is Badajos, where after a successful siege the British soldiers were given free rein. The Spanish still haven't forgiven them. Even 200 years later, when a British Regiment wanted to put up a monument to their achievement, the people of Badajoz refused them because of their behaviour after the siege. It was similar at San Sebastian a couple of years later, where again the British troops had been given free rein.

Another example is the way prisoners are treated. This has varied through the years and from culture to culture, from allowing them to go home, through keeping them in camps for varying periods of time to killing them. There is no real development over time here. Apart from the Geneva Conventions, which both before and afterwards various armies have ignored, there is no clear linear development to the better treatment of prisoners. Henry V ordered them killed in 1415; English Civil War prisoners were usually allowed to go home (except for officers), prisoners taken during the Peninsular War were often kept in awful conditions (Dartmoor prison was built for French prisoners). In World War I most prisoners were kept in relatively good conditions, but in World War II it depended whose side you were on. The Germans looked after British and French prisoners but allowed Russian prisoners to die. The Russians treated the Germans in a similar way, and after the war only released the last prisoners in 1955. The Japanese treated their prisoners terribly.

Methodological issues

Writing this book has sometimes been very difficult. As a psychologist with some knowledge of historical methods (rather than the other way round) my focus has been on attempting to understand behaviour based on the evidence available. An historian would have attempted to understand what happened and then try to understand the why, whereas I wanted to understand why people did what they did and how they felt about it, with no deep concern for historical truth. The focus is somewhat different. When I interviewed Normandy veterans, as a psychologist I was interested in the impact their experiences had on them, not whether they were telling the truth. As previously argued, I know some were confabulating, but psychologically that does not really matter. For historians, it does.

The evidence historians have to piece together a story is often weak. Trying to develop an understanding of a battle such as Agincourt – very well-known and regularly written about over the centuries – is hard to do for the historian. Apart from archeological evidence there is probably very little more to find out; and there is still debate about many aspects of the battle. the numbers involved, the actual site and tactics, and so on. For the psychologist it becomes almost impossible, as the evidence is not psychological. Attempting to draw anything from the evidence, trying to piece together something of the experiences of the ordinary soldier and how he functioned, drawing on what was said at the time and our understanding of fundamental human behaviour, we still do not get very far. This of course brings in the other problem, that of universality and culture. Much of human behaviour is universal across time and culture but much is also culturally specific. The problem is, we are not precisely clear about which is which, even from modern day research. Looking back at the chapters, there is far less psychological evidence about the period of the Hundred Years War than any of the later wars considered.

Even drawing on Shakespeare's writing about the period, if we say that having nightmares is evidence of traumatic stress, we are extrapolating a long way from what was being described at the time, i.e., nightmares. We are assuming that other symptoms of PTSD are present even though they are not described. This is not a valid assumption. As I have noted elsewhere, the changing nature of the perception of the individual may lead to different patterns of symptoms. We know that this is the case when simply comparing the present day pattern of symptoms described as PTSD with the often very different symptoms experienced by men in the trenches of World War I who were diagnosed with various often poorly described disorders such as shell shock or neurasthenia.

As we progress through the book, the evidence for psychological impact becomes stronger. Even at the point of the Civil Wars of the mid-seventeenth century we have a great deal more information to go on, even though – as in all the chapters – I have only touched on the subject. There is much more in the archives for the psychologists to glean, many writings which will tell us something of the psychological impact of the Civil Wars. The Battle of Sedan is a good illustration of how much psychologists have to rely on fiction to get the psychology of war. While Zola's account is not meant to be factual – it is a novel – it is built on good evidence, that of Zola walking the battlefields, meeting people who were involved and talking to them. Zola's novels are perhaps more social documentary than novel, with only the characters themselves being fictional.

I spent relatively little time on the period of the World Wars as these are well-documented and understood, though as mentioned previously, the psychological consequences of these wars could be understood more thoroughly.

The future of war trauma and narrative

There is a growing awareness that war trauma cannot be explained simply by employing PTSD. PTSD is a useful construct in that it provides a framework for clinical practice (and indeed a diagnosis that often makes it possible to provide treatment), for theoretical developments and the testing of treatment methods, and for demonstrating that there are similarities in the ways people respond to traumatic or difficult circumstances, whether they have experienced war, rape or sexual abuse, or a manmade or natural disaster or serious accident. People tend to have similar reactions, and they can be treated in similar ways – though there are questions about the effectiveness of the techniques that we use.

PTSD is very helpful when there is a single traumatic event. When there is a car accident, a death, some sort of disaster, and the traumatic reaction is not too complex. When it comes to war it is just not enough. People display a whole series of responses to the experiences of war. War itself consists of a wide range of experience, from active fighting – firing weapons and/or being fired at – to long periods of nothing happening, to the destruction of homes and the killing of friends and family. Rape is common in war, maiming through landmines, bombs or shells, other enemy activity, and so on. Wars can last for years. A person can go through a lot in a few years. The range of experiences and the impact they have is very complex, and if a person experiences significant symptoms of mental ill-health, it is often not something that can be readily treated using a relatively simple formula.

Narrative

This is where we return to the notion of narrative. We all have life biographies, the stories of life we construct, reconstruct, and share with other people. These narratives are generally coherent. We continually monitor them to help us make sense of our experiences in the world. For many people the life narrative is generally positive, so new experiences are interpreted positively – generally. For others there is a less positive tone to our narratives, so new experiences may be interpreted less positively. At the most basic this may separate the optimists and the pessimists. If a life narrative is very negative it can mean depression, with new events being interpreted in such a negative way that the person finds them difficult to deal with.

War disrupts people's lives, their narratives, their biographies. Their lives are never going to be the same again. If someone is traumatised then whatever treatment is received can only mean learning to manage, to cope with life. Research with World War II veterans (Hunt, 1996) showed that war trauma and the effects of war are lifelong. This needs to be recognised, and can be best recognised through narrative. If people are going to rebuild their lives after war, they are going to have to rebuild their narratives about life. As mentioned earlier, there is also the societal or cultural master narrative to consider. The way society thinks about war and the people who have taken part in a war will have an impact both on society itself and on the participants. The classic example is the U.S. soldier returning from Vietnam who was spat on and called a murderer. He is not likely to quickly resolve any problems he has as a result of that war. He is likely to remain traumatised without the support of his social system.

The narrative approach is the key way of understanding the impact of war. It helps explain why wars start in the first place. It helps understand the conduct of the war. It helps with the consequences of the war. It helps at all levels, from culture and society through to relationships and the individual. If we can begin to piece these parts together, our understanding of war and the impact of war will be the greater.

Classically, war trauma disrupts a person's autobiography by introducing elements that are difficult to incorporate into the narrative. For instance, someone who did think that generally people are good may find that many are not good, or if they trusted themselves to behave in an effective manner in a difficult situation and they find they did not act in what they see as an appropriate manner, may have difficulty incorporating this new information into the life narrative. If they had a life-threatening experience then the memory of this experience may be fragmented, so it is difficult to give it meaning. These disruptions to the life narrative can last a long time, and the person may find it difficult to resolve them, to make the narrative coherent again.

Narrative problems can be resolved through thinking, talking, having therapy, writing, drawing, or any means whereby the person makes sense of their experiences. It is perhaps why people have always told stories of war to their friends and community.

This narrative disruption is also seen at the societal (master narrative) level, where there are conflicting master narratives. This was seen in the British Civil Wars, where King Charles and Parliament had fundamentally different master narratives at the start of the war, and the war itself probably made the conflict between the master narratives worse. It was not until a generation or more later that the wounds in society healed – it might be said they have never really healed but been reinterpreted into right-wing and left-wing ideologies. It is the same with the consequences of the Spanish Civil War. It is only now that the participants are generally dead that society can start to heal the wounds.

The wounds of the 30 Years War of the twentieth century's, which continued through to the Cold War separation of East and West Europe, was functionally healed by the existence of the European Union, which at the time of writing appears to be starting to fall apart. Societal narratives too need resolution in a similar way to individual narratives. Societies have to find ways of mending, of creating new meaningful narratives, whether that is the memory law of Spain or the European Union.

The role of memorials, commemorative events and remembrance was included because it forges the link between those who took part and those who did not, and also between the individuals who took part and society. The larger-scale commemorative events such as Remembrance Day are there to demonstrate to individuals that society has a coherent narrative that recognises the contributions of those who took part in a war. Though, as I argued earlier, the commemorative events we hold relating to World War I are hardly representative of the average person in the UK, being militaristic (which we are not), Royalist (which we have conflicting narratives on) and Christian (which most of us are not, and some of us are of a different religion); which it is the right time to remove or change this event. That is not to say that the memorials to individual events should be removed. They perform a useful historical purpose in showing where events took place. It is the larger events, and perhaps the war cemeteries themselves (at least any up to and including World War I), for the reasons argued earlier, that should go. If you remember the 2 up 2 down theory mentioned in Chapter 4 then you may agree that it is time to make changes to our commemorative stance.

Concluding statement

The book has shown, I hope, that there are close links between disciplines when it comes to understanding the psychological response to war. I have tried to argue that traditional psychological approaches are insufficient to explain how people respond to and deal with war, that we need to draw on the work of people in many other disciplines, whether they are sociologists, archaeologists, historians or others, that they all contribute to the *psychological* understanding. I hope I have also shown that by visiting battlefields themselves and walking or driving in the footsteps of those who took part, we can gain a much greater understanding of both the battles and the people.

I have not attempted to explain each battle with detailed accounts from the various data sources (with the odd exception) but I hope I have shown there is scope for much further psychological research using these – for psychology – unusual forms of data. I hope the book will function as a heuristic for others to conduct more comprehensive psychological research into the psychological understanding of these and other battlefields. In the end, I hope to have shown that historians need psychologists and that psychologists need historians.

REFERENCES

Abdul-Hamid, W.K. & Hacker Hughes, J.G.H. 2015. Integration of religion and spirituality into trauma psychotherapy: An example in sufism. *Journal of EMDR Practice and Research*, 9, 150–156.

Aeshchylus. *Agamemnon*. http://www.open.ac.uk/people/sites/www.open.ac.uk.people/files/files/aeschylus-agamemnon-definitive.pdf. Accessed 27 May 2019.

Alexander, J.C., Eyerman, R., Giesen, B., Smelser, N.J. & Sztompka, P. 2004. *Cultural Trauma and Collective Identity*. Berkeley: University of California Press.

Alghamdi, M., Hunt, N. & Thomas, S. 2015. The effectiveness of narrative exposure therapy with traumatised fire-fighters in Saudi Arabia: A randomised controlled study. *Behaviour Research and Therapy*, 66, 64–71.

Al-Hadethe, A., Hunt, N., Al-Qaysi, G. & Thomas, S. 2015. Randomised controlled study comparing two psychological therapies for post-traumatic stress disorder (PTSD): Emotional freedom techniques (EFT) vs narrative exposure therapy (NET). *Journal of Traumatic Stress Disorders and Treatment*, 4(4).

American Psychiatric Association. 2013. *The Diagnostic and Statistical Manual of Mental Disorders*, 5th Ed. Washington, DC: Author.

Andrews, M. 2014. *Narrative Imagination and Everyday Life*. Oxford: Oxford University Press.

Andrews, M., Bagot-Jewitt, C. & Hunt, N. 2011a. *Lest We Forget: How we Remember the Dead*. London: History Press.

Andrews, M., Bagot-Jewitt, C. & Hunt, N. 2011b. Introduction: National memory and war. *Journal of War and Cultural Studies*, 4, 283–288.

Andrews, M., Squire, C. & Tamboukou, M. 2013. *Doing Narrative Research*, 2nd Ed. London: Sage.

Army Field Manual (FM) 3-0. 2001. *Operations*. Washington DC: Headquarters, Department of the Army.

Atherton, I. & Morgan, P. 2011. The battlefield war memorial: Commemoration and the battlefield site from the Middle Ages to the modern era. *Journal of War and Cultural Studies*, 4(3), 289–304.

Barash, J.A. 2016. *Collective Memory and the Historical Past*. Chicago: University of Chicago Press.

Barham, P. 2004. *Forgotten Lunatics of the Great War*. New Haven: Yale University Press.

Battlefields Trust. 2009. Finding Bosworth. *Battlefield*, 14(4), 9–11.

Baxell. 2012. *Unlikely Warriors: The British in the Spanish Civil War and the Struggle against Fascism*. London: Aurum Press.

Beevor, A. 2012. *The Battle for Spain: Spanish Civil War 1936–1939*. London: Weidenfeld & Nicolson.

Belfield, E. & Essame, H. 1967. *The Battle for Normandy*. London: Pan.

Bentley, S. 2005. Short history of PTSD: From Thermopylae to Hue soldiers have always had a disturbing reaction to war. *The VVA Veteran*, March/April.

Blakeley, G. 2008. Politics as usual? The trials and tribulations of the law of historical memory in Spain. *Revista Interdisciplinar*, 7, 315–330.

Braun, V. & Clarke, V. 2006. Using thematic analysis in psychology. *Qualitative Research in Psychology*, 3, 77–101.

Bruner, J. 1986. *Actual Minds, Possible Worlds*. Harvard: Harvard University Press.

Bull, N. & Panton, D. 2000 Drafting the Vimy Ridge charter for conservation of battlefield terrain. *Managing Cultural Landscapes*, 31,5–11.

Burne, A.H. 1950/2005. *The Battlefields of England*. Barnsley: Pen & Sword.

Burnell, K., Coleman, P. & Hunt, N. 2006. Falklands War Veterans' perceptions of social support and the reconciliation of traumatic memories. *Aging & Mental Health*, 10(3), 1–8.

Byrne, E. 2013. Were the pulverised bones of soldiers and horses who died at the battle of Waterloo sold as soil fertiliser? Retrieved 08/08/18 from: https://www.historyextra.com/period/were-the-pulverised-bones-of-soldiers-and-horses-who-died-at-the-battle-of-waterloo-sold-as-soil-fertiliser/

Carman, J. 2013. *Archaeologies of Conflict*. London: Bloomsbury.

Carr, G. 2010. The archeaology of occupation, 1940–2009: A case study from the Channel Islands. *Antiquity*, 84(323), 191–174.

Castell, E. & Falco, L. 2002. Across the river: Interpreting the Battle of the Ebro or battlefields as a didactic resource. In: Doyle P. & Bennett M. (Eds). *Fields of Battle: Terrain in Military History*, pp. 257–264. London: Springer.

Chronis, A. 2005. Coconstructing heritage at the Gettysburg storyscape. *Annals of Tourism Research*, 32(2), 386–406.

Clarke, V. & Braun, V. 2013. *Successful Qualitative Research: A Practical Guide for Beginners*. London: Sage.

Clausewitz. See von Clausewitz.

Collins, J.M. 1998. *Military Geography for Professionals and the Public*. Washington DC: National Defence University Press.

COMEBE. 2001. http://www.batallaebre.org/app/index.php?page=comebe. Accessed 3 March 2019.

Cooper, A. 1660. *Stratologia: Or, the History of the English Civil Warrs, in English Verse*. London.

Costello, E. 2005 *Rifleman Costello – The Adventures of a Soldier of the 95th (Rifles) in the Peninsular and Waterloo Campaigns of the Napoleonic Wars*. London: Leonaur.

Covel, W. 1659. *A Declaration unto the Parliament, Council of State, and Army, Shewing Impartially the Causes of the Peoples Tumults, Madness, and Confusions*. London.

Crocq, M.-A. & Crocq, L. 2000. From shell shock and war neurosis to posttraumatic stress disorder: A history of psychotraumatology. *Dialogues in Clinical Neuroscience*, 2(1), 47–55.

Curry, A. 2000. *1415 Agincourt: A New History*. London: The History Press.

Da Costa, J.M. 1871. On irritable heart: A clinical study of a form of functional cardiac disorder and its consequences. *The American Journal of the Medical Sciences*, 61, 18–52.

Daly, R.J. 1983. Samuel Pepys and post-traumatic stress disorder. *British Journal of Psychiatry*, 143, 64–8.

Danieli, Y. (Ed). 1998. *International Handbook of Multigenerational Legacies of Trauma*. New York: Plenum.

Davis, G.J. 2014. *Gilgamesh, The New Translation*. London: Lulu.

Delano-Smith, C. & Kain, R.J.P. 1999. *English Maps: A History*. Toronto: University of Toronto Press.

D'Errico, D. & Hunt, N. 2019. Place responsiveness: IPA walking interviews to explore participants' responses to natural disasters. *Qualititative Research in Psychology*. DOI: 10.1080/14780887.2019.1604929.

Dixon, N.F. 1976. *On the Psychology of Military Incompetence*. London: Vintage.

Donagan, B. 2001. The web of honour: Soldiers, Christians, and gentlemen in the English Civil War. *The Historical Journal*, 44(2), 365–389.

Donaldson, J. 1841. *Recollections of n Eventful Life of a Soldier*. London: A & C Black.

Douglas, J. 1997. *Douglas' Tale of the Peninsular and Waterloo*. Barnsley: Leo Cooper.

Doyle, P. & Bennett, M.R. 1997. Military geography: Terrain evaluation and the British Western Front, 1914–18. *Geographical Journal*, 163, 1–24.

Doyle, P. & Bennett, M.R. (Eds). 2002. *Fields of Battle: Terrain in Military History*. London: Kluwer.

Dunkley, R.A., Morgan, N.J. & Westwood, S. 2011. Visiting the trenches: Exploring meanings and motivations in battlefield tourism. *Tourism Management*, 32(4), 860–868.

Ehlen, J. & Whisonant, R. 2008. Military geology of Antietam battlefield, Maryland, USA: Geology, terrain and casualties. *Geology Today*, 24(1), 20–27.

Esdaile, C.J. 2009. *Peninsular Eyewitness: The Experience of War in Spain and Portugal 1808–1813*. Barnsley: Leo Cooper.

Espinosa Maestre, F. 2013. *Shoot the Messenger?: Spanish Democracy and the Crimes of Franco: From the Pact of Silence to the Trial of Baltazar Garzon. Translated by Richard Barker*. East Sussex: Sussex University Press.

Evans, J. & Jones, P. 2011. The walking interview: Methodology, mobility and place. *Applied Geography*, 31, 849–858.

Evelyn, J. 1661. *A Panegyric to Charles the Second Presented to His Majestie the XXXIII of April, Being the Day of His Coronation*. London.

Figes, O. 2011 *Crimea*. London: Metropolitan Books.

Fitchett, W.H. 1900/2009. *Wellington's Men*. Kindle.

Fletcher, I. 2012. *Salamanca 1812: Wellington Crushes Marmont*. Oxford: Osprey.

Foa, E. 2009. *Effective Treatments for PTSD*, 2nd Ed. New York: Guilford Press.

Foard, G. & Curry, A. 2013. *Bosworth 1485: A Battlefield Rediscovered*. Oxford: Oxbow Books.

Foster, H. 1643. *A True and Exact Relation of the Marchings of the Two Regiments of the Trained-Bands of the City of London*. London.

Francois, P. 2013 'The best way to see Waterloo is with your eyes shut': British 'histourism', authenticity and commercialisation in the mid-nineteenth century. *Anthropological Journal of European Cultures*, 22(1), 26–41.

Froissart. 1978. *Contemporary Chronicles of The Hundred Years' War. Edited and translated by Geoffrey Brereton*. London: Penguin.

Glover, G. 2015. *Waterloo in 100 Objects*. London: The History Press.

God. *The Bible*. London: King James.

Gonzalez-Ruibal, A. 2007. Making things public: Archaeologies of the Spanish civil war. *Public Archaeology*, 6(4), 203–226.

González-Ruibal A., Ayán Vila X. & Caesar R. 2015. Ethics, archaeology, and civil conflict: The case of Spain. In: González-Ruibal A. & Moshenska G. (Eds). *Ethics and the Archaeology of Violence. Ethical Archaeologies: The Politics of Social Justice*, vol. 2. New York, NY: Springer.

Goodrich, T. 2014. *Hellstorm: The Death of Nazi Germany, 1944–1947*. Aberdeen: Aberdeen Books.

Goya, F. 1863. *The Disasters of War*. Madrid: Spain.

Grogan, S. 2014. *Shell Shocked Britain: The First World War's Legacy for Britain's Mental Health*. Barnsley: Pen and Sword.

Halbwachs, M. & Coser, L.A. 1992. *On Collective Memory*. Chicago: University of Chicago Press.

Hall, C. 2019. *British Exploitation of Germans Science and Technology, 1943–1949*. London: Routledge.

Harris, B. 1848/1970. *Recollections of Rifleman Harris*. London: Military Book Society.

Hastings, M. 1984. *Overlord: D-Day and the Battle for Normandy 1944*. London: Pan.

Herodotus. See Rawlinson.

HMSO. 1922. *Report of the War Office Committee of Enquiry into 'Shell Shock'*. London: HMSO.

Hogg, M.A. 2006. Social identity theory. In: Burke, P.J. (Ed). *Contemporary Social Psychological Theories*, pp. 111–136. Stanford University Press.

Horowitz, M. 2005. *Treatment of Stress Response Syndromes*. New York: Aronson.

Howitt, D. 2010. *Introduction to Qualitative Research Methods in Psychology*. London: Pearson.

Hugo, V. 1862/1982. *Les Miserables*. Lonndon: Penguin.

Hunt, N. 1996. *The Long Term Psychological Effects of War Trauma*. Unpublished Thesis, University of Plymouth.

Hunt, N. 2004. Representations of trauma in All Quiet on the Western Front. *European Psychiatry*. 19, 489–493.

Hunt, N.C. 2010. *Memory, War and Trauma*. Cambridge: Cambridge University Press.

Hunt, N.C. 2011. Recuerdo la Guerra Civil España: Turning forgotten history into current memory. In: Andrews, M., Bagot-Jewitt, C. & Hunt, N. (Eds). *Lest we Forget: How we Remember the Dead*.

Hunt, N.C. & Gekenyi, M. 2005. Comparing refugees and non-refugees: The Bosnian experience. *Journal of Anxiety Disorders*, 19, 717–723.

Hunt, N.C. & Robbins, I. 1998. Telling stories of the war: Ageing veterans coping with their memories through narrative. *Oral History*, 26(2), 57–64.

Hunt, N.C. & Robbins, I. 2001a. The long term consequences of war: The experience of World War Two. *Aging and Mental Health*, 5(2), 184–191.

Hunt, N.C. & Robbins, I. 2001b. World War Two veterans, social support and veterans' associations. *Aging and Mental Health*, 5(2), 176–183.

Hutton, R. 2004. *Debates in Stuart History*. London: Palgrave MacMillan.

Jones, E. 2006. Historical approaches to post-combat disorders. *Philosophical Transactions of the Royal Society of London: Series B Biological Sciences*, 361, 1468.

Jones, M. 2005. *24 Hours at Agincourt*. London: W.H. Allen.

Jones, E., Vermaas, R.H., McCartney, H. et al. 2003. Flashbacks and post-traumatic stress disorder: The genesis of a 20th-century diagnosis. *British Journal of Psychiatry*, 182, 158–63.

Kamrani, K. 2007. The Discover Magazine interview with Jane Goodall. https://primatology.net/2007/04/07/the-discover-magazine-interview-with-jane-goodall/. Accessed 20 February 2019.

Keegan, J. 1978. *The Face of Battle: A Study of Agincourt, Waterloo and the Somme.* London: Random house.

Keegan, J. 1982. *Six Armies in Normandy: From D-Day to the Liberation of Paris.* London: Cape.

Kershaw, R. 2014. *24 Hours at Waterloo: 18 June 1815.* London: Casemate.

Laszlo, J. 2008. *The Science of Stories: An Introduction to Narrative Psychology.* London: Routledge.

Leese, P. 2002. *Shell Shock: Traumatic Neuroses and the British Soldiers of the First World War.* New York: Palgrave MacMillan.

Lowenthal, D. 1975. Past time, present place: Landscape and memory. *Geographical Review,* 65(1), 1–36.

McAdams, D.P. 2008. Personal narratives and the life story. In: O. John, R. Robins & L.A. Pervin (Eds). *Handbook of Personality: Theory and Research,* pp 241–261. New York: Guilford Press.

McCawley, M. 2015. *Origins of the Cold War 1941–1949.* London: Routledge.

Miller, G.A. 1956. The magical number seven, plus or minus two: Some limits on our capacity for processing information. *The Psychological Review,* 63, 81–97.

Mitchell, C.W. & Gavish, D. 1980. Land on which battles are lost and won. *Geographical Magazine,* LII(12), 838–840.

Mott, F.W. 1919. *Neuroses and Shell Shock.* London: Hodder & Stoughton.

Murray, M. 2003. Narrative psychology. In: Smith, J.A. (Ed). *Qualitative Psychology: A Practical Guide to Research Methods,* pp. 111–131. London: Sage.

Myers, C.S. 1915. A contribution to the study of shell shock(1), being an account of 3 cases of memory, vision, smell and taste, admitted to the Westminster War Hospital, Le Touquet. *Lancet,* Feb, 317–320.

Myers, C.S. 1940. *Shell Shock in France, 1914–1918.* Cambridge: Cambridge University Press.

Orwell, G. 1938/2000. *Homage to Catalonia.* London: Penguin Classics.

Pearce, S. 2005. The materiel of war: Waterloo and its culture. In: Bonehill, J. & Quilley, G. (Eds). *Conflicting Visions: War and Visual Culture in Britain and France, c. 1700–1830.* Aldershot: Ashgate.

Peters, E. 2016. Trauma narratives of the English Civil War. *Journal for Early Modern Cultural Studies,* 16(1), 78–94.

Pierce, E. 1660. *Anglorum Singultus: Or, the Sobbs of England, Poured Out, to Be Presented to his Excellency Generall George Monke.* London.

Plamper, J. 2017. Fear: Solders and emotion in early twentieth century Russian military psychology. *Slavic Review,* 68(2), 259–283.

Preston, P. 1984. *The Spanish Civil War: 1936–1939.* London: Weidenfeld & Nicholson.

Rawlinson. 1910/1992. *Histories: Herodotus.* London: Everyman.

Reid, F. 2010. *Broken Men – Shell Shock, Treatment and Recovery in Britain, 1914–30.* London: Continuum.

Reig Tapia, A. 1999. *Memoria de la Guerra Civil: Los Mitos de la Tribu.* Madrid: Alianza.

Remarque, E.M. 1929. *All Quiet on the Western Front.* London: Little, Brown & Co.

Remarque, E.M. 1931. *The Road Back.* Little, Brown & Co.

Richards, D.S. 2002. *The Peninsular Years: Britain's Redcoats in Spain and Portugal.* Barnsley: Pen and Sword.

Richards, R.L. 1910. Mental and nervous diseases in the Russo-Japanese war. *Military Surgeon*, 26, 177.

Russell, W.H. 2014. *Battles of the Crimean War*. London: Amberley Publishing.

Sarbin, T. 1986. *Narrative Psychology: The Storied Nature of Human Conduct*. London: Praeger.

Sargant, W. & Slater, E. 1944. *An Introduction to Physical Methods of Treatment in Psychiatry*. Edinburgh: E & S Livingstone Ltd.

Schama, S. 2004. *Landscape and Memory*. London: Harper Perennial.

Scott, D.D. & McFeaters, A.P. 2011. The archeology of historic battlefields: A history and theoretical development in conflict archeology. *Journal of Archeological Research*, 19(1), 103–132.

Seaton, A.V. 1996. Guided by the dark: From thanatopsis to thanatourism. *International Journal of Heritage Studies*, 2(4), 234–244.

Seaton, A.V. 1999. War and thantourism: Waterloo 1815–1914. *Annals of Tourism Research*, 26, 130–158.

Shackel, P. 2003. *Memory in Black and White: Race, Commemoration and the Post-Bellum Landscape*. Oxford: Altamira Press.

Shakespeare, W. 1623. *Henry IV Part I. Mr. William Shakespeare's Comedies, Histories, & Tragedies (The First Folio)*, London: Edward Blount and William and Isaac Jaggard.

Sharpley, R. & Stone, P.R. 2009. *The Darker Side of Travel: The Theory and Practice of Dark Tourism*. Bristol: Channel View Publications.

Shay, J. 1991. Learning about combat stress from Homer's Iliad. *Journal of Traumatic Stress*, 4(4), 561–579.

Shay, J. 1994. *Achilles in Vietnam: Combat Trauma and the Undoing of Character*. New York: Pocket Books.

Shay, J. 2003. *Odysseus in America: Combat Trauma and the Trials of Homecoming*. Washington: James Bennett.

Shepherd, B. 2002. *A War of Nerves: Soldiers and Psychologists, 1914–1994*. London: Pimlico.

Smith, V. 1998. War and tourism: An American ethnography. *Annals of Tourism Research*, 25, 202–227.

Socrates (440 BCE) Ajax. http://classics.mit.edu/Sophocles/ajax.html Accessed 27 May 2019.

Stamp, G. 2010. *The Memorial to the Missing of the Somme*. London: Profile Books.

Stone, P.R. 2012. Dark tourism and significant other death: Towards a model of mortality mediation. *Annals of Tourism Research*, 39(3), 1565–1587.

Stoyle, M. 2003. Memories of the maimed: The testimony of Charles I's former soldiers, 1660–1730. *History*, 88, 204–226.

Tajfel, H. 1970. Experiments in intergroup discrimination. *Scientific American*, 223, 96–102.

Tancock, L.W. 1972. *Introduction: The Debacle*. London: Penguin.

van der Kolk, B. 2015. *The Body Keeps the Score: Brain, Mind and Body in the Healing of Trauma*. London: Penguin.

Verani, H.J. & Clarke, D.D. 1982. Octavio Paz and the language of space. *World Literature Today*, 56(4), 631–635.

Von Clausewitz, C. 1832/2008. *On War*. Oxford: Oxford University Press.

Wanke, P. 2005. *Russian/Soviet Military Psychiatry, 1904–45*. London: Cass.

Whittington, K.E. 2016. *The Social Impact of the Hundred Years War on the Societies of England and France*. Dissertation: Orlando, Florida: University of Central Florida.

Willard, P., Frost, W. & Lade, C. 2011. Battlefield tourism: The visitor experience. *CAUTHE 2011: National Conference: Tourism: Creating a Brilliant Blend, 1359–63.* Adelaide, School of Management.

Wither, G. 1661. *Campo-Musae: Or, the Field-Musings of Major George Wither, Touching on His Military Ingagement for the King and Parliament.* London.

Xue, C., Ge, Y., Tang, B., Liu, Y., Kang, P., Wang, M. & Zhang, L. 2015. A meta-analysis of risk factors for combat-related PTSD among military personnel and veterans. *PLoS One*, 10(3).

Zang, Y., Hunt, N. & Cox, T. 2013. A randomised controlled pilot study: The effectiveness of narrative exposure therapy with adult survivors of the Sichuan Earthquake. *BMC Psychiatry*, 13(1), 41.

Zola, E. 1892. *La Debacle.* Les Rougon-Macquart. France: Charpentier.

INDEX

Entries in **bold** indicate chapter topics.

Printed in Great Britain
by Amazon